DISCOVER RUSSIA, CENTRAL ASIA AND THE CAUCASUS

Reader's Digest

PUBLISHED BY THE READER'S DIGEST ASSOCIATION LIMITED

LONDON   NEW YORK   SYDNEY   MONTREAL

DISCOVER RUSSIA, CENTRAL ASIA AND THE CAUCASUS

Translated and edited by Toucan Books Limited, London
for Reader's Digest, London

Translated and adapted from the French by John Man

For Reader's Digest
Series Editor: Christine Noble
Editorial Assistant: Lucy Murray
Prepress Accounts Manager: Penny Grose

Reader's Digest General Books
Editorial Director: Cortina Butler
Art Director: Nick Clark

First English language edition Copyright © 2002
The Reader's Digest Association Limited
11 Westferry Circus, Canary Wharf, London E14 4HE
www.readersdigest.co.uk

Reprinted with amendments 2004

We are committed to both the quality of our products and
the service we provide to our customers. We value your
comments, so please feel free to contact us on 08705 113366,
or via our web site at www.readersdigest.co.uk
If you have any comments about the content of our books,
you can contact us at gbeditorial@readersdigest.co.uk

ISBN 0 276 42517 0

Discover the World: RUSSIA, CENTRAL ASIA AND THE CAUCASUS
was created and produced by
ML Éditions, Paris for Selection Reader's Digest S.A., Paris,
and first published
in 2000 as *Regards sur le Monde: LA RUSSIE, L'ASIE CENTRALE
ET LE CAUCASE*

©2000 Selection Reader's Digest, S.A.
212 boulevard Saint-Germain, 75007, Paris

CONTENTS

RUSSIA

KAZAKHSTAN

GEORGIA

ARMENIA

AZERBAIJAN

UZBEKISTAN

TURKMENISTAN

KYRGYZSTAN

TAJIKISTAN

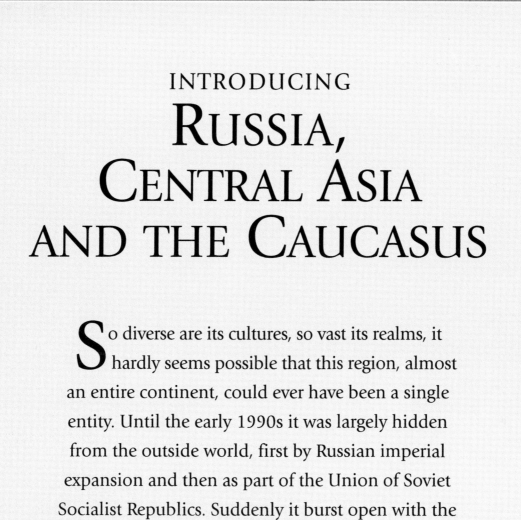

INTRODUCING
RUSSIA,
CENTRAL ASIA
AND THE CAUCASUS

So diverse are its cultures, so vast its realms, it hardly seems possible that this region, almost an entire continent, could ever have been a single entity. Until the early 1990s it was largely hidden from the outside world, first by Russian imperial expansion and then as part of the Union of Soviet Socialist Republics. Suddenly it burst open with the collapse of communism. Fifteen independent nations emerged from the rubble of the USSR. These new nations revealed an extraordinary mosaic of peoples, landscapes and cultures extending from the Baltic to the Pacific, from the Arctic to Afghanistan.

Young nations

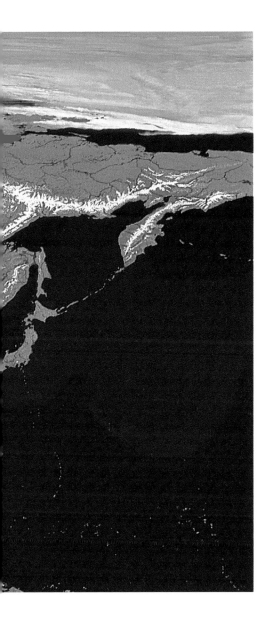

The Russian Federation is the largest and most dominant of the 15 nations born when the Soviet Union collapsed. Territorially, it constitutes only two-thirds the size of the old Union of Soviet Socialist Republics, and it remains the world's largest country at 6.5 million sq miles (17 million km²). It is almost twice the size of the next largest, Canada.

Russia's size defines its destiny, as its tsarist and Soviet rulers discovered. As soon as expansion started in the 16th century, the endless landscapes inspired a particular sort of development, based on the assumption that resources were inexhaustible. The exploitation of these vast domains went hand in hand with a tendency towards aggrandisement. Great construction projects – such as the growing of cotton on the semideserts of Uzbekistan or the ploughing of the Kazakh grasslands – served to express the power of the state. They also helped to redistribute a population weighted heavily towards the urbanised west at the expense of the sparsely inhabited wilds of Siberia. Without this drive to overcome the hideous extremes of climate and geography, the nation's assets would probably have remained untapped.

The Urals, the traditional frontier between European Russia and Siberia, and between Europe and Asia, were never a barrier to settlement. Their highest peak is Mt Narodnaya at only 6250 ft (1905 m). It is to the east that the real challenge lies, where climate and ecology combine to form three different types of wilderness. In the far north lies the treeless tundra, which tops the Eurasian landmass in a 2500 mile (4000 km) cap of permanently frozen subsoil (permafrost). Farther south, a swathe of forest, the taiga, gives way to grasslands so huge that the Russian word for them – steppe – has been adopted throughout Central Asia. Across this whole region, some 2000 miles (3500 km) from polar

A vast estate   In a composite satellite photograph, Russia and its former empire span almost half the Northern Hemisphere.

waste to its southern fringes, the brutal winters and brief summers allow little respite for agriculture. Almost all the great rivers flow northwards. Other than the Amur, no river offers an easy east-west route, and most of them are frozen solid for six months of the year. Only to the south-west of the Urals, in the dark, fertile soils of the Volga and Kuban rivers, is farming viable.

Uniquely among the world's great empires, Russia had no accessible oceanic coast lines. Northern seas are frozen for much of the year – over half the Arctic Ocean is Russian – and southerly coasts fringe inland seas. Of the many themes in Russian history, two stand out: the need for trade links by sea and the need for adequate defences on land.

In the early 18th century, St Petersburg was built as Peter the Great's 'window on the West'. In the 19th century, Russian foreign policy was dominated by the desire to lengthen its western border and the need for access to the Mediterranean through the old Ottoman Empire, via the Black Sea. These enduring concerns explain why, in the post-communist breakup, the independence of the Baltic States, with their long coastline bordering the West, and the Ukraine, with its Black Sea coastline, were seen as such heavy blows. The parallel obsession with a secure land frontier explains why the loss of Central Asian areas was such a threat – it reopened them to Russia's ancient foes, the Turks, and their Islamic neighbours.

Russia's 145 million citizens and the 137 million people of the ex-Soviet empire now face two of the greatest challenges in their history. The first is to prevent financial ruin, as they move from state-controlled to market-led economies. Second is the need to create and assert their national identities. After acting as conqueror and superpower for centuries, Russia is confronting the difficult task of renouncing dominion over its former vassals. Meanwhile, the young independent nations are striving to make independence work and maintain freedoms in the face of political extremism. This is no easy transition.

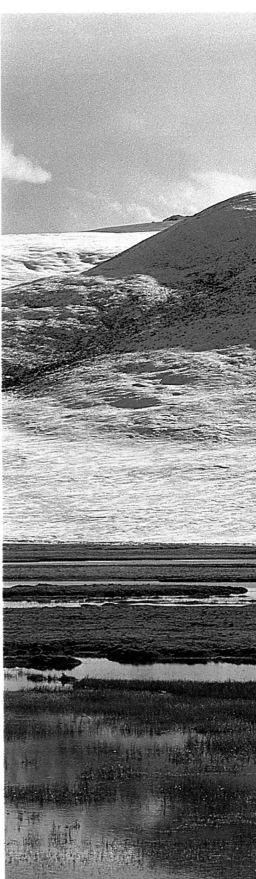

Walrus paradise *Wrangel Island, lying 100 miles (160 km) off Siberia's north-east coast, is a haven for seals, polar bears and walruses, and home for a few hardy zoologists. The island was claimed by Canada, until Russian settlers secured it in 1924.*

Ice-free zone *A frozen cape reaching into a clear sea reveals why the Baltic Sea is so vital to Russian interests. Russia's Baltic coastline is only 100 miles (160 km) – a mere fraction of the country's 5600 miles (9000 km) of ocean frontage – but it is ice-free almost all year round. Russian ships can sail from St Petersburg to the North Sea. In addition, they can use lakes, rivers and canals to cut north across the Kareliyan isthmus to the White Sea, also ice-free for six months of the year. Other canals lead southwards to the Volga and the Black Sea. Access to the Baltic has another advantage – Baltic herring is a popular food in Russia.*

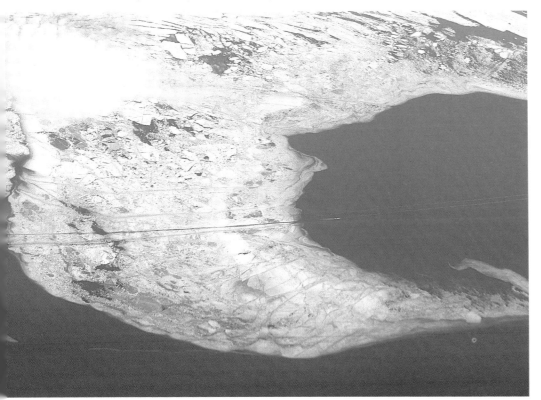

Southern heights *In Central Asia, grasslands and deserts extend to the plateaus and foothills of great mountain ranges – the Tien Shan, the Pamirs, the Karakorams. In Kazakhstan, Tajikistan, Kyrgyzstan and Uzbekistan, pastoral nomads still tend herds on the lower slopes.*

Disputed marvels These spectacular 'organ pipes' of basalt are on the Kuril Islands off Siberia's far eastern coast. The 56 islands have 100 volcanic peaks, of which 38 are active, making an unstable division between the Pacific and the Sea of Okhotsk. They run for 750 miles (1200 km) from the Kamchatka Peninsula across to the Japanese island of Hokkaido. Though chilly, foggy and subject to earthquakes, they have been the subject of an unending dispute. In the 18th century, Russia and Japan colonised the chain, and their inhabitants, the Ainu. By agreement, Japan took possession in 1875. On Japan's defeat in 1945, Russia seized them. Japan continues to demand their return.

Volcanic wonderland Geysers dot the Kamchatka Peninsula, which juts out from Russia's east coast for 750 miles (1200 km). Lying on a fault line, the peninsula is a geological showcase, with dozens of geysers, hot springs and mud volcanoes, all brought to boiling point by subterranean heat. Some 150 volcanoes, a third of them active, are dotted along two parallel mountain ranges.

A break in the desert The Red Canyon is one of the curiosities of Turkmenistan. Most of the country is flat desert, but in the far south, on the Afghan border, the little River Kushka flows northwards below cliffs that it cut into the desert floor millennia ago, when it was far larger.

Living sands *Two tortoises in Turkmenistan's Karakum ('Black Sands') prove the truth of an Uzbek proverb: 'The sun burns up everything but life.' Despite their seeming sterility, the deserts and semideserts of Central Asia have a wide variety of life: not only snakes, lizards, scorpions and spiders, but also mammals – antelope, long-eared hedgehogs and several species of rodent, which hide in deep burrows from the sun's heat and from predators.*

Salty wastes *Along the River Tedzhen in southern Turkmenistan, salt, scattered trees and saxauls stripe the landscape white, green and brown. Saxauls are little gnarled trees that can suck up moisture from deep below the surface. They give life to this arid land (75 per cent of Turkmenistan is desert). The salt is washed out of the Iranian and Afghan highlands to the south. Decades of attempted development and irrigation using the mineral-rich waters has resulted in ever-increasing deposits of salt, which are gradually poisoning the land.*

Desert crossing Camels are the only form of transport in the shifting sands of Uzbekistan's Kyzylkum ('Red Desert'). This desolate landscape covers two-thirds of the country, extending for 300 miles (480 km) between the Aral Sea and Tashkent. Uzbekistan and its once rich cities of Bukhara and Samarkand were crossroads on the great Silk Road from the east.

The roof of the world In the Pamirs an isolated Tajik village clings like lichen to a rocky foreshore. Tajikistan is 90 per cent mountains; the average altitude of the country is 11 500 ft (3500 m). The Pamirs is a young and angular range, spilling over into Afghanistan and China. It was born some 60 million years ago when India, then a separate continental plate, collided with Asia. The process continues, creating a convoluted landscape in which herdsmen raise goats and yaks amid the ravines and rushing rivers.

Rugged isolation *Tortuous ravines and dense forests keep the Georgian enclave of Abkhazia isolated from its neighbours in the Caucasian massif. The Caucasus forms a 750 mile long (1200 km) frontier between the Caspian and Black seas. At the Caspian in the east, it forms the Apsheron Peninsula. In the west, it follows the course of the River Kuban to the north-east coast of the Black Sea. Its granite and crystalline mountains include Europe's highest peak, Mt Elbrus, 18 510 ft (5642 m), and three others of more than 16 500 ft (5000 m) high: Dykh-Tau, Koshtan-Tau and Kazbek. The impenetrable landscape helped to forge the ferocious independence of its many peoples: Georgians, Chechens, Armenians and Azerbaijanis.*

Golden mountains *Deep in the Altai, the Katun and Biya rivers flow together into this lake to create the source of the Siberian giant, the Ob. The Altai Mountains fan out for 600 miles (1000 km) from Russia into Kazakhstan, China and Mongolia. Compared to their neighbours in the Tien Shan, the mountains of the Altai are modest, reaching no higher than Mt Belukha's 14 783 ft (4506 m). Steppe-lands extend up to 3300 ft (1000 m), where conifers and birches take over, giving way to high pastures. This knot of mountains, with their heavily eroded central plateaus, is the source of another great river, the Yenisey, which like the Ob flows northwards across Siberia to the Arctic. The Altai is rich in resources – its name in Mongol means 'possessing gold'. Other deposits include coal, zinc, lead, iron, copper and tin.*

Siberian treasures If there is one tree that symbolises Russia, it is the birch (berioza), a favourite subject for Russian artists. There are 12 species, which grow almost everywhere across the Northern Hemisphere, not only in temperate zones. The European birch is common in Siberian forests, the taiga, and even on the tundra, where few other trees grow. With its grey-white bark and silvery leaves, the birch has countless uses. The fine-textured grain of the wood makes it ideal for making furniture, floors, buildings and poles. From its bark peasants made shoes called 'lapti'. The sap, sometimes used to make a sort of wine, was also an ingredient in traditional folk remedies, and the raw material for the manufacture of a type of turpentine, known as 'Venetian turpentine', which turns into a rich brown resin when exposed to sunlight. Commonly used to preserve wood, the resin gives old Siberian buildings a characteristic burnished colour.

Vast resource *Coniferous forest, known by its Russian name 'taiga', spans the world's land masses between the tundra to the north and the steppe to the south. Through its spruces, firs and pines, and deciduous birches roam fur-bearing animals, reindeer and scattered populations of nomads. But deforestation in some areas threatens the region's ecology.*

Brief blooms *Like the American prairies, the Asian steppe, with its slight rainfall and poor soils, is the domain of grasses. The wind scatters pollen freely across this treeless expanse, creating a paradise for herbivores. After the spring rains, the steppe bursts into colour with a carpet of short-lived wild flowers, such as buttercups, anemones and poppies (pictured left). In summer, when midday temperatures reach more than 30°C (86°F), the flowers die and the grasses fade into a uniform mat of grey-green before the onset of winter. Then everything is frozen for six months.*

A brief history

Burial tent *A yurt-shaped Central Asian funerary urn in terracotta, 4th century BC.*

The eight states of Central Asia and the Caucasus have one feature in common: they owe their existence to Russia. In its three manifestations – tsarist, communist and post-communist – Russia has either annexed or, as today, maintained a close interest in its southern neighbours: Armenia, Azerbaijan, Georgia, Kazakhstan, Kyrgyzstan, Tajikistan, Turkmenistan and Uzbekistan. Together with Russia, they are now all members of the Commonwealth of Independent States formed in 1991.

Peace and turmoil

The Central Asian steppes, from the Caspian Sea to Mongolia, saw a succession of different empires and cultures, most of them created by the westward drift of nomads from eastern Asia. Independence was always temporary, depending on the ebb and flow of conquest.

The history of Central Asia has many gaps owing to a scarcity of written records. It was part of the Persian Achaemenid Empire in the 6th century BC, conquered by Alexander the Great in 329 BC, then ruled by the Greek Seleucids. In 247 BC the Seleucids fell to the Parthians, who created an independent kingdom on the eastern shores of the Caspian, expanding south into present-day Iran and Iraq. Bactria, a nation extending from the desert

Scythian gold

The Scythians were recorded by the Greek historian Herodotus. They migrated from Central Asia in the 8th to 7th centuries BC, but they remained a shadowy people until the Russians began to retrieve their works of art from graves in the 20th century. Mainly small-scale items made of wood, leather and metals, including gold, they reveal a fascination for animals: panthers, tigers, boars and horses. Stags were particularly popular, perhaps because they were symbols of power.

Animal magic *Scythian stag of wood, gold and copper.*

regions beyond the Aral Sea to north-west India, became independent. In the eastern and northern areas, nomadic tribesmen left their marks: the Scythians (8th century BC); Sarmatians (7th to 4th centuries BC); Kushans (from China, 2nd century BC to 3rd century AD); Huns (from Manchuria), ancestors of the Turks; and Mongols in the late 12th century. In the 16th century, Russia began its conquest, absorbing Central Asia in the 19th century.

Caucasian mosaic

The Armenians first settled in eastern Anatolia and the south-west Caucasus in the 7th century BC. They came from Asia Minor (today's Turkey) and inherited the

Secret histories *Toprak Kala, Uzbekistan, was part of the kingdom of Khorezm in the 3rd to 4th centuries. Other than these remains, virtually nothing is known of this period.*

Islamic wonder   The gem-like mausoleum of Bukhara's emir Ismail Samani (892-907) is one of the few buildings in Bukhara to survive the Turkish invasion in 999. It is made of clay bricks bound with egg-yolks and camels' milk.

ancient kingdom of Urartu, which controlled much of present-day Armenia, Georgia, Azerbaijan and eastern Turkey. On the borderlands of several empires, the region came under the influence of the Assyrians and the Medes, as well as steppe-land peoples such as the Parthians, who disputed the area with the Romans. A turning point came in about AD 300, when St Gregory, known as 'the Illuminator', converted Tiridates III to Christianity. After being fought over by the Persians and Constantinople's Greek rulers, the Caucasus fell to the Arabs in the 7th century and the Seljuk Turks in the 11th century. It experienced a brief renaissance under Georgia in the 12th century. Imperial rulers came and went: the Mongols, the Persians, the Turks again (now ruling in Constantinople). From the 17th century, the Russians advanced into the area in search of outlets to the Black Sea and the Mediterranean.

Russian origins

For many centuries, the great plain of eastern Europe was crisscrossed by numerous nomadic tribes, all wanderers from farther east. In the 6th century, the Slavs, an Indo-European people migrating westward, left behind the ancestors of the Russians. They settled, becoming slash-and-burn farmers. Those who settled on the Dniepr found they were on the 'River Road' that led from the North Sea to the Black Sea. Reborn as traders, they faced threats on three sides: from the Khazars of Central Asia, from Constantinople's Byzantine Empire and from the Varangians of Scandinavia, better known as the Vikings. Despite these ever-present threats, the Slavs never united. The monkish chronicler Nestor relates how in the 9th century the northern Slav princes agreed to call in a Swedish Varangian prince, Rurik, as their overlord. In Nestor's words: 'There was no law among them, but tribe rose against tribe ... They said to themselves, "Let us seek a prince who may rule over us and judge us according to the Law."'

Nestor's story may be a legend, but however it happened, around 860 Rurik established Novgorod, which was to form the core of the Russian state.

Founding father   The 9th-century Varangian prince Rurik is regarded as the founder of the first Russian state. His dynasty, the Rurikids, lasted until 1598.

Nomadic tapestry   The Scythians left numerous artefacts such as this felt hanging, 5th century BC.

The growth of the Kievan state

Rurik and his successors consolidated their hold on Slav lands while developing their trade links. Rurik's heir, Oleg, moved south to Kiev, which he declared should be the mother of Russian cities. But it was the coming of Christianity that provided the emergent empire with its cultural foundations. In 957, the formidable regent Olga had herself baptised in Constantinople. Her grandson, Vladimir, seeing the political benefits of conversion, had his people baptised *en masse*. From then on, Russia became Orthodox, deriving its rites, art and architecture from Byzantium. Vladimir left

Missionary brothers *In the 9th century, the Greek brothers Cyril and Methodius modified Greek script to record the Slavic tongue and convert the Slavs. This script evolved into the modern 'Cyrillic' alphabet.*

12 sons who fought bitterly over the succession. Yaroslav emerged victorious, and in a long reign (1019-54) imposed peace, codified laws, turned Kiev into a prestigious city and extended Russian rule to the Gulf of Finland. When he died, Kievan Russia was the largest kingdom in Europe, stretching from the Baltic to the Black Sea. But the unity that Yaroslav established proved fragile. He divided his realm between his five sons, ensuring intense dynastic feuding for the next two centuries.

The Tartar yoke

In this divided state, the Russians were no match for the menace that now swept out of the unknown regions beyond the eastern steppes. In 1223, the Mongols attacked. These warriors on horseback were like nothing the Russians – or any other European – had seen before. They were a devastating and pitiless fighting machine, and they swept across Russia like an avenging wind. An initial foray in 1223 was followed by an all-out assault in 1236-42. Ryazan, Moscow, Vladimir and Kiev all went up in smoke.

Settling in the open grassland of the lower Volga, the heirs of Genghis Khan established a kingdom that was known as the 'Golden Horde' (from the Mongol word for palace).

The heathen Mongols dominated Russia for the next 250 years, a period known as the 'Tartar yoke' (Tartar is another word for Mongol). For all that time, the Russian princes had to pay taxes to the Tartar khan. Meanwhile, the country was isolated from cultural developments in Western Europe – the Renaissance passed it by.

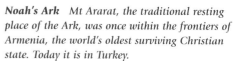

Noah's Ark *Mt Ararat, the traditional resting place of the Ark, was once within the frontiers of Armenia, the world's oldest surviving Christian state. Today it is in Turkey.*

The rise of Moscow

Moscow began to grow in importance in the early 14th century, despite an extended power struggle with the rival principality of Vladimir. In 1328, Ivan I – Ivan Kalita, or 'Moneybags' – unified the two, still under Tartar control. Fifty years later, the Muscovite prince Dmitry Donskoi engaged the Tartars at the momentous Battle of Kulikovo and – to his and everybody's astonishment – defeated them. The Mongols, it turned

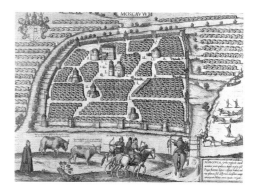

Walled city *In the 14th century Grand Prince Ivan Kalita ('Moneybags') fortified Moscow with stone walls and erected the first stone buildings.*

Moscow's expansion, 14th to 16th centuries.

Georgia's high point

Golden ruler *Queen Tamara of Georgia (centre) in a 12th-century mosaic.*

After six centuries of Arab rule, King David II, known as 'the Builder', reclaimed independence for Georgia in 1122. But it was Queen Tamara (1184-1213) who took Georgia to its zenith. With an empire stretching across the Caucasus, she presided over a golden age of prestige and artistic creativity.

out, were no longer unbeatable. Moscow became the centre of the Russian Church as well as the political heart of the growing state. The loss of Constantinople to the Turks in 1454 left Moscow as the pre-eminent Orthodox city – 'the third Rome'. A seal was set on its authority when Ivan III married Sophia, daughter of the last Byzantine emperor. In 1480, with the Tartars weakened by internal divisions, Ivan defeated both them and a new challenge from Lithuania. He secured other regions: Novgorod, Tver, Vyatka and Pskov. Nothing now seemed to stand in Moscow's way. Ivan IV (1533-84) turned Russian power eastwards, with the ruthlessness that gave him his nickname, Grozny – 'the Terrible'. He was

Fearful tsar Ivan the Terrible in a modern oil-and-collage portrait by Ilya Glazunov, 1989.

The Silk Road

The Silk Road is a term coined in the 1870s for the trade network that linked East and West since Roman times. After the Romans first saw silk in 53 BC, demand grew. It was made in the West from the 3rd century. Furs, ceramics and spices also moved westwards, in exchange for gems, ivory, glass and perfume. The routes led from Xian in China across 1875 miles (3000 km) of desert and mountain to the great market towns of Central Asia: Samarkand, Bukhara and Tashkent. The challenges and the potential profits inspired explorers such as Marco Polo. In the 15th century, new sea routes bypassed the Silk Road, but it still remains a lure for travellers.

Italian traveller Marco Polo, the 13th-century explorer, in Mongol robes.

the first ruler to name himself a tsar, from the Latin *caesar*. In the 1550s, he took Astrakhan and Kazan and advanced into Siberia. In the west, he waged war against Sweden and Poland, and concluded trade treaties with England. At home he imposed autocratic rule on local aristocrats, the boyars, banning the inheritance of land and the right to raise taxes. In his paranoid desire to crush all opposition he sentenced the entire population of Novgorod to death in 1570.

Time of troubles

In 1598, the death of the last Rurikid, Fyodor I, ushered in 20 years of strife known as the 'Time of Troubles'. The new

tsar was a boyar, Boris Godunov, rumoured to have killed Ivan the Terrible's heir, Dmitri. In the words of historian Bernard Pares: 'It seems that a band of hooligans entered the small town [Uglich] and dispatched Dmitri, whereupon the inhabitants rose in anger and killed the murderers. The regent Boris sent down one of his intimates, Kleshin, who was commonly supposed to have planned the murder, to investigate the matter. The investigators asked all the wrong questions, called none of the right witnesses, and declared that Dmitri had died in a fit of apoplexy by falling on a knife.'

The murder did not damage Godunov's ambitions. His fellow boyars voted him on to the throne. Though a talented ruler, he lived in fear of treachery and unrest, which was exacerbated by famines and foreign intrusions. The Poles invaded, backing a pretender, a 'False Dmitri' claiming to be Ivan's murdered heir. When Godunov died in 1605, Russia was left leaderless and defenceless. Smolensk fell to the Poles, Novgorod to the Swedes. By 1612, the Poles even occupied Moscow.

The coming of the Romanovs

In 1613, a new and lasting dynasty came to power, the Romanovs. Under the rule of Mikhail (1613-45), great nephew of Ivan the Terrible, and his son Alexei (1645-76), Russians enjoyed 50 years of peace. They

Alexander Nevsky: victory on ice

Alexander, prince of Novgorod, was a hero to the Russians. He secured the country's borders, first with his defeat of the Swedes on the River Neva in 1240, which won him an enduring nickname: Nevsky. Then, in 1242, he crushed the knights of the Teutonic Order, crusaders fighting to expand Prussia. His victory on frozen Lake Peipus became a symbol of resistance, immortalised in Eisenstein's 1939 film, *Alexander Nevsky* (below).

secured their frontiers with Sweden and Poland and looked to the West for specialist help in developing industry and training the army. As Russia began to look outwards, so foreigners came to settle in Moscow. Siberia, with all its riches, began to be opened up by colonists and explorers.

A tsar looks west

Alexei's spirit of openness paved the way for his son, Peter the Great. More than any of his predecessors, Peter I (1689-1725) determined to modernise his country. He was well suited to the task, with a fine build – 6 ft 6 in (2 m) tall – immense energy and a technical mind. In an unprecedented step he set off on a tour of Europe in 1697. Above all he wanted to study shipbuilding, as he knew that a modern navy would be the key to Russia's taking its place among the leading European nations. He sought out experts in

England and Holland and engaged craftsmen and military specialists to work in Russia. On his return, he crushed a rebellion by the murderous Streltsy (palace guard) with a ferocity worthy of his predecessor Ivan the Terrible. He then turned to his major task, war with Sweden. Having

Divine support In a painting of 1710, Peter I rules with angelic backing.

Armed bands Rebellious Cossacks led a peasants' revolt in the 1770s.

Successful dynasty As this commemorative poster shows, the Romanov dynasty lasted for 300 years. But in 1913, Romanov rule had only four more years to run.

wrested from Sweden a boggy mosquito-infested stretch of seaboard, Peter set about building his 'window on the West', the city of St Petersburg. The city became a showcase for Peter's modernising pro-Western projects: men were forced to shave their precious beards and go clean shaven in the Western style. A civil service, with a meritocratic system of ranks and promotions, was instituted.

Catherine II

The next ruler to take her country fully in hand – after an intervening period of 37 years and six monarchs – was Catherine II (1762-96). Of German origin, she was the wife of the ineffective Peter III, whom she deposed, and possibly

Cossacks in revolt

In 1773, Catherine II was threatened by an uprising of the Cossacks of the Don. It was led by Emelyan Pugachev, who claimed to be Peter III, the futile husband she had exiled, and perhaps had murdered in 1762. The peasants' revolt spread from east of the Volga, capturing town after town, until Pugachev's 30 000-strong rabble threatened Moscow. There, the mob, hungry for reform, delighted in the news that Pugachev had hanged 500 priests. Catherine's army stopped them. Pugachev was brought to Moscow in an iron cage; he was beheaded in Red Square in 1775.

Cossack hero Pugachev, the pretender and Cossack rebel, inspired Pushkin's novel, The Captain's Daughter (1836).

power base. Serfs became the property, in effect the slaves, of their masters, who had the right to banish them to Siberia.

Reform and repression

In contrast to his mother, Catherine's son, Paul I, ruled as a military dictator. He was assassinated in 1801. His son, Alexander I (1801-25) began his reign with promises of reform, working towards a constitutional monarchy. He made the first moves towards liberating the serfs. But these fine intentions were swamped by war

assassinated. Under her stern rule, Russia seized part of Poland and won access to the Black Sea across Crimea and Georgia.

Catherine was an odd mixture: she had taste, style and intelligence; she studied philosophy and natural history; she loved poetry and corresponded with Voltaire and Diderot; she also wrote a new law code, based on the work of the French philosopher Montesquieu. She founded hospitals and paved the way for primary education. Yet rebellion seethed around her. Despite her humanitarian interests, Catherine acted the authoritarian. A revolt by the Cossacks, under their leader Emelyan Pugachev (see box, left), was crushed. The discontented were sent to Siberia, notably to the mines of Nerchinsk. Peasant unrest was suppressed with the aid of the rising class of gentry, which supplied Catherine's

Favourite adviser Catherine's closest minister, Grigory Potemkin, played a crucial role in the conquest of the Crimea in 1783. As a reward for his services, he was made a prince.

Russian expansion, 1689-1900.

The Russian State in 1689
Territories annexed to the Russian Empire

- 1689 to 1800
- 1801 to 1815
- 1816 to 1860
- 1861 to 1900
- Territory acceded to Russia under the treaty of Aigun, 1858
- Vassal Khanates
- Extent of the Russian Empire in 1900

Doomed duchess In a 17th-century incident recalled by this 19th-century painting, an aristocratic Old Believer is carted off to a slow death by entombment.

The Old Believers

After the Time of Troubles in the early 17th century, the reforms brought in by Peter the Great included revisions to the Orthodox liturgy, backed by the Patriarch Nikon. Apparently minor points, such as a misspelling of the name of Jesus, and a dispute over whether to use two or three fingers when giving the blessing, aroused bitter controversy. Resistance by the so-called Old Believers (Raskolniki) was led by the Archpriest Petrovich Avvakum, who regarded Peter as the Antichrist. The dispute split the Church. Avvakum's followers were excommunicated, and he was finally burned at the stake in 1682. The Old Believers survived in many different sects, some of which still practise their faith in remote Siberian communities.

with Napoleonic France. In 1812 the French invaded, but Napoleon had misjudged both the resolve of the Russian people and the perils of the northern winter, which proved fatal for his troops. He was forced to retreat. Russia emerged victorious and in 1815, by the Treaty of Vienna, occupied the whole of Poland.

Alexander's death in 1825 sparked an attempted coup by the reforming Decembrists (see box, below). They were crushed by his successor, the reactionary Nicholas I (1825-55). Nicholas ruled through his bureaucrats and his political police, but secret societies kept liberal ideas alive.

Russia continued to press outwards. In Poland, an attempt at revolution in 1830-1 was put down, taking Russia to the borders of Germany, to the consternation

of Western powers. In Central Asia, Russian advances were driven by the need to offset British imperial expansion from India. In the south, Russian ambitions were blocked by the Anglo-French victory in the Crimea (1854-6).

The Tsar Liberator

Nicholas's son, Alexander II (1855-81), was a determined reformer. In 1861, in the wake of the disastrous defeat in Crimea, he took the historic decision to liberate Russia's 20 million serfs. Land was distributed through village communes. Schools and railways were built and provincial elected assemblies introduced.

In 1864 Alexander also reformed the legal system, but he blocked pressure from radicals for a constitution. Revolutionary groups were on the increase and several attempts were made on his life. In the 1870s one such group, the People's Will, sentenced Alexander to death. He was making plans to introduce a more liberal government

Freedom fighter In the Caucasian mountains, the priest-prince Shamil of Dagestan directs resistance against the advancing Russians. Russia's victory in 1859 opened the way for complete control of the Caucasus.

when, in 1881, a bomb was thrown at him in his carriage in St Petersburg. He died of his injuries.

An empire on ice

His son Alexander III (1881-94) turned with ever greater ruthlessness against radicalism. Reinforcing censorship and the secret police, he imposed Russian rule and persecuted his empire's ethnic and religious minorities (particularly the Jews of the Ukraine). At the same time, industry boomed, and new railways linked the new coal and iron fields. But in the appalling conditions, the growing proletariat of factory workers provided fertile soil for

The Decembrists

In 1816, young Russian officers, fired by French revolutionary ideals, set up a 'Society of Salvation' to fight for reform. Most wanted freedom for the serfs, some wanted a republic, others a liberal monarchy. The death of Alexander I in December 1825 provided them with the opportunity to stage a coup. Backed by 2000 rebels, they gathered in Senate Square, St Petersburg. Tsarist troops opened fire, killing 80 rebels. Their leaders were hanged or sent to Siberia. The coup collapsed, but the 'Decembrists' remained an inspiration to many subsequent revolutionaries.

Disastrous retreat After their failure to force Russia to capitulate, French troops struggle home through the bitter winter of 1812. Stragglers fell victim to Russian guerrillas.

Hypnotic monk Grigory Rasputin wielded influence through Empress Alexandra. He alone appeared able to control the bleeding of the haemophiliac Prince Alexei. Eventually, he vetted appointments and policies. He was assassinated by Prince Felix Yusupov in 1916.

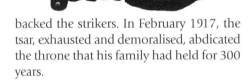

Vanished from history In a family portrait taken in 1906, Nicholas II and Alexandra pose with Olga, Tatiana and Maria (back row), while Anastasia holds hands with two-year-old Alexei (front row). The Bolsheviks murdered the family in Yekaterinburg in July 1918. Their bones were ceremoniously reburied in 2000.

revolutionary ideas. Alexander grew ever more isolated from his people, relying for advice on a moribund nobility and an all-powerful Church.

Nicholas II (1894-1917), who was an intelligent but weak man, continued along the same road, unable to prevent looming catastrophe. Although ranking fifth among the world's industrial powers, at home Russia was a social anachronism: 85 per cent of the population lived on the land, in primitive conditions, while a rich minority maintained themselves by dominating the poor majority.

The humiliating defeat of the Russian fleet by the Japanese at Tsushima in the Russo-Japanese War (1904-5) shocked the nation. Russia was supposedly a rival to other Western nations, yet she became the first European nation to be defeated by an Asian power since the days of Genghis Khan. Malcontents were further united by the regime's despotism and remoteness, symbolised by this stunning defeat.

The end of the tsars

In November 1904, Nicholas permitted a meeting of St Petersburg's *zemstvo* (district assembly), which made demands he had no intention of satisfying. On January 22, 1905, unarmed protesters who had gathered to call for reforms were brutally scattered, and 70 died in the skirmish. 'Bloody Sunday', as it was known, inspired many other protests: naval mutinies led to a general strike; workers formed councils (*soviets*) in St Petersburg and Moscow.

Forced to concede, Nicholas announced the creation of a Duma, an elected assembly. From 1906, collapse seemed to be checked by the prime minister, Peter Stolypin – but he was assassinated in 1911. With the royal family's isolation marked by reliance on the advice of an illiterate monk, Grigory Rasputin, events spun out of control.

Bound by a network of treaties to support Britain and France, and oppose Germany and Austria-Hungary, Russia entered the First World War. She was totally unprepared. Human and material losses were vast, reinforcements inadequate, desertion common. An estimated 1.7 million people died and almost 5 million were wounded in the three years of war. Soldiers called upon to suppress strikes backed the strikers. In February 1917, the tsar, exhausted and demoralised, abdicated the throne that his family had held for 300 years.

The October Revolution

The new Provisional Government was unable to tackle fundamental social problems and was at loggerheads with the soviet (workers' council) in St Petersburg. The exiled Bolshevik leader, Vladimir Ilyich Lenin, returned to Russia, aiming to turn

Medieval v. modern In Baku, Russia's main oil-producing centre, carters work at the oil derricks that made Russia a modern industrial power.

Humble thanks Serfs in St Petersburg kneel to Alexander II, who gave them their freedom in 1861.

Humiliation in the East

By 1903, the Trans-Siberian Railway gave Russia access to China, Manchuria and Korea, the independence of which was guaranteed by Japan. In 1904, Japan attacked. The loss of Port Arthur in China galvanised Russia into despatching a naval force, which was sunk by the Japanese in the Strait of Tsushima in May 1905. The blow to Russian pride was immense and the public reaction helped to spark the mini-revolution of 1905. Desperate to preserve its power, the regime redoubled repression at home, but by now the downfall of tsarist autocracy was perhaps inevitable.

the chaos to the advantage of his party. An attempted coup in the summer of 1917 failed. On October 25-26 the Bolsheviks struck.

They took control of the main government building, the Winter Palace, and seized other key points in and around Petrograd (St Petersburg). Alexander Kerensky, the leader of the provisional government, fled.

Inadequate response Two tsarist soldiers guard a St Petersburg strongpoint during the strikes of March 1917.

The Bolsheviks quickly seized control of the machinery of power, bullying the opposition parties into compliance.

Civil war

At once, lands and factories were nationalised and the Gregorian calendar was introduced, aligning Russian history with the rest of Europe's and shifting dates back two weeks. The Bolshevik government made a costly peace with the Germans (much to the fury of imperial Russia's Western allies), freeing Lenin's hand to deal with problems closer to home.

Within months, the Bolsheviks faced civil war with a broad coalition of anti-Bolsheviks backed by Britain and France. The struggle with the 'Whites' raged on several fronts – in the Crimea, the Ukraine, the Baltic, the Caucasus and Siberia. The Reds won, but at huge cost to the economy. Famine was widespread and in these terrible years, from 1918 to 1922, some 10 million people lost their lives.

Lenin's more liberal New Economic Policy of 1921 was a tactical retreat which allowed a market economy to grow for a while. His death in 1924 unleashed a fierce power struggle.

Lost leaders 'White' generals like these were never able to coordinate action against the Reds. The Cossack leader Anton Denikin, Nicholas Yudenitch in the Baltic and Admiral Alexander Kolchak in Siberia were among those who, with allied support, carved out their own brief empires, until they fled or were shot.

Spellbinding orator Vladimir Ilyich Ulyanov, better known by his revolutionary name of Lenin, harangues a Petrograd (St Petersburg) crowd during the summer build-up to the 1917 revolution. On his left stands Lev Trotsky, leader of the Petrograd soviet.

Heroes of industry

The Soviet economy depended crucially on industrial workers. In factories, the political leaders designated some people as 'shock workers': their task was to inspire the workforce to ever-higher production records. The archetype was a miner, Aleksei Stakhanov, who allegedly dug 102 tons of coal in one shift – 14 times in excess of his normal output.

'Stakhanovites' were honoured by having their portraits hung in a hall of fame. These heroes became propaganda stars, with holidays in the best Crimean hotels and access to shops reserved for the elite.

Hall of fame Collective farm heroes.

Rule through terror

Lenin left a triumvirate of rulers – Stalin, Kamenev and Zinoviev – among whom the General Secretary, Stalin, was the best placed to take power. Born Joseph Djugashvili, he was the son of a Georgian cobbler. He had not lived abroad, had little interest in political theory and was well schooled in conspiracy. But it was he who controlled

Farming revolution Happy agricultural workers call upon their countrymen to join the collective farms (kolkhozy). In reality, peasants were forced into collectives – whether they liked it or not.

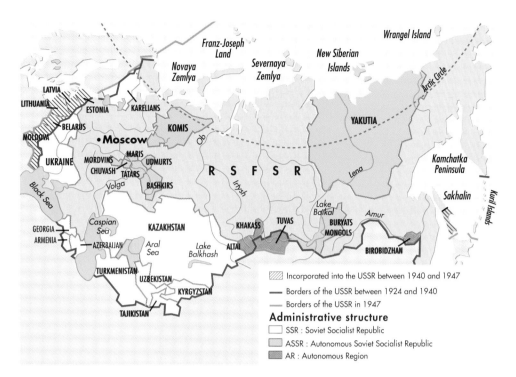

Franz-Joseph Land
Novaya Zemlya
Severnaya Zemlya
New Siberian Islands
Wrangel Island
Arctic Circle

LATVIA
LITHUANIA
ESTONIA
KARELIANS
BELARUS
MOLDOVA
•Moscow
KOMIS
YAKUTIA
UKRAINE
MORDVINS
MARIS
CHUVASH
TATARS
UDMURTS
Volga
BASHKIRS
Ob
Irtysh
Lena
R S F S R
Kamchatka Peninsula
Sakhalin
Kuril Islands
Black Sea
GEORGIA
ARMENIA
Caspian Sea
AZERBAIJAN
KAZAKHSTAN
Aral Sea
Lake Balkhash
KHAKASS
TUVAS
ALTAI
Lake Baikal
BURYATS
MONGOLS
Amur
BIROBIDZHAN
TURKMENISTAN
UZBEKISTAN
KYRGYZSTAN
TAJIKISTAN

Incorporated into the USSR between 1940 and 1947
Borders of the USSR between 1924 and 1940
Borders of the USSR in 1947
Administrative structure
SSR : Soviet Socialist Republic
ASSR : Autonomous Soviet Socialist Republic
AR : Autonomous Region

Forging the USSR

In 1918, the All-Russia Congress of Soviets proclaimed a republic of soviets, made up of deputies from the workers, soldiers and peasants. In July, Russia became the Russian Soviet Federated Socialist Republic. Other Soviet republics followed: Ukraine, Belorussia (Belarus), Transcaucasia. In 1922, these joined Russia to form a Union of Soviet Socialist Republics (USSR). Three Central Asian areas joined in the 1920s. By the 1924 Constitution, the republics were equal (although each ruled by its own party, controlled by Moscow). Foreign affairs, defence and economic planning were centrally controlled. Other minor changes were confirmed by the 1936 Constitution, which also split the Caucasus into Georgia, Armenia and Azerbaijan.

the key appointments. In 1927, Stalin sidelined 'Leftists', exiling Trotsky, the party's most authoritative figure. He then turned against the idea of international revolution to focus on 'socialism in one country'. He ended Lenin's New Economic Policy, with its toleration of private ownership.

A succession of five-year plans were introduced to develop heavy industry. Peasants were forced into collective farms and well-to-do farmers (*kulaks*) were criminalised. All opposition was brutally crushed. But from its low base, industry surged forward: output rose 20 per cent in 1929, and 38 per cent in 1930, with new industrial towns springing up in Siberia. By 1931, 60 per cent of land had been 'collectivised'. Education became universal.

When millions died

Astonishing progress came with astonishing cost. Collectivisation was bitterly resisted by the peasants, who believed that it meant taking back the land which the revolution had given to them. It resulted in famines in which millions died. Seeing enemies everywhere, Stalin purged a third of his million-strong party. Untold numbers – millions – were arrested and shot, or consigned to the gulag. On the eve of the

Red tsar Stalin (1879-1953), the Georgian who succeeded Lenin, set up a totalitarian system based on a compliant bureaucracy, ideological conformity and the ruthless use of terror.

Street fighting Soviet soldiers battle for Stalingrad, the turning point of the Second World War.

Second World War, 90 per cent of the Red Army's officer corps was purged and the country was paralysed by terror.

When Hitler launched 'Barbarossa', his invasion of Russia in June 1941 the Soviet Union was drawn into the Second World War. The human cost was greater than for any other country – more than 20 million lost their lives.

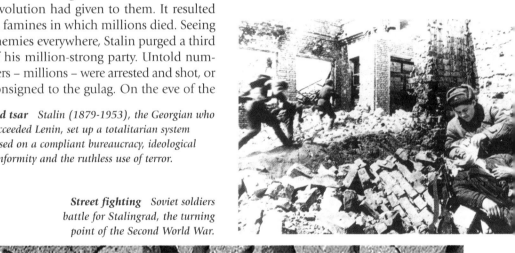

The Great Patriotic War

Stalin had not planned for war, and hoped to avoid it by signing a non-aggression pact with Hitler in 1939. But Hitler had no intention of sticking to it. When the Germans attacked on June 22, 1941, Stalin refused for several hours to believe that he had been duped. Then he turned patriot and demanded supreme sacrifices of his country, and the Russians responded. Bitter winter weather came to their aid, as it had done in 1812. The German advance faltered at Leningrad and at Moscow. In February 1943, the Soviet victory in Stalingrad, after six months of bitter street fighting, marked a turning point. From then on Hitler's armies were on the retreat. Two years later the USSR emerged as co-victor with her Western allies, but at a terrible cost. At least 20 million people had died, 1700 towns and 70 000 villages had been flattened and 40 000 miles (65 000 km) of railway track were destroyed. The scars would endure for decades.

Cold War and high hopes

In 1953, with Russia controlling an empire and dependencies of a size undreamed of by the tsars, Stalin died. Millions set aside his brutalities and recalled only his heroic stature. The whole country mourned as he was buried beside Lenin in the mausoleum in Red Square.

Yet three years later, at the 20th Party Congress, his successor, Nikita Khrushchev, delivered a bombshell: Stalin was a monster, he said, guilty of frightful crimes and ideological errors, most notably that of indulging in a cult of personality. Stalin's embalmed corpse was removed from Lenin's mausoleum and his name was erased from the streets and buildings.

Khrushchev promised a new world of technological advance, with the 'virgin lands'

Damning the past
In 1956, Nikita Khrushchev condemned Stalin's 'cult of personality' and opted for 'peaceful coexistence' with the West rather than world revolution.

of Kazakhstan feeding all, and the USSR beating the USA into space. From 1957, a series of 'firsts' in space – first satellite, first man in orbit, first unmanned lunar landing – symbolised the new era. The camps were opened and there was an end to arbitrary terror. But Khrushchev's thaw was no revolution. The 'virgin lands' turned to dust bowls, and in 1956 an uprising in Hungary was crushed with traditional ruthlessness. Khrushchev's ambitions reached a sudden and dramatic limit when in 1962 he was forced by the USA, under the threat of nuclear war, to remove missiles from Cuba. He fell from power in 1964.

The big freeze

After the brief thaw, the Soviet Union entered another ideological ice age, under the unimaginative rule of Leonid Brezhnev

Ice warrior For 18 years (1964-82), Leonid Brezhnev's frozen features symbolised a regime that was unable to escape from the social, political and economic shackles of centralisation.

(1906-82). The next two decades were years in which critics were criminalised, banned or incarcerated in psychiatric hospitals. The economy faltered: central planning fed a bureaucratic elite, not the people. In the wider Soviet empire, unrest came to a head with a revolution in Czechoslovakia; the 'Prague Spring' was crushed in August 1968 when the Red Army tanks rolled in. In 1979, the Soviet army invaded Afghanistan. This was, it seemed, an empire that could succeed only with force.

Reform and collapse

A thaw of a different kind started with the accession of Mikhail Gorbachev in 1985. On May 17, 1985, Gorbachev stood in the Smolny Institute, Leningrad, where Lenin had proclaimed the victory of Bolshevism

---

Afghanistan: the 'Soviet Vietnam'

In December 1979, Russian troops poured across the border into Afghanistan. The aim was to shore up the fragile Marxist government, ensuring Soviet influence in the Islamic world. It was the latest roll of the dice in the 'Great Game' which, over 150 years, had pitched Russia against the British Empire, and then the Soviet Union against the USA. It was an equivalent of the British invasion of Afghanistan in 1841 and the US involvement in Vietnam, and equally disastrous. A modern army once again proved no match for guerrillas. In 1989, Gorbachev pulled the troops out. Some 13 000 deaths and 35 000 wounded – not counting the unknown Afghan losses – left a fearful scar on Russian psyches and on national pride.

Retreating forces Russian troops pull out of the Afghan captial, Kabul, on May 16, 1988.

Assessing the Commonwealth

Springing from the ruins of the USSR in 1991, the 12-strong Commonwealth of Independent States includes all the old Soviet republics except the Baltic States. It consists of the three giants – Russia, the Ukraine and Belarus – together with the smaller Armenia, Azerbaijan, Georgia, Kazakhstan, Kyrgyzstan, Moldova, Uzbekistan, Tajikistan and Turkmenistan. Russia dominates the group. There is no centralised administration, but the aim of the Commonwealth is to coordinate economic and strategic policies. After a period of inactivity, the organisation has been revitalised by Putin, but it remains to be seen how successfully the large problems of inflation, racketeering and inter-ethnic conflicts are dealt with .

Caucasian mafiosi
Chechens are arrested in Moscow in 1999, when war between Russia and Chechnya resumed. The first war began in 1992 after Chechnya declared independence from the Russian Federation.

After the failed coup of August 1991 the Soviet Union itself fell apart. One by one, the republics broke away.

A new nightmare

But the euphoria of freedom soon gave way to sombre economic and political realities. Ethnic violence killed or displaced thousands in Azerbaijan, Armenia, Georgia, Tajikistan and Chechnya. In Russia, the market economy has been 'banditised': officials stripped their businesses and funnelled cash abroad; hyperinflation undermined jobs and income; production nosedived. Yeltsin's successor, Vladimir Putin, has been left with the task of restoring economic stability at home and confidence in his nation abroad.

Welcome visitor *Mikhail Gorbachev stands with USA President Ronald Reagan on a visit to New York. As the realist who unwillingly accepted the USSR's collapse, Gorbachev was understandably popular in the West.*

in 1917, and announced a new revolution: 'We must all change our attitudes, from the worker to the minister!' His reforms were to be based on policies summarised by two catchwords: *perestroika* (reconstruction) and *glasnost* (openness). Perestroika implied a radical shake-up of the economy, and also a war on beauracracy, corruption and vodka-driven absenteeism; glasnost meant that the press was free – within limits – to report on the failings of

the Soviet system and to make constructive suggestions.

The original intention was never to introduce a Western market economy, still less to abolish the socialist regime. But when, in 1990, the Communist Party relinquished its monopoly, and other parties were allowed to campaign for the newly empowered Congress of People's Deputies, reformers far more radical than Gorbachev himself seized their moment.

A leading 'democrat' was Boris Yeltsin, only recently promoted within the Communist Party by Gorbachev. He was elected president of the Russian Federation in June 1991, a couple of months before the USSR ceased to exist. As new master of the Kremlin, Yeltsin presided over the uncontrolled meltdown of the economy. The empire began to unravel, a collapse trumpeted in November 1989 when protesters smashed down the Berlin Wall.

Turning the clock back? *With the economy in perennial crisis, miners and communists join forces during a demonstration in Moscow in 1998.*

New ruler *In January 2000, Boris Yeltsin (right) ceded the premiership to Vladimir Putin, 20 years his junior. The former KGB officer faced two major tasks – to reassert the rule of law and negotiate or impose peace in Chechnya.*

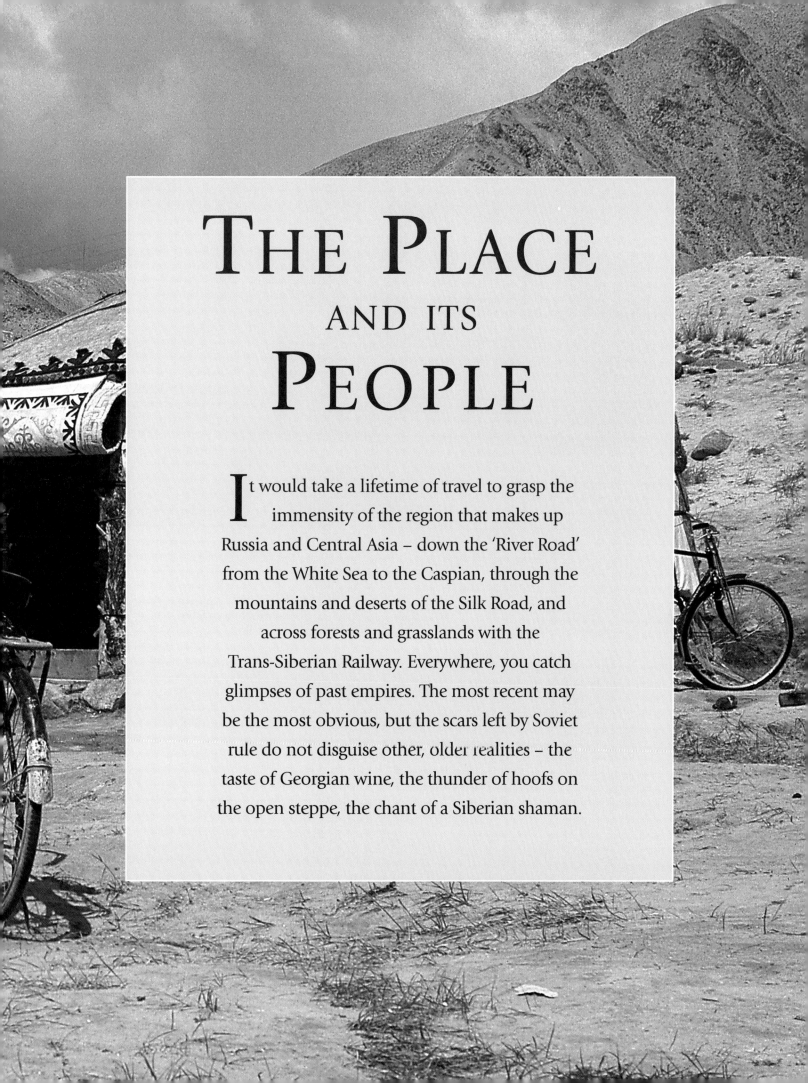

THE PLACE
AND ITS
PEOPLE

It would take a lifetime of travel to grasp the immensity of the region that makes up Russia and Central Asia – down the 'River Road' from the White Sea to the Caspian, through the mountains and deserts of the Silk Road, and across forests and grasslands with the Trans-Siberian Railway. Everywhere, you catch glimpses of past empires. The most recent may be the most obvious, but the scars left by Soviet rule do not disguise other, older realities – the taste of Georgian wine, the thunder of hoofs on the open steppe, the chant of a Siberian shaman.

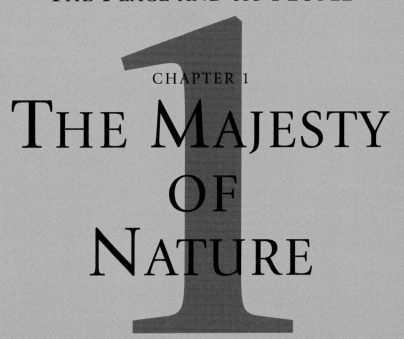

CHAPTER 1

THE MAJESTY OF NATURE

Beyond the smokestacks and oil fields of industrial Siberia, there is a different world – an untouched virgin wilderness protected by its size and remoteness. From the Arctic plains to the towering peaks of the Pamirs and Tien Shan, from the stunted ranges of the Urals to the forest fastnesses of Manchuria, these are the domains of a mass of rare animals. They include polar bears, brown bears, Siberian tigers and snow leopards, and Lake Baikal's unique freshwater seals. The tundra provides a summer playground for thousands of birds; the steppe blooms with spring flowers. Mighty rivers snake their way across the landscape. Soviet planners saw all this as a resource to be plundered. In the future, perhaps, it will be treasured for its own sake.

An early frost dusts a fire-ravaged field near Kazalinsk, Kazakhstan.

Baikal, Siberia's inland sea

Lake Baikal is a glorious crescent of water, 394 miles (635 km) long but only 30 miles (48 km) wide. It fills a 25 million-year-old rift in the Earth's crust, and it still echoes with the violence of its origins. Hot water springs gush from its bed and tremors often stir up its surface. No wonder the local Buryat people revere it as the domain of angry gods.

Baikal is the world's eighth largest lake by surface area, but it is the deepest and the greatest by volume. Three hundred and thirty-six rivers flow into it, but only one, the Angara, flows out. In theory, its waters should become too mineral-rich to sustain life; but its immense depth ensures stability – the water temperature remains at a steady 4°C (39°F) below 700 ft (200 m) – and supports a unique ecology.

Lake Baikal is often called 'the pearl of Siberia', and in summer, its surface reflects the blue sky like a jewel in a jade clasp. Its water is so clear that you can spot the glitter of a dropped coin at a depth of 130 ft (40 m). But Baikal's storms are notorious: as autumn draws on, winds lash the lake, beating its surface into oceanic waves. Then winter descends, locking the water under a thick carapace of ice. In the depth of winter, the frozen surface is easily strong enough to support the weight of a lorry.

The tourist economy

Lake Baikal's economy used to be dominated by the flow of trade goods between the two lines of the Trans-Siberian Railway, which touch its northern

Relict species The Baikal seal, the only freshwater species in the world, may have evolved after the lake's early link to the salty Arctic broke and its waters became fresh.

Ice fishing In winter, Baikal's fishermen cut holes in the ice and use horses to haul in their catch of local salmon.

34

Winter chill *Snow falls on Baikal from October. The lake is frozen from January to May.*

Baikal in profile

Lake Baikal is about 25 million years old – possibly the world's oldest lake. It has a surface area of 12 160 sq miles (31 500 km²) and its coastline is 1245 miles (2000 km) long. The lake is situated on an enormous north-south fault line in eastern Siberia and is more than a mile (1.6 km) deep. It holds some 5500 cu miles (31 500 km³) of water, equal to all the Great Lakes of North America, and amounting to one-fifth of the world's fresh water.

and southern points. It is busier in the south, where the two cities of Irkutsk and Ulan Ude provide markets. But 'busy' is a relative term: for city-dwellers, this is pristine wilderness, and nowadays tourism is a significant factor in the post-Soviet economy. Nature lovers come to admire mountains up to 8200 ft (2500 m) high, outcrops of bare rocks, sheer cliffs, and sandy or pebbly beaches that make good swimming spots in high summer.

A world of rarities

The animals are the greatest attraction: of the 1700 species recorded here, two-thirds are endemic, including the world's only fresh-water seal. One of the lake's 50 or so species of fish, the omul, has always been a prime resource. It belongs to the salmon family, and until recently made up half of the 100 000 tons fished from the lake every year. It is a popular delicacy with the local people. One family of fish have a particular claim to fame – the oil-fishes or golomyanka (*comephoridae*), which bear live young and have evolved a transparent body that makes them virtually invisible in the lake's clear waters. Giant sponges carpet the lake floor and

Beached on ice *A fishing vessel is frozen in place, while in the background a van is driven across the thick layer of ice.*

A world apart *Of Baikal's 18 substantial islands, the largest is Olkhon, which is big enough to include farms and a mountain which rises to 4186 ft (1268 m).*

armies of tiny algae-eating crayfish and shrimps ensure the lake's cleanliness – or did so until recently, when pollution began to threaten permanent change.

The threat of pollution

The pollution comes principally from the giant cellulose-making complexes of Baikalsk and it is intensified by the hydroelectric works on the River Angara. Biologists warn that if the factory is not closed, Baikal's delicate ecology will be damaged beyond repair. But no one has yet come up with a means of compensating the 3000 employees, or of purifying the environment.

Baikal's own people

The Buryat Mongols peopled the Baikal region long before the arrival of the Russians in the 17th century. The Buryats put up fierce resistance to Russian colonisation. Many of them retain their stockbreeding traditions, while some became lumbermen, and others man the factories of the capital of their republic, Ulan-Ude. Although their language and culture nearly died out in the Soviet era, Ulan-Ude has remained a centre of Buddhism and their faith has witnessed a revival in recent years.

Nomads no more *Many Buryats have moved away from traditional Mongolian gers (felt tents) and settled into wooden houses.*

The frozen, teeming northland

The most northerly point of the Eurasian landmass – indeed the most northerly piece of mainland anywhere – is the Taymyr Peninsula. This bare knob of tundra, apparently dead in winter, becomes vibrant with life in the brief summer.

Coping with cold *The Dolgan know how to protect themselves from cold that can freeze exposed skin in minutes.*

Here, between the mouths of the Yenisei and the Khatanga rivers, Siberia runs out into the Arctic Ocean. Beyond lies nothing but the ice-capped, uninhabitable islands of the Severnaya Zemlya Archipelago. On the coast itself, Cape Chelyuskin, at 77°45′ N, is the world's most northerly chunk of mainland, some 300 miles (500 km) beyond Canada's northernmost point. Across Taymyr's 156 000 sq miles (400 000 km²) – three times the size of England – live some 60 000 people, among them a few surviving indigenous Yakuts and Dolgans, who hunt and herd reindeer.

From icy waste to summer wonderland

The Taymyr Peninsula extends 700 miles (1100 km) north of the Arctic Circle. It looks like a frozen desert in winter, when blizzards snowblast the treeless waste. In the months of polar darkness, the only light comes from moon and stars, the dim glow of the sun below the horizon, and the occasional ghostly flickering of the aurora borealis (northern lights).

In summer, a brief two months in which the sun never sets, the landscape bursts into vibrant life. When the thermometer reaches 10°C (50°F), the frozen surface turns to mush, providing an ideal breeding-ground for mosquitoes. Ice ridges wrinkle the ground, and as the dips fill with meltwater, they form a honeycomb of polygonal pools. In a rug of mosses, herbs and grasses, small flowers glint blue and pink. Lake Taymyr reflects the blue sky, and the gentle slopes of the Byrranga Mountains edge the horizon. Salmon

Out of the freezer *At the approach of winter, Dolgan reindeer-herders head south with their felt-covered tents.*

Paradise for hunters

Protection for threatened species is hard to enforce in the huge expanses of Siberia. Trappers are free to go after rare creatures such as lynx and sable, much prized for its pelt. The two most endangered species – both protected – are the snow leopard of the southern Siberian mountains and the Siberian tiger. They are found in the Amur region in the far east. The Siberian tiger, the largest of all the big cats, weighs up to 880 lb (400 kg). A large male has been known to eat 120 lb (50 kg) of meat in a single meal. Hunters are advised to avoid polar bears, which can turn into man-eaters if they are wounded.

Wide-ranging hunter *The Siberian tiger may hunt over 4000 sq miles (10 000 km²).*

Arctic giant *A polar bear weighing half a ton stands 8 ft (2.4 m) tall when it rears up.*

and char swim up the rivers to breed. Polar bears and wolves track herds of wild reindeer. Walruses and seals play inshore, while farther out beluga whales feed.

Birds by the million

Near the town of Khatanga is a nature reserve covering 3.2 million acres (1.3 million ha). It was set up in 1993 to provide a secure home for 150 species of migratory birds. As the brief summer ends and the young mature, vast flocks take to the air, heading for Europe, southern Asia and even Africa. June skies are full of gulls, ducks and other smaller species. Some cover immense distances to reach the reserve: golden plovers arrive from the Pacific, swallows from South Africa. The Arctic tern has the most astonishing journey of all, wintering near the South Pole and then flying north for eight months to spend summer in the Taymyr.

Swimming birds are here *en masse*: white-beaked divers, white-feathered mergansers, swans, gulls, skuas, curlews and geese. Small waders nest near marshes and ponds, where they gorge on fish and insects. Some passerines, like the sparrow-sized snowbunting, nest right on the ground, at the risk of having their nestlings snatched by foxes or by birds of prey, such as buzzards, peregrine falcons or snowy owls. For self-protection, the ptarmigan, a permanent resident on the peninsula, moults from white in winter to brown in summer as a year-round camouflage – about the only trait that distinguishes it from its

White predator *Unlike other owls, the snowy owl nests on the ground and is active through the day.*

more southerly cousin, the grouse. But this is not a totally reliable defence, for the Arctic fox, with its small ears and blunt face, has evolved the same disguise, turning from grey in summer to white in winter (a changeover that produces the 'blue' fox fur much sought after by traders). The ptarmigan also have to beware of lynxes, which can snatch a low-flying bird out of the air.

The mammoth hunters

The permafrost makes an excellent deepfreeze, which has preserved the remains of mammoths since they became extinct around 12 000 years ago. As in other parts of Siberia, tusks and bones are often found eroded from their frozen graves. In 1898 a complete carcass was discovered on the River Berezovka. The local Dolgan, a group of mixed Tungus, Yakut and Russian origin, traditionally used mammoth ivory for their belt buckles and reindeer harnesses. Nowadays, the trade in ivory is banned, but a black market thrives.

Curving streams *The Taymyr Peninsula is crossed by rivers meandering northwards across the low-lying tundra.*

A world bound by rivers

Swollen by countless tributaries, subject to massive surges and forming vast floodplains, Russia's mighty rivers are its lifeblood. They meander for immense distances, linking the remote interior to the coasts and inland seas, providing vital transport and trade routes and a valuable source of energy.

Rivers were the thoroughfares for conquerors, explorers and traders as they penetrated deep into the heart of Russia and Central Asia. They were the natural sites for towns and formed important supply routes. Now their dams supply much of Russia's energy and their waters are tapped for irrigation.

The mother river

The Volga's progress across the country is never less than stately. Its gentle gradient of only 1.5 in per mile (6 cm per km) ensures a sluggish current that makes it easily navigable for its whole length – at least it does in summer, when its upper reaches are free of ice. Rising north-west of Moscow, at only 726 ft (220 m) above sea level, it flows to the Caspian 2300 miles (3700 km) away. It is Europe's longest river – almost 600 miles (1000 km) longer than the Danube.

The challenge for boatmen comes from its changing volume. In winter, it delivers 72 000 cu ft (2000 m³) per second; in spring, this flow increases 30-fold. On a single day, the river may rise by 33 ft (10 m). Even

before Ivan the Terrible secured it with a line of forts, the Volga was the main 'River Road' that linked Russia's central plains with the regions to the south.

Vikings used the Volga long before Russia existed as a state, making a bridge between Scandinavia and the Islamic world (some 85 000 Arabic coins have been found in Scandinavia). In the Soviet era, dams controlled its flow and canals turned it into a transcontinental waterway, from the Baltic and the White Sea south to the Caspian, and – through 13 huge locks that join it to the Don – to

Kolyma's gold

Though it is Russia's sixth longest river (1600 miles/2500 km), few had heard of the Kolyma until the 1930s, when gold was found. Magadan opened to the south and the area became infamous for its labour camps. The camps have gone, but the mining continues.

High water Swollen by melting snow and ice, the River Neva rises by 13 ft (4 m) in spring and inundates parts of St Petersburg.

the Black Sea. Compared to the Volga, the Dniepr seems a mere stream, but it is Europe's third-longest river (1437 miles/2300 km long). It rises near Smolensk and flows through Belarus and Ukraine to the Black Sea. Both the Don (1162 miles/1870 km) and the Pechora (1100 miles/1800 km) are longer than the Rhine.

The River Ural rises on the west side of the Ural Mountains, placing it in Europe, but empties into the Caspian Sea, 1560 miles (2500 km) away in Asia. Among Russia's Asian rivers, it ranks fifth; if counted as a European river, it is second only to the Volga.

River highway The Volga's width, length and placidity make it ideal for shipping. One-third of Russians live in its basin.

Radiation alert on the Yenisei

The River Yenisei has its sources in the mountains of Tuva, north of Mongolia. As it makes its way northwards, it steadily widens until it reaches the lowlands at Krasnoyarsk, the largest city on its banks. Here it is bridged by the Trans-Siberian Railway. Soviet planners constructed an immense dam here between 1956 and 1971. Since then, the Yenisei has backed up to form a lake 156 miles (250 km) long. They also built a nuclear power station, which discharged its plutonium-rich effluent straight back into the river with catastrophic effects for 1000 miles (1600 km)

downstream. Readings of riverbed contamination exceed those taken near Chernobyl in Ukraine after explosions at the nuclear plant in 1986. The Yenisei plant was closed in 1990, but the effects will endure for decades.

The Asian giants

There is no dispute, though, that the Western rivers pale by comparison with the titanic rivers of Siberia. The Ob-Irtysh – the two rivers are usually combined – is the fifth longest in the world and the second in Asia after the Yangtze. It runs for 3460 miles (5570 km) from the Altai Mountains north to the Arctic – and that excludes its drowned lower reaches, now a 500 mile (800 km) gulf. Wandering over the Siberian plains, it spreads into countless lakes and channels, joining up only 100 miles (160 km) from its mouth.

Many other Siberian rivers rank among Asia's top ten. The Yenisei, with its tributary the Angara, is more than 3000 miles (5000 km) long; the Amur and Lena are more than 2500 miles (4000 km) in length.

Historically, two of the greats are the Syr-Darya and Amu-Darya, which rise in the Pamirs and Tien Shan and water the Central Asian deserts. Now, though, they have been tamed by dams and irrigation. In its lower reaches, where it once fed the Aral Sea, the Amu-Darya is a trickle. The Aral is half its original size and has become a shrinking salt pan – one of the modern world's greatest ecological catastrophes.

Highland origins The Lena cuts through the mountains north of Lake Baikal, creating imposing rock formations, before emerging on to the Siberian plains.

The great Siberian forests

Half of Russia is covered by the band of forest known as taiga. Predominantly conifers and birches, it covers 2.5 million sq miles (6.5 million km²), extending from the Baltic to the Bering Strait, from the Arctic Circle to the central Siberian highlands north of Lake Baikal. Birds, bears and sable are among its wildlife.

Golden pelt *The sable of eastern Siberia is prized for its thick, soft fur.*

At first glance, especially from the air, the taiga seems inhospitable, mysterious, empty of people, immense and unvarying. Experience on the ground would allow you to put a tick against the first four, but make you query the last. Given enough time, the visitor will discover a vast range of sub-ecologies.

A universe of conifers

In the taiga's more temperate zones, silver birches and aspens predominate. To the north, where the more extreme cold (down to –30°C/–22°F) favours needles over leaves, conifers take over. These are mainly spruces and pines, with a scattering of deciduous birches, which shed their leaves in autumn. Even farther north, the forest begins to thin, forming the so-called sub-Arctic taiga, which in turn gives way to the treeless matting of the tundra. Only conifers can endure the extreme conditions on the fringes, where winter temperatures of –70°C (–94°F) have been recorded. The changes dictated by latitude combine with the effects of fires, which are a natural part of the ecology. In a world in which cold inhibits rotting, fires accelerate the return of carbon to the soil. In burnt areas, the first new shoots are those of aspen and birch. These areas are popular with animals – and researchers studying the region's wildlife – because the fires eliminate the normally ubiquitous swarms of mosquitoes for a year or so.

In the dim world beneath the canopy grows a range of totally different plants. In higher and drier areas, the floor cover is made up of fallen pine needles and lichens. Damp and low-lying spots – marshy hollows, peat bogs, lakes and river banks – encourage

Forest canopy *Mature taiga in central Siberia displays a range of tree species. Firs, spruces and pines are particularly resistant to the year-round dryness and the biting winters.*

Siberian beauty *The Bohemian (or boreal) waxwing, 7-8.5 in (18-21 cm) in length, has sleek and silky plumage. It lives on berries and buds.*

mosses and a great variety of shrubs and ground plants. These include the bearberry, crowberry and bilberry, as well as a host of other berry-carriers. They all provide food for the summer wildlife populations that stream up from the south.

Millions of birds

Despite the cold and the snow that covers the ground for up to eight months of the year, the taiga supports an astonishing range of wildlife.

Birds are everywhere, especially near flowing water and marshes. Here the bilberry bushes produce dark blue fruit, which is much sought-after in high summer by birds such as the hazel hen, bullfinch and waxwing. Waxwings sometimes gorge themselves on so many berries that they are unable to fly for a time.

Many of the species found here are the same as in temperate forests – eagle owls, sparrowhawks, magpies, thrushes, tits, chaffinches, goldfinches.

Others, such as pine grosbeaks, crossbills and nutcrackers, are adapted to the rigours of the climate, eating conifer seeds and cones. These birds have four-footed rivals for their food sources,

Forest and river   *The taiga, seen here touched with autumnal shades, is crisscrossed by rivers that are frozen solid for more than half the year.*

among them voles and several species of squirrel. The undergrowth is also home to a huge variety of rodents, which are prey for owls and bats.

Land of bears and reindeer

Like the birds, many of the taiga's mammals are common to temperate regions. The brown bear is one of the most important species. Among others that prowl and forage over the forest floor are lynx, deer, boar, wolves, hedgehogs, silver foxes, badgers, weasels, ermines, martens, sables, beavers and otters. Wolverines are particularly vicious predators. Despite being no more than 3 ft (1 m) long, they are capable of killing a young deer, or even driving a wolf or bear from a kill and gorging on the carcass.

Larger animals include moose and reindeer, which are the commonest of the mammals. Living off the white lichens that colonise clearings and undergrowth, they are found both in the wild and as domestic animals (unlike the North American caribou, which have never been domesticated). From their herds of reindeer, Siberians get fur, milk, leather and meat. The reindeer are also used as draught animals, pulling the sledges of country-dwellers.

The brown bear

Of the estimated 40 000 to 50 000 Eurasian brown bears, three-quarters live in Russia. The taiga suits the bear well. Foraging alone for berries and hunting small mammals, mature bears are the forest's biggest carnivore, weighing up to 440 lb (200 kg). They are no match, though, for a polar bear or an American grizzly. In the past, the only thing Siberia's bears had to fear was the hunter in pursuit of its meat, its fat and its skin. Now it faces another threat – deforestation, which with hunting has reduced the species by 50 per cent in the last 150 years and virtually eliminated the bear population in western Europe.

On top of the world

The sharp crests of the Pamirs and the Tien Shan straddle the borderlands between Tajikistan and Kazakhstan to the west and the Chinese province of Xinjiang. Punctuated with glacial ravines, lakes and plateaus, these bitter, windswept peaks range up to 23 000 ft (7000 m). Little inhabits this barren landscape where even the lake-side sand dunes are frozen.

Griffon vulture

The Pamirs and the Tien Shan owe their height to the forces unleashed by a titanic collision of continental plates. Some 60 million years ago, India, shifting northwards, began to drive into Asia. Across a vast zone, rocks buckled, thrusting downwards and upwards. The Tibetan plateau rose by about 2 miles (3 km), and waves of mountains rolled up and out, forming today's mighty ranges: the Himalayas, the Hindu Kush, the Karakorams, the Tien Shan and the Pamirs.

Sculpting the landscape

The process continues, as earthquakes testify, and the changes are mixed with those imposed by climate: the grinding of glaciers; the steady erosion of rain and frost; the effects of silt-laden rivers. In the

Ancient tracks   A camel caravan crosses a valley in the Tien Shan, following one of the old Silk Road routes.

Warmly clad   *Though mostly domesticated, yaks sometimes roam wild, protected from the cold by their multilayered coats.*

Pamirs alone, there are more than 1000 glaciers covering 3000 sq miles (8000 km²). The Fedchenko in Tajikistan, one of the longest glaciers in the world, stretches for 43 miles (70 km). It is fed by ice from two huge mountains with names that recall a vanished time – Revolution Peak and Communism Peak.

On the plateaus above 11 550 ft (3500 m), the eternal cold and rarefied air place severe limits on life. Marco Polo rode this route in 1272. 'You ride across it for 12 days together,' he recorded, 'finding nothing but a desert without habitations or any green thing, so that travellers are obliged to carry with them whatever they have

High and mighty The Tien Shan's highest peak, Pobedy (Victory) overlooks Kyrgyzstan, Kazakhstan and China.

need of. The region is so lofty and cold that you do not even see birds flying.' In Soviet times, this desolation of rocks, moraines and ice was out of bounds. Today, hardy travellers can reach spots virtually unknown to outsiders, such as the frozen sand dunes that surround Lake Kara-Kol, the Black Lake, the world's highest at almost 13 000 ft (3915 m), created by a meteorite impact some 10 million years ago.

The Tien Shan, too, holds many surprises, such as Lake Ysyk-Kol, the world's largest mountain lake (2400 sq miles/6200 km²). Nearby mountains include Victory Peak (Pik Pobedy) and Khan Tengri, the second highest in the former USSR. Constantly replenished from glaciers, its level is readjusted by evaporation, which forms a localised climate of rain and snow-clouds.

Wild sheep Marco Polo's argali is noted both for its size (up to 330 lb/150 kg) and its horns, which may reach 6 ft (1.8 m).

Highland landscape Lakes punctuate the stark ranges of Central Asia.

Exploring the peaks

For centuries the Pamirs and the Tien Shan were totally unknown, except to the people who lived there, to a few Buddhist monks and to the Silk Road merchants. Only in the late 19th century, when Russian and British explorers penetrated the region, was detailed information gathered. In 1871, the Russian Alexei Fedchenko crossed the Alai Range on the borders of Kyrgyzstan and Tajikistan, giving his name to one of the world's longest glaciers. British expeditions followed in 1874, followed by the Swedish explorer Sven Hedin and George Nathaniel Curzon, later viceroy of India, in the mid 1890s. The Tien Shan was equally resistant: the Russian Peter Semyonov was the first European explorer in the area, in 1857. He led an expedition to the base of Khan Tengri ('King of the Sky'), which at 20 989 ft (6398 m) was thought to be the range's highest peak, until in 1943 a Soviet expedition found Pik Pobedy – Victory Peak – (24 406 ft/ 7439 m), naming it after the Russian victory over the Germans at Stalingrad.

Of birds and animals

Lower down, the meltwater brings fertility. The birches and firs that grow at 6500–9500 ft (2000–3000 m) give way to larches and ashes at 5000 ft (1500 m). Copses shelter numerous birds: ibises, bar-headed geese, Asian and long-tailed tits – as well as the predatory species such as the griffon vulture, which can soar above the highest peaks.

Mammals most commonly seen in summer are the marmots, but they hibernate for the winter months in deep burrows. Yaks are well adapted to survive

Upward thrust Movement below ground created the jagged Pamirs.

in the open all year round. They can be found in every village, carrying people, transporting goods and providing meat, milk, wool and leather. Persian gazelles and argali, the local wild sheep, migrate up into the mountains at the onset of summer, providing easy prey for the snow leopard.

The barren tundra

It sits like a cap on top of the Eurasia landmass. The tundra is a bitter and desolate wilderness reaching from the tree line north to the Arctic Ocean. The intense cold and the long nights of winter limit the opportunities for life, but mosses, lichens and fish survive in this impoverished ecology. Humans, too, have adapted to the extremes.

Giant estuary   The Lena's shallow delta is 11 500 sq miles (30 000 km²) of honeycombed tundra and sandbars.

Where the trees end, the tundra begins, running north for up to 400 miles (650 km) before it reaches the Arctic Ocean. But this is a vague zone, ill-defined in the south by a straggling transition from stunted larches and spruces to mosses, lichens and a scattering of dwarf shrubs – willows, birches and heathers.

Moulded by cold

It is the temperature that sets the rules for life on the tundra. The year-round average is about –10°C (14°F), but this disguises a range from –40°C (–40°F) in winter (which can drop much lower in a high wind) to 10°C (50°F) in July. The three months of summer are not enough to thaw more than the top few inches of soil. Below that is the permafrost, a solid foundation reaching down to some 300 ft (100 m) – and often much more. Even if trees could adapt to the tundra's cold, their roots could not penetrate far enough to support them. In summer, the melting surface cannot drain, and turns to a mush of bogs and marshes. The regular freezing and thawing, and the constant presence of ice just beneath the surface creates peculiar effects. Water forms puddles, at the

The northern lights

During the winter months, the Arctic seas freeze solid and the hours of daylight dwindle to nothing. At this time a ghostly glow may come from the aurora borealis (northern lights). The effect is made when solar particles dive along the Earth's lines of magnetism and interact with the upper atmosphere, creating electrical discharges that flicker yellow and green. The curtains of light are 1.8 miles (3 km) wide

and 300 miles (500 km) high, with their lower borders at a height of about 60 miles (100 km).

edges of which it merges into ice, and refreezes. As water expands when it freezes, the process creates ridges and bumps. In some areas the whole landscape develops into a latticework of puddles and ridges, ranging from 1 ft (30 cm) across up to 300 ft (100 m). In marshy areas, the frozen water accumulates into 'pingos', ice-domes that may rise to a height of more than 200 ft (70 m), and dot the landscape like little mountains.

Reindeer, wolves and nomads

There is little to sustain large animals in this sparse land. On the true tundra, only reindeer can scrape a living, eating marsh plants and the lichen that is commonly known as 'reindeer moss'. The reindeer live in herds and migrate with the seasons, often attracting the attention of wolves.

The 300 000 nomads of the tundra – the Tungus, Lamuts, Yakuts and Nentsy (or Samoyed) – usually live off herds of a 100 or so reindeer, though the Nentsy may handle up to 1000. All share a similar way of life that follows a seasonal pattern: in the summer they settle on the coast to fish and in the winter they retreat southwards on sledges to the edge of the taiga, where the forest provides forage.

The most populous of the northern nomads are the Yakuts. Migrating from the Lake Baikal region in historical times, they assimilated other, smaller groups, such as the Tungus and Yukaghir. Most of them live in the taiga, but some herd reindeer on the tundra, using tepee-like tents of skin and birch bark during migrations.

Blurred borderland On the divide between taiga and tundra, stunted trees give way to mosses, lichens and low bushes.

The rise and fall of industry

The Soviets began to take a close interest in these remote regions when Stalin decided to shift the nation's industrial bases eastwards, out of the reach of Nazi Germany. They were aware of Siberia's immense deposits of coal and minerals – Yakutia in particular is rich in platinum and diamonds – and wood was in plentiful supply. Investment poured in under Stalin and river and coastal forts sprouted factories. Siberia's population, only 6.5 million in 1920, had increased to 30 million, mostly concentrated in towns, when the Soviet Union collapsed in 1991.

In the late 20th century, development shuddered to a halt, then reversed. Workers, often unpaid, were left to tend antiquated, underfunded industrial complexes. Assets were sold off by former Soviet officials eager to obtain dollars. Many people fled, leaving remote communities struggling to survive without any means of employment.

Arctic predator When driven by hunger, the wolf becomes a ruthless hunter, preying on reindeer roaming the tundra.

Nomad campsite In north western Siberia, tents and sledges mark a stopover during a seasonal migration of the Nentsy people.

The coldest town on Earth

Verkhoyansk, 80 miles (130 km) north of the Arctic Circle in eastern Siberia, is no place for holidays. This little mining community of 2000 people is the coldest town on Earth. Its record is -67.7°C (-89.9°F), recorded on February 5 to 7, 1892 (matched later by the outpost of Oymyakon in 1933). The local Yakuts, like the Inuit of northern Canada, are proficient at keeping out the cold by the expert use of furs and tepees.

Survival expert A Yakut, one of the 236 000 who form Siberia's largest ethnic group.

Destruction from below

Moulded by stupendous tectonic forces, the Asian continent is still subject to the Earth movements that first raised its mountains. From Kazakhstan to the Pacific coast, few places are free of the grumble of a coming earthquake, the sight of rippling roads, and the effects of shattered buildings and infrastructure.

Homeless   *Earthquake victims, 1988.*

For the past century, the region once covered by the Soviet Union has endured two major seismic disasters every year on average. One of the worst quakes of recent years occurred in Armenia in 1988. It was centred on the town of Spitak. Most of the residents were killed as the buildings collapsed on top of them. Since the quake hit mid-morning, nearly all the children of Spitak died in their classrooms. This natural catastrophe came at the end of a terrible year for Armenia: in March there had been appalling outbreaks of ethnic violence against Armenians in Azerbaijan (and also against Azeris in Armenia) and ethnic war was brewing between the two Soviet republics.

Desperate search   *After Armenia's quake, survivors search notices asking for help to trace relatives lost in the ruins.*

But the immediate reaction to the earthquake was sympathetic and humanitarian. Gorbachev launched a desperate rescue effort, and aid poured in from the West. As the dust settled it became clear that the high human toll of the earthquake – 25 000 dead, 30 000 injured, half a million homeless – was due, in part, to poor construction made worse by corruption in the Soviet building industry.

Tashkent, the capital of Uzbekistan, was devastated by an earthquake in 1966, when the local geological fault, the Talasso-Fergana, slipped. Half the city was shattered, leaving 300 000 homeless. But its story of reconstruction was very different from that of Armenia 22 years later. Tashkent was an ancient Muslim city of 70 000 when the

Miraculous find   *A girl is carried out of ruins in Leninakan, Armenia.*

Measuring quakes

Seismologists use two scales to measure earthquake tremors. The first, devised in 1902 by the Italian geologist Giuseppe Mercalli, grades earthquakes on a 12-point scale of destruction, from 'not felt' to 'damage total'. The scale was modified in 1931, but remains problematical because it is subjective. A more objective scale, which is in common use, was devised by American seismologist Charles Richter in 1935. His 10-point scale measures magnitude as recorded by a seismograph. In what is known as a logorithmic progression, each point on the scale represents a tenfold increase in energy. So far no earthquake has reached 10: the most powerful ever recorded was 8.6 (Alaska,1964).

Russians seized it in 1865. In the 20th century, industrialisation boosted the population to half a million. Wartime evacuation of the Soviet Union's western industries further increased the population. At the time of the earthquake 2 million people lived in Tashkent. In a supreme effort, all the Soviet empire rallied to help

Lone survivor   A single apartment block stands largely undamaged amid houses shattered in Sakhalin, off the east coast of Russia, after an earthquake in 1995.

in the rebuilding. Each republic took responsibility for an area. Their efforts are reflected in the names of today's suburbs – for example, the Kiev, Riga and Ashkhabad districts.

Reading the warning signs

Russian researchers analyse statistics, the Greeks focus on sub-surface electrical anomalies and the Chinese observe the behaviour of snakes, but no one has been able to come up with a fail-safe method to predict earthquakes. While anecdotal evidence does indeed suggest that animals sense impending catastrophe, scientists prefer to search for more reliable indications of an impending quake. Warnings may come from tiny pre-quakes, or from changes in rock structure that hint at a build-up of subterranean pressure. Lasers and magnetometers can record what is happening, but to date no reliable prediction has been made in time to save lives.

A checklist of catastrophes

These are just two catastrophes of recent years, but there have been many others. Ashkhabad, Turkmenistan's capital, suffered earthquakes in 1893, 1895 and 1929, finally falling victim to a massive earthquake in 1948, which killed 11 000 and levelled most of the city. Kamchatka had severe shocks in 1954, 1984, 1987 and 1997. Almaty, or Alma-Ata, as it used to be, was all but flattened in 1887 and 1911, and suffered badly again in 1956. In 1995 the northern region of Sakhalin island was shaken, destroying the town of Neftegorsk.

Relief operation   When an earthquake hit the Armenian town of Spitak in 1988, international aid workers set up a relief operation.

Still standing   A cast-iron Lenin contemplates the ruins of Neftegorsk, northern Sakhalin, after the 1995 earthquake.

The challenge of the steppe

The steppe is a vast belt of open grassland which extends from the Black Sea to Manchuria. For centuries it was home to fiecely independent nomads and their livestock, and a westward route for migrating tribes and Mongol invaders. The nomads may have settled in towns, but the steppe has not lost its character.

Grassland grazer The saiga antelope, once common on the steppe, is now a rarity.

Grassland herding is a specialised and demanding life, which breeds toughness and rugged independence. It also breeds a love-hate relationship with settled culture. Nomads cannot afford to be burdened with material goods, but they like the benefits of urban life.

Nomad conquests

Historically, rivalries kept nomads in small groups, but when a great leader arose, they would burst out of their homelands and override settled peoples from China to Europe. The Turks were Central Asians who drifted west in this way, and the Mongols left the marks of Ghengis Khan's empire across Eurasia. The rise of nation-states put an end

Key to the steppe A herd of horses skirts a river in eastern Kazakhstan. Soon after the horse was domesticated in about 2000 BC, pastoral nomads developed methods of exploiting the grassland, which was of no use to traditional farmers.

Dairy-based economy Milk from mares and other domestic animals is used to make 'milk beer', yogurts and curds.

to nomad conquests, and the steppes and its peoples were tamed.

But the steppe's ecology remains intact in many places, particularly in Kazakhstan, a nation the size of all western Europe. Here 90 per cent of the country is grassland. To outsiders, some of the border areas in Uzbekistan and Turkmenistan may appear barren, but the animals of the steppe are accustomed to grazing over what looks like desert, as long as it supports a scattering of grasses and bushes.

Extreme conditions

The steppe is high and dry and far from the moderating effects of any ocean. Temperatures may rise to 40°C (104°F) in summer, and drop below –40°C (–40°F) in winter. Once the snow melts in April and May, the grass forms a carpet of green dotted with wild

Rich pickings In a Turkmenistan cotton field, women tend a new crop. Irrigation and hot summers make for perfect conditions for cotton, but in the long run soil fertility is at risk.

flowers such as irises, peonies and bellflowers. In the height of summer, under clear skies, cattle and horses grow thin as the grasses begin to wilt and turn brown.

Exploiting the virgin lands

Today, in the former Soviet empire, nomads are rare. Like all settled cultures, the Russians despised and feared nomads, and saw in the steppes the potential for development. Wells were drilled, canals built, crops planted, and nomads were turned into farm workers. In Tajikistan, Uzbekistan and Turkmenistan, 7.5 million acres (3 million ha) of land were turned over to cotton production and cattle fodder on Stalin's orders, while 1.2 million acres (0.5 million ha) raised tobacco, fruits and vegetables. Azeris, on the Caspian's barren shore, grew grapes. In Kazakhstan, under Khrushchev's grandiose scheme for the so-called 'virgin lands', 62 million acres (25 million ha) became wheat fields.

New pastures A Kazakh herdsman leads a mare and foal back home.

These schemes worked, for a time. In 1927, the USSR imported 41 per cent of its cotton, and five years later only 2.6 per cent. But long-term returns proved illusory. The prairies of Kazakhstan turned to dust. To irrigate the cotton fields of Uzbekistan took so much water from the Amu Darya and Syr Darya that they bled to death. The Aral Sea shrank and is now less than half its original size, leaving behind a salty wilderness. Draining the water tables beneath the

Springtime carpet Flowers merge with grasses to form part of Kazakhstan's 1 million sq miles (2.5 million km²) of steppe.

steppes has caused irreparable chemical changes to the soil. It seems likely that much of the steppes and their desert borderlands will one day simply revert to their pre-industrial state.

Animals seen and unseen

Yet in untouched areas, the steppe retains its original wildlife, predominantly rodents such as ground squirrels, marmots, voles, hares and mice. Most of them live in colonies and burrow to escape the cold, the heat and predators such as foxes, polecats, martens, buzzards and falcons.

Larger mammals are fewer in number, but easier to see. Gazelles are the commonest, particularly the Persian gazelle, which can reach a speed of almost 30 mph (50 km/h). The saiga antelope, under threat because its horns are valued in Chinese medicine, still survives in some areas. Two-humped Bactrian camels are widely used as domestic animals, but their wild cousins survive only in remote spots in Mongolia and China.

Ships for seas of grass and sand

The two-humped or Bactrian camel is perfectly equipped for both the steppe and semidesert. Its thick coat protects it from the rigours of winter. In spring it moults, providing its owners with wool that has for centuries been vital for clothing and blankets and as an item of trade. The camel can survive for long periods without water, storing up to 20 gallons (100 litres) at a time in the fat of its humps. It can live off thorn bushes and saline plants. It is even able to close its sphincter and nostrils, both to conserve humidity and to protect itself from dust storms. It also makes an extraordinary range of noises, which include stomach rumbles and groans that carry across the grasslands like foghorns.

CHAPTER 2

PEOPLE AND RESOURCES

The end of the Soviet Union was a seismic political event that brought the whole economy tumbling down. The system that had promoted itself as an alternative to capitalism was now revealed as bankrupt. Without effective institutions and laws, the switch to a market economy was brutal. Production and purchasing power plummeted, while the loss of wages created an economy based either on barter or Mafia-controlled criminality. In 1995, Russia ranked 11th in the world by GNP, but 61st in terms of productivity per person. One-third of the population now lives in abject poverty. However, the picture is not one of total gloom. Russia is among the world's top ten countries in the production of natural gas, petroleum, coal, aluminium, iron, copper, nickel, platinum, palladium and diamonds – a bounty that could yet be the salvation of the whole region.

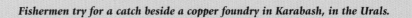

Fishermen try for a catch beside a copper foundry in Karabash, in the Urals.

Siberia's empire of gas

The conquest of western Siberia's frozen wastes continues, thanks to its rich supplies of gas. The Yamalo-Nenets district, lying between the northern Urals and the lower Yenisei, has been turned into a corporate empire by Russia's national gas company, Gazprom.

Final link *Completing a 62 000 mile gas pipeline.*

Resting on the frozen ground of the Yamal Peninsula, huts mark the track of one of Gazprom's next big advances. Beneath the tundra, where the Nenets still pasture their reindeer, stretches a promising deposit of natural gas. In 2010, if all goes to plan, the gas will start to flow along a pipeline via Minsk to Berlin.

An extended empire

Exploitation has steadily advanced northwards since the 1960s, when oil was first discovered in the Ob basin. In its wake came pipelines, derricks and roads, all built under the most extreme conditions. Whole towns sprang into existence: Novy Urengoy, Nadym, and finally Yamburg at the mouth of the River Taz. Now 23 000 people, attracted by high wages, work in this city 125 miles (200 km) north of the Arctic Circle. The place belongs entirely to Gazprom, and no one is allowed in without permission.

Oil-tank houses *Gazprom workers living in temporary accommodation.*

The other gas giant

Gas is the main resource of Turkmenistan. Its reserves bordering the Caspian Sea are estimated at 2000 cu miles (8000 km³), the world's fourth largest oil field. The problem is transport. A pipeline runs into Iran, but Western nations have vetoed an extension. Turkmenistan has had to depend on the Russian pipeline to Europe, which has been problematic. Seen as a competitor, Gazprom imposed limits and in 1997 a dispute led to Turkemistan being denied access to the system. However since 1999, exports have increased greatly.

The Gazprom monopoly

Gazprom, the child of the old Ministry of Gas, was privatised in 1991. As a commercial company it came into being with a monopoly on extracting, processing and selling natural gas. Since Russia has around one-quarter of the world's natural gas reserves and is responsible for 28 per cent of the world's gas production, Gazprom's potential could be enormous. The same goes for the power of its directors – the *gazparatchiks*. One of their number,

High-rise *Gazprom's headquarters dominates its section of Moscow.*

Viktor Chernomyrdin, was prime minister under Yeltsin. His successor at Gazprom, Rem Vyakhirev, is among the richest men in the world, according to the business magazine *Forbes*.

A company with clout

Since it is the principal supplier of gas to the nations of the former Soviet Union, Gazprom is a key element in Moscow's politcal dealings with its near neighbours. No less vital are the company's economic and social roles as a source of income from exports, and as an employer of hundreds of thousands of people, whom it provides with social benefits such as housing, healthcare and holidays. Its wealth also allows it to help other companies in financial difficulties.

Industrial Urals

Around the rich mineral deposits of the Ural Mountains is a vast industrial landscape inhabited by 20 million people. This is the backbone of the Russian economy. The entire region is undergoing a massive restructuring operation to bring it into the 21st century.

I n the Soviet era, the Urals has staged an industrial epic worthy of the grandest of social realistic frescoes. But the industrial exploration of the east began much earlier, when Peter the Great founded Yekaterinburg in 1723.

Muck and brass The Urals industrial 'corridor' is one of the most polluted areas on Earth.

Forging the new industries

The first chapter was written by 18th-century ironworkers, who began to forge the Urals' first towns and their dozens of factories. This wave of tsarist-era industrialisation ran out of steam in the late 19th and early 20th centuries.

Then came the Soviet era, when entire cities such as Magnitogorsk ('The Magnetic Mountain') were planted like saplings in the empty Siberian wastes. As well as iron and coal, the Urals harboured copper, manganese, nickel, zinc and rarer metals such as vanadium and ruthenium. By the 1930s, the region had become a powerhouse of heavy industry, second only to the Donbass in Ukraine. Giant factories arose, and railway networks linked the Urals to Siberia's coal-rich Kuznetsk Basin (Kuzbass) around Novosibirsk, Tomsk

Gas masks A worker in the Karabash copper refinery wears a mask to avoid breathing in lead, arsenic, nickel and zinc.

and Krasnoyarsk. Together they form one giant conglomerate which is known as the Ural-Kuzbass.

The most glorious chapter in this epic was written in the Second World War. When German armies advanced into the Russian heartland, seizing the Donbass, more than 1000 factories were dismantled, transported by train and rebuilt in the Urals. Many factories began turning out tanks as the factory walls were built around them.

Lungs of steel

Having contributed so much to the wartime economy and to Soviet victory, the Urals remained one of the most dynamic industrial regions, with a growth rate that was steadily above the national average. The oil and coal reserves of western Siberia and Central Asia boosted the chemical industry, which from the early 1980s produced a quarter of the Soviet Union's fertiliser. In addition, factories in the Urals turned out a quarter of the country's iron, a third of its steel and a fifth of its electricity.

These remarkable achievements have exacted their toll: towns in the Urals are among the most highly polluted in the country. Clouds from the Karabash copper refinery, 45 miles (70 km) northwest of Chelyabinsk, were remarked on by orbiting cosmonauts.

Seeking renewal

In the post-Soviet economic crisis of the 1990s the Ural-Kuzbass dissolved in chaos: Magnitogorsk's iron ran out and the heavy industries that were mired in organisational rigidity and technical obsolescence found it impossible to keep up production. Unemployment and poverty were particularly marked in the Urals. Only mining continued to sustain exports, and may yet provide local industrialists with their trumpcard. On a positive note, pollution levels may drop as industrial activity declines.

Soviet legacy Former state-run heavy industrial complexes, such as this one at Magnitogorsk, are not economically viable today.

Gambling for Caspian oil

The existence of huge oil fields beneath the Caspian Sea has turned the region into a diplomatic and economic battleground. Negotiations between governments and multi-national corporations are just part of a much larger game of strategy in which Russia, the United States of America and Iran are the major players.

High hopes *Workers in a Caspian oilfield drill for a rich future.*

While the Soviet installations gradually decay, garish buildings of glass and granite jostle for space between the bristling derricks that hem the Azerbaijan capital of Baku. Multinational firms have moved in to exploit the oil-rich Caspian. The seafront promenade is now lined with the German limousines of the *nouveau riche*. Bars, restaurants and clubs by the dozen cater to expatriate Westerners.

Black gold

Baku looks like Turkey, but it smells like Texas. The town reeks of oil, and there is a permanent greasy sheen on the still waters of the Caspian. Azerbaijan is cashing in on the fabulous wealth beneath its feet. The rush began in the final years of the Soviet empire, when Mikhail Gorbachev approached the American giant Chevron to develop Kazakhstan's Tengiz oil fields.

Without even completing offshore research, geologists estimated the Tengiz reserves at 25 billion barrels. This was enough to inspire dreams of another Persian Gulf. But the oil rush really began when the newly independent republics of Azerbaijan, Kazakhstan and Turkmenistan invited other major oil companies to share in their treasure. They were aiming to build support against the two powers that had traditionally dominated them: Russia and Iran. Baku filled up with Westerners, mostly American oil

Offshore roads *Baku's Naft Dachlari (Petroleum Rocks) covers an area of 43 sq miles (110 km²).*

Suntan oil *With a fine view of oil platforms, Azeri holidaymakers have a constant reminder that they have gained little from the oil boom but pollution.*

Self-sufficiency Workers' housing at Naft Dachlari. The oil complexes are a closed world: the foreign companies import all essential supplies for their workforce.

entrepreneurs, who toured the ancient nodding derricks outside the city, then went back to their hotels to drink warm beer and do their sums. But the expected bonanza failed to materialise. Technical problems had to be overcome, such as the high sulphur content of the Kazakh reserves. The fluctuating level of the Caspian Sea is another difficulty: after dropping 10 ft (3 m) between 1935 and 1977, it then rose by 7 ft (2 m) in a decade, at which point it stabilised – but for how long?

At present, total reserves – still disconcertingly vague – are estimated at between 75 billion and 200 billion barrels, the higher figure being equal to the proven reserves of Iran and Iraq combined. With the offshore discovery in 2000 of one of the largest oilfields of the last 30 years, known as East Kashagan, and the opening of the first major pipeline from the Tengiz field, prospects for the area are looking much improved from the earlier slump.

Playing for high stakes

Commentators compare the jockeying for power in the region with the 'Great Game' of diplomacy and espionage played by the Russians and British as they vied for control of Central Asia in the 19th century. In today's Great Game, however, geopolitical issues take a back seat to economic ones. Oil has played a crucial role in the conflicts that have engulfed the Caucasus. Georgia and Chechnya are crossed by the two pipelines leading from Baku to the Black

Sea ports of Novorossiysk and Batumi. Both areas are totally dependent on Russia for their supplies of energy.

The United States is the latest entrant in the latter-day Great Game, backing a southerly route for a pipeline, following the western end of the Silk Road across Turkey to the Mediterranean – a route that offers the supreme advantage of avoiding both Russia and Iran. The USA is eager to ensure political stability in the region – and the end to drug trafficking and outright banditry – to enable an uninterrupted flow of oil. It was for this reason that in 2000 the director of the CIA toured Uzbekistan and Kazakhstan.

The China connection

Kazakhstan is a particular object of international attention, too, because it is in a position to look either east or west – or even both ways at once.

Indeed, it was virtually forced to do so in the early 1990s, when Russia under President Yeltsin practised what has been termed 'involuntary disengagement'. Though rich in oil fields, Kazakhstan has no petrol, because 85 per cent of its oil goes to Russian refineries. To escape this historic bind, in 1998 Kazakh officials signed a treaty with China to build a pipeline into Xinjiang. This caused concern in Russia: it has a 3750 mile (6000 km) border with Kaz-akhstan and it cannot afford to be 'disengaged' from its neighbour. For that reason President Putin has sought to ensure continued influence over the region.

Drilling by numbers Derricks in Bayil, Azerbaijan, testify to the importance of oil in the country's precarious economy.

Rival line In 1999, to counter the US-backed pipeline running through Turkey, the Russians opened this line from Baku to Supsa, Georgia.

Black gold in the East

On his way to China in the 13th century, Marco Polo heard about Baku's oil: 'On the confines towards Georgiana there is a fountain from which oil springs in great abundance, insomuch that a hundred shiploads might be taken from it at one time. The oil is not good to use with food, but 'tis good to burn, and is also used to anoint camels that have the

mange. People come from vast distances to fetch it.' Exploitation started in 1871, at the behest of the Nobel brothers. At the time of the German invasion in 1941, Baku was a prime objective. After the Soviet victory, Baku's oil and subsidiary supplies from Sumgait became the nation's prime source, until the wells of the 'second Baku' opened up on the Volga.

The diamonds of Sakha

Eastern Siberia is a far-reaching wilderness with a brutal climate, a sparse and scattered population and untold wealth lying hidden beneath the permafrost.

Sparkling exports *Sakha, an area the size of India, produces about 10 per cent of the world's diamonds.*

The republic of Sakha (Yakutia) is the largest in the Russian Federation, it is also the emptiest – just one person per square mile (3 km²) – and the coldest at –72°C (–97°F) in the depths of winter. However, its main claim to fame is that it is a major source of diamonds.

Nationalism on the rise

Life for the Evenki of Sakha may consist of herding reindeer across the taiga, but for most people it is more likely to involve coping with the dust and relentless noise of machinery biting into the frozen earth. Except for a few meagre trees that huddle in valleys, the landscape is a surreal one of open-cast diamond mines. It is pitted with gaping holes up to half a mile (800 m) across and 1300 ft (400 m) deep, around which tracks spiral from rim to floor.

In Soviet times, Sakha (Yakutia) kept a mere 1 per cent of the wealth it produced. When the Soviet Union broke up, the Yakuts objected to this arrangement, and on March 31, 1992, they signed an

A city built on diamonds

Mirny is a town defined almost entirely by its open-cast mine, a crater that plunges 4000 ft (1200 m) to diamond-bearing rock. Starting operations in 1959, the mine now produces some 10 million carats a year. It was named Mir (Peace), from which the town takes its name – Peaceful. As well as coping with the difficulties imposed by bitter winters, high prices and draconian conditions, the local minority population of Yakuts, Evenki, Yukaghir and Chukchi, are also victims of a power struggle for control of the riches. Sakha (Yakutia) is allowed to keep only a quarter of the mine's total production.

agreement that gave them control of 20 per cent of gemstone diamonds and total control of industrial diamonds. Production is almost totally managed by the South African company de Beers, which markets 80 per cent of the world's diamonds and 95 per cent of those from Russia. As part of the deal, Yakut legislators claimed for their republic the right of self-determination, public ownership of all resources and the freedom to establish commercial links directly with foreign partners.

A brighter future?

The last clause of the deal is of particular significance because Sakha is as close to Beijing and Tokyo as it is to Moscow. The results are already apparent. Japan buys 90 per cent of the coal exported by Sakha (Yakutia) on the two rail links, the Baikal-Amur Magistral (BAM) and the Trans-Siberian Railway. A second agreement with the Japanese is currently transforming the diamond industry. It is part of a portfolio of changes that will make the name Sakha Republic (Yakutia) better known than it is at present.

Totting up *Workers assess diamonds prior to cutting them and preparing them for export.*

Buried treasure *Mirny's giant Mir mine is the tip of a pipe of kimberlite, the rock in which diamonds form, 60 miles (100 km) beneath the surface.*

Krasnoyarsk Krai

Laptev Sea

East Siberian Sea

Tiksi

Arctic circle

Verkhoyansk

Zyryanka

Mirny

Yakutsk

Magadan Oblast

Lensk

Lena

Irkutsk Oblast

Aldan

Chita Oblast

Amur Oblast

Resources
◇ Gold
◆ Tungsten
▽ Diamonds
■ Coal
△ Petro-chemicals

100 km

The threatened taiga

The ruthless exploitation of Siberia's subterranean resources – gold, diamonds, copper, oil, gas – has released industrial pollution that threatens both its forests and the animals that inhabit them.

Awaiting despatch *Cut trees are piled up for floating down river.*

Siberia is almost unimaginably vast. A train journey from one side to the other feels like a sea voyage in which the stations are scattered islands in a green and wooded ocean. Siberia feels inexhaustible and indestructible, but that impression is illusory: the forests are being used up much too fast, the extraction of minerals is causing pollution and the ancient ecology of the taiga is changing irreversibly.

Victim of industry

The thick forest (taiga) consists of birch, spruce and fir. Exploitation of the wood has spread in all directions, from the Baltic across the Urals and on to the River Amur in eastern Siberia. First it followed the route of the Trans-Siberian Railway, then of its northern branch, the BAM – the Baikal-Amur Magistral – which circles north of Lake Baikal.

In eastern Siberia, where the forest reserves are of particular importance for the ecology of the region, several huge industrial complexes were established at the instigation of Stalin. Political prisoners sent to the Siberian *gulags* (prison camps) and peasants deported to work in these remote regions cut thousands of acres of forest to supply mines with pit props and paper mills with their raw material. Little care was taken in felling, and there was no programme of reforestation.

Endless vista *In the Yenisei valley, the taiga rolls to the horizon.*

Soft gold – at a price

Furs have provided wealth for the nomadic trappers of the taiga, who sold them to Russian traders. Most furs are now farmed, and 80 per cent of them are sold in the St Petersburg auction houses. 'Soft gold' they call it, of which the top grade is ermine. But sable, Siberian lynx, silver fox, white wolf, beaver and mink all fetch a good price.

Industrial pollutants

Today, lumberjacks take their chainsaws to the remotest regions – to the great Far Eastern forest massifs of the Kamchatka Peninsula and Sakhalin island. Over-exploitation, combined with slow climatic change, has torn more and more holes in the tree canopy across the length and breadth of the northern forests.

Norilsk, some 60 miles (100 km) to the east of the lower Yenisei, is a nickel-processing area with a particularly vile reputation. The release of sulphur compounds has completely devastated 1.2 million acres (500 000 ha). Airborne pollution and chemical effluents have intensified the losses.

Georgia the joyful

People first settled in Georgia some 10 000 years ago, seduced by its gentle climate and its fertile soils. There they discovered the secret of making wine. Still as faithful as ever to their old ways, Georgians maintain their vinicultural traditions and their reputation for good living.

Georgia's superb white and red wines are the products of some 500 vineyards that bask on the chalky slopes of the Kakheti region in the east and in subtropical Imereti, in central Georgia. Except for the muscats, European varieties are uncommon. The dry *petits vins* from Kakheti – around places such as Napareuli, Tsinandali and Qvareli – are popular locally and much prized abroad. Georgians also enjoy making wines for themselves, from the bunches that weigh down the vines growing in their gardens.

Oceans of vines   Planted in waves across the landscape, varieties such as saperavi *and* rkatsiteli *produce grapes that make excellent wines. Here the fruits ripens in a Kakheti vineyard.*

The story of Armenia's 'cognac'

In 1877, experts from the Hexagon, the seven subdistricts of the Cognac region, began to make a brandy in the distillery of Yerevan, the Armenian capital, labelling it as a 'cognac'. With a distinctive aroma derived from the local soil, combined with that of the barrels in which it was fermented, the 'cognac' acquired an international reputation. After gracing the tables of Russian royalty, it became the jewel in Armenia's economic crown. By then, the term 'cognac' had been copyrighted by the French region. In 1998, the French company

Pernod-Ricard bought the Yerevan distillery, modernised it, gave its bottles a new look and relaunched the drink as a brandy, not a cognac, named Ararat. It is now exported to 60 countries.

Bottling machine   *Ararat rolls off the production line in Yerevan.*

Wine-making, Georgian style

Georgians use two rather special techniques that differ from the European method of making wine. They both involve letting the skin ferment with the juice (what is known as 'must'), and there are local variations. In Imereti, for example, the process specifies a partial fermentation of grape juice and skins in earthenware jars, *kvevri*, which are buried in the ground. In Kakheti, the skins and the juice are allowed to ferment together for three to five months. The bouquet of these products may not be to all tastes, but Georgians have no doubt at all about their superiority.

Charming wine   A Georgian leaves a wine cellar clasping a bottle of his country's best. As the French novelist Alexandre Dumas recorded on a journey to the country: 'In Georgia, it confers honour to drink more than one's neighbour … God has given Georgian drinkers Kakhetian wine, a wine of charm.'

The toastmaster's art

Georgian wine goes with any meal from a banquet to family picnic. A traditional meal unfolds to a succession of toasts delivered by the *tamada*, the master of ceremonies, whose job is to make elaborate and eloquent toasts to entertain the guests at the feast and to flatter the hosts.

Caspian caviar

A one-time money-spinner, Caspian caviar will soon disappear from the menu. Production is in free fall, sturgeon are dying, and experts predict that there will be no more caviar from the Caspian by 2015.

Fish and grab *Masked poachers snatch a harvest of caviar from their latest haul.*

The sturgeon, like the salmon, is a nomad. Every three years they make the journey from the depths of the Caspian to the Volga delta where they breed. They have long been a favourite food of Russians, but it is its roe – the fabled caviar – which makes sturgeon the king of fish. Caviar, everyone agrees, is an acquired taste. Russians like it best on hot, buttered white toast, and see it as the classiest, most perfect accompaniment to a shot of ice-cold vodka. Another favourite caviar occasion is 'maslenitsa' – Shrove Tuesday – when the salty little black beads are wrapped in buckwheat pancakes and smothered with thick sour cream.

Off to the market *Once removed, the roes are cleaned and salted with fine sea salt. Most of the preparation is done aboard ship.*

From tight control to free for all

In the 20th century, the two nations sharing the Caspian coastline, the Soviet Union and Iran, agreed to split the caviar trade and put it under tight state control.

Three new independent states emerged on the shores of the Caspian Sea (Azerbaijan, Kazakhstan and Turkmenistan), joined by two autonomous regions (Dagestan and Kalmykiya), all of them claiming a share in the proceeds of the caviar trade.

Most of the sturgeon are now caught too young, before they have had a chance to produce enough eggs to breed. This problem is exacerbated by the detrimental effect of dams built in the middle River Volga, which have changed the water level in the Caspian, increased its salinity and introduced pollutants.

The governments concerned have taken precautionary measures, but according to the Fisheries Research Institute in Astrakhan, the number of Caspian sturgeon has dropped tenfold in the last decade. The figures speak for themselves: in 1985, the caviar harvest was 25 000 tons. By 1997 it had dropped to 1200 tons and in 1999 it was 320 tons. If this trend continues, it will not be long before supplies dry up.

Of icons and sturgeon

Before sturgeon were caught for their eggs, they were in great demand from icon painters. Boiling their fins produced a sort of glue, which, when diluted and mixed with chalk, could be used as a foundation layer. With this mixture spread over the baseboard, the iconographer could sketch his outline and apply his colours.

A rare dish from a rare fish

Of the 20 or more species of sturgeon – all of which forage the seafloor for food – only three types are caught in the Caspian. They give their names to three different types of caviar. With its hint of hazelnut and its big, moist grains, beluga is the most refined, the most sought-after. It is the rarest and most expensive caviar, costing almost £3000 per kilogram. Osetra, with firm, golden grains and a saltier taste, sells for £1480 per kilogram. With its medium-sized, grey grains and a well-balanced taste, sevruga is the commonest and cheapest caviar, going for about £1300 per kilogram.

Mighty catch *Azerbaijani fishermen prepare their catch.*

The horses and camels of Turkmenistan

Turkmenistan is the most southerly, the hottest and the sandiest of the former Soviet republics. Oil and gas production are the mainstay of the new economy, but camels and horses still have an impotant role to play.

Life force   For Turkmens, camels are symbols. One reassuring proverb runs: 'When the camel train does an about-turn, the last camel takes the lead.'

Industrialisation came late to Turkmenistan, but today it is one of the world's leading suppliers of gas and oil. Eighty per cent of Central Asian oil requirements come from here, and its capital, Ashgabat, provides 33 per cent of Russia's gas.

Living traditions

Technological advance has not destroyed the centuries-old traditions that formed the country's character. Even if horsemen and nomads are rarities these days, Ashgabat's market is still stacked high with carpets made in Bukhara. Towering above the hubbub are the immense, shaggy hats of the Tekes, the main Turkmen tribe. They adopted settled ways only in the 17th century, having rivalled other tribes for control of the Silk Road, a 5000 mile (8000 km) route leading from the Mediterranean across Persia and Turkmenistan to China. The Tekes put up the main resistance to imperial Russia's advance through Central Asia towards British India in the 1860s and 1870s.

The Tekes have not forgotten their nomadic past, and it is their clans rather than their towns that hold the keys to power. Camels are the mainstay of their traditional economy. They have recently recovered from a low point and now number more than 100 000. Used both for transport and for pumping water from wells, each camel supplies 5 lb (2.5 kg) of wool at every shearing, 9 pints (5 litres) of milk a day, and 900–1300 lb (400–600 kg) of meat. Horses

are another reminder of the great days of the caravan trade. Once traded along the Silk Road, along with jade and ivory, horses have now lost much of their economic value, but still confer prestige.

When the country's president, Saparmurad Niyazov, visited London in March 1993, he offered prime minister John Major a horse, a reminder that Central Asian peoples pioneered horse-breeding and remain proud of the fact.

The Turkmen horse

Turkmenistan raises pure breds for export to many countries. One of the world's oldest breeds, the Akhal-Teke, much favoured by the mounted warriors of the east, is a direct descendant of the original Turkmen horse. Raised in tough conditions, it is noted for endurance – a reputation justified when several of them were ridden the 2500 mile (4000 km) journey from Ashgabat to Moscow. The Akhal-Teke is also admired for its aristocratic profile and its glorious golden coat. The Don breed, prized by the Cossacks and still found wild on the steppes, has been crossed with the Turkmen horse to produce a new and much admired lineage: the Karabakh.

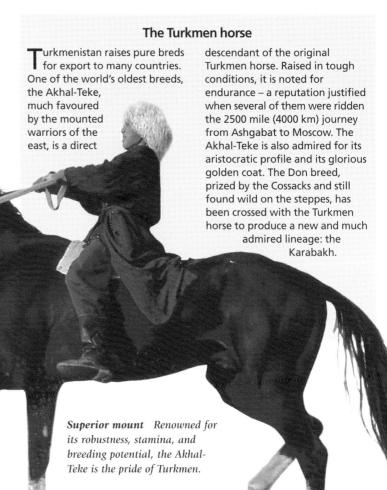

Prize horse
The Akhal-Teke is one of the oldest and purest breeds.

Superior mount   Renowned for its robustness, stamina, and breeding potential, the Akhal-Teke is the pride of Turkmen.

Classroom aid *Near Samarkand, schoolchildren help out with the cotton harvest.*

Uzbekistan's cotton

Cotton fields stretch as far as the eye can see across the baking landscape of Uzbekistan. For better or for worse, Uzbekistan and its economy are governed by the seasonal rhythm of its 'white gold'.

The sun-burned plains that cover most of Uzbekistan were virgin lands when the Russians arrived at the end of the 19th century. In the 20th century, huge irrigation works covered these 'hungry lands' with plantations, making cotton Uzbekistan's main resource. Of the 8.6 millon acres (3.5 million ha) that are cultivated, 70 per cent is artificially irrigated.

One-crop land

Growing some 3 million tons of fibre and seeds every year, Uzbekistan has been one of the top five countries in the world for cotton production in past decades. Recently, the export revenue from this crop has fallen significantly, but it remains the principal earner at around 25 per cent of revenue.

The Soviet Union turned Uzbekistan into a prime cotton producer that supplied two-thirds of the USSR's production, but at the cost of imposing a single crop and creating a dependency on imported food. Now the country imports much of its cereals, meat, potatoes and milk products. In the late 1990s, a decline in the price of cotton, the major source of foreign exchange, intensified a monetary crisis and accelerated economic decline.

Brezhnev's cotton galore

In the 1970s, the Soviet leader Leonid Brezhnev declared cotton his major weapon in an economic war. To irrigate the new fields, his plan – thankfully unrealised – was to divert the River Irtysh from its northward route into Siberia. Whole mountainsides were covered with giant slogans visible from miles away: 'Seven million tons of cotton for the Motherland!' Now independent, Uzbekistan maintains a monopoly of cotton processing. At harvest time in September, the government dragoons an army of pickers into action and some 2 million people work the fields for a month.

Weighing in *Once gathered, the cotton is put into sacks and weighed. The workers are paid by the kilogram.*

Harvest time *The cotton is sowed in April or early May and harvested in September.*

Life after the collective farm

In world production rankings, the Soviet Union always had a high place in both agriculture and saltwater fishing. When the communist regime fell, so did output.

Potato production is about the only commodity that has increased over the past decade in Russia. As the country's most basic food, potatoes are the first and most essential vegetable to be grown on the individual plots that allow millions of families in both town and countryside to live at subsistence level.

Living off the allotment

The allotments, gardens and communal orchards that have sprung up in urban areas play an increasing role in food production. They provide almost 90 per cent of the country's potatoes, half of the other vegetables, 40 per cent of the meat and as much as one-third of the milk.

In part, it is the dramatic fall in purchasing power that explains this phenomenon, which is something entirely separate from the catastrophe that has hit the farms. Deprived of state aid, let alone tractors – the production of which has plummeted along with everything else – farmers are unable to modernise their equipment. And, just as demand dropped, they had no choice but to accept a brutal hike in the cost of energy, fertilisers and pesticides.

Cutback in cattle

Cattle farmers were severely affected: between 1990 and 1994, meat production halved, and the vast herds raised on collective farms soon diminished for lack of fodder. In Soviet times the cattle were raised on American cereals imported by the state at great expense. Today Russia still imports cereals, but only in proportion to its much reduced budget and its declining reserves of foreign currency.

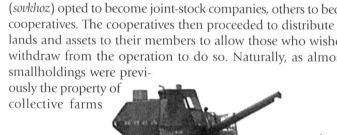

Ancient ways In the Pamirs, a herdswoman milks her cattle.

The failures of privatisation

During Gorbachev's liberalisation in the 1980s, the state started to restructure and reorganise the collective farms. But the farms were never geared to producing for the open market, and the task proved too difficult.

In 1991, new laws on private property gave rights to individual farmers. This meant changing the status of the collective farms, both state farms and cooperatives. Some of the old state farms (*sovkhoz*) opted to become joint-stock companies, others to become cooperatives. The cooperatives then proceeded to distribute their lands and assets to their members to allow those who wished to withdraw from the operation to do so. Naturally, as almost all smallholdings were previously the property of collective farms

Tea harvest Workers tend a tea plantation in Azerbaijan, where half the population depend on traditional agriculture.

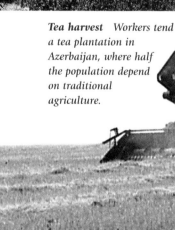

Military aid   In 1998, soldiers were called upon to help out with the vital potato and carrot harvest in the Moscow region.

of some kind or another, the number of small farms jumped – from 64 000 in January 1992 to 280 000 in 1995. But with no access to credit, no possibility of upgrading and no marketing mechanisms, the average farm of about 100 acres (40 ha) was just too small to cope. A large proportion of the overburdened and inexperienced owners simply gave up at the first bad harvest.

A disastrous legacy

In practical everyday life, nothing much changed. The same structures set up to collectivise the farms had now been thoroughly ossified by decades of intensive agriculture, monoculture and centralised control of ordering and marketing.

Considering that Russian peasants had only ever been allowed to own land between 1861, when serfdom was abolished, and the consolidation of Soviet power after the Revolution, the force of character of those who took on the challenge of running their own farms was truly remarkable. There was simply no tradition of private ownership: those five decades were too short a time for a significant class of peasant landowners to emerge – and any that did come to the fore were eliminated by Stalin, along with their expertise. Agriculture, more than any other sector of the economy, is now paying the price of its past.

The trouble with fishing

The fishing industry is hardly any better off. It is not that the Russian fishing fleet is small, for it makes up half the world's total tonnage. Behind the blankets of ice that enclose the northern coasts for most of the year, great ports, from Murmansk (in the well-

The riches of Kamchatka

Its scientific name is *Paralithodes camtschatica*, and the factory ships of Kamchatka drag up 50 tons a day from the icy depths of the Sea of Okhotsk. This is the domain of the king crab, whose mighty legs, which can span up to 4 ft (1.3 m), contain a prodigious mass of meat. The crab ranges from the Sea of Japan to the coast of British Columbia. Together with tourism, which is expanding now that the peninsula has been opened to the world, the king crab is Kamchatka's principal asset. Hopes are high that it will bring prosperity to the region, as it has to the fishermen of Japan and Alaska.

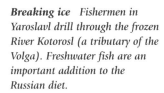

Breaking ice   Fishermen in Yaroslavl drill through the frozen River Kotorosl (a tributary of the Volga). Freshwater fish are an important addition to the Russian diet.

stocked Barents) to Okhotsk on the Pacific coast, shelter all the old Soviet factory ships. These range the oceans, returning laden with herring from the Atlantic and salmon and crab from the far side of the Pacific.

But the catches have been declining, from 11.2 million tons in 1992 to 4 million tons today. This has meant Russia dropping from second place in the world league of fishing nations to fifth. Over-exploitation, which also affects Russia's rivals, is not solely responsible for this fall. Once again, it is the financial crisis that is largely to blame, making it impossible to renew a dilapidated fleet or pay a crew enough to make the work worthwhile.

Golden grains   An armada of combines harvest wheat in Kazakhstan. Despite huge agricultural developments, the Soviet Union never reached self-sufficiency in cereal production, and nor have its successors.

CHAPTER 3

CUTTING-EDGE TECHNOLOGIES

The explosion of the first Soviet atomic bomb in 1949 and the launch of the first artificial satellite in 1957 gave the world the impression that the USSR was way ahead of its US rival in scientific innovation. It was inconceivable that such mastery might go hand in hand with underdevelopment at home. The Soviet propaganda machine was adept at hiding the failures of a system that could spend billions of roubles on advanced military and industrial projects, yet ignore ideologically suspect areas, such as information technology and genetics. Today, Russia is striving to reverse the situation and has successfully sought international collaboration on ground-breaking projects. But restructuring industry to meet modern needs is proving a challenge.

Workers in St Petersburg check a nuclear power plant.

Baikonur: the heart of the space programme

Russia has been reaching for the stars from the Baikonur Cosmodrome since the 1950s. First it was in direct competition with the USA, but times have changed and today Russia is a major collaborator in an international space programme.

World hero *Yuri Gagarin, first man in space, was fêted around the world. He died in 1968 in a plane crash.*

I t was only a little bleeping sound, but when picked up by radios around the world it was enough to announce the start of a new era – the conquest of space. The fact that the sound came from a Soviet spacecraft was enough to tell the world that the USSR had made its bid to take over as the dominant superpower.

Moon probe *Russian Moon exploration has relied on machines rather than humans.*

Sputnik's message

It was night-time on October 4, 1957, when the giant R-7 rocket blasted off from Baikonur in Kazakhstan. The rocket, far more powerful than anything the Americans possessed, had been developed by the head of the Soviet space programme, Sergei Korolev, to carry nuclear warheads. In its nose it carried a grapefruit-sized aluminium sphere weighing 183 lb (83.6 kg). After five minutes, Sputnik (meaning 'travelling companion') was in orbit, transmitting its reassuring beep-beep sound. As the official newsagency TASS announced the following day, it was a triumph for communism, and capitalism had better beware. The USSR had proved that its rockets could reach the USA within minutes. Besides being a technological leap forward, Sputnik's launch opened an arms race and a space race that would dominate the next 20 years.

From first space-dog to first spaceman

A month later, the USSR confirmed its lead by launching Sputnik 2, with another first: the first living creature in space, a dog named Laika. The journey ended a week later in a fiery re-entry and the dog died. The USA countered by orbiting its first satellite, Explorer 1. Then, after two other firsts (first to strike the Moon, first to circle it), the USSR capped its successes with the first man in space, Yuri Gagarin, on April 12, 1961. Gagarin orbited the Earth in Vostok I, an expedition that lasted 108 minutes from launch to landing. He

International venture *Claudie André-Deshays (top), a French astronaut, poses with Russian crew members on the Franco-Russian Soyuz TM-24 mission of August 1996.*

Star graduates   These Soviet cosmonauts in Star City outside Moscow are two of the 200 people, including 15 foreigners, who have trained here.

was followed by the first woman in space (Valentina Tereshkova) and the first space walk (Alexei Leonov). Tereshkova's 1963 space flight lasted three days during which she orbited the Earth 48 times.

Meanwhile, the USA had established its dominance, ending with the manned lunar landing in 1969. The Soviet space programme continued to build on its experience, sending satellites into orbit using its 'workhorse' launcher, the Soyuz, which, since its introduction in 1963, has become the world's most frequently flown launch vehicle. In 1971, Salyut I became the first space station to be sent into orbit. Then in 1975, in an early spirit of cooperation, the USSR's Soyuz 19 and the USA's Apollo 18 linked in space.

A huge Shuttle-type launcher called Buran was left unfinished when the Soviet Union collapsed, and space exploration was forced to take a back seat. But the space station Mir (1986-2001) lived up to its name (peace), becoming a symbol of a new era of space cooperation with its old rival, the USA.

International programme

Since the 1990s Russia has been working with the USA on the development of an International Space Station. The Americans were right to involve the Russians in this project. In addition to their experience in manned space flight, the Russians had several well-proven rockets, including Proton and Energiya, and both the Soyuz

Space heroine   Valentina Tereshkova was the first woman in orbit.

Space headquarters   The Baykonur Cosmodrome in Tyuratam, Kazakhstan, first used in 1957, is now run jointly by Russians and Kazakhs.

Mir: an epic of endurance

When Mir was launched in 1986, the space station was designed to last for five to six years. But its successor was cancelled, so Mir soldiered on and grew bigger as extra modules – Kvant 1, Kvant 2, Kristall, Spektr, Priroda – were added to make it the largest space station to date. With the USSR's collapse in 1991, Russia sought international help. Some 30 crew members flew in it, including, in 1988, Musa Manarov and Vladimir Titov, who spent 365 days aboard. Astronauts from France, Britain, the USA, Poland, Germany and Japan also joined the space station. But Mir was plagued by disasters. In 1997, the crew had to deal with a fire and the first space crash, when a supply module made a hole in it. In the late 1990s the International Space Station began to take shape and Mir's days were numbered. After surpassing its expected life by ten years, the battered hulk was brought down over the South Pacific in 2001.

manned spacecraft and the unmanned Progresses were useful means of transport into orbit. In late 1998 the first two modules of the International Space Station were launched and assembled – one was Russian, the other American. The third was also Russian: the Zvezda Service Module, launched in July 2000 to provide the first living accommodation. Two of the three crew members who arrived in November 2000 were Russian. After the American space shuttle disaster in 2003, the only contact with the International Space Station was through Baikonur. The station is scheduled for completion in 2006.

Russian involvement in the space programme is a vital part of President Putin's policy of re-engaging in Central Asia, in particular in Kazakhstan. In January 2004, Kazakhstan's President Nazarbayev and Putin agreed to extend Moscow's lease of Baikonur Cosmodrome until 2050. Space technology is once again a lever to ensure Russian influence in the heart of Central Asia, as well as internationally.

Rebuilding the military machine

The army once had the pick of Soviet industrial output. Great swathes of the economy were devoted to fulfilling its needs. Now the armed forces are reforming, and the industries that served it are finding new ways to be profitable.

The first reform instituted by the new Russian army was a grand symbolic gesture. In 1991, as the communist regime collapsed, the post of political officer was abolished. This structural change marked the death of the commissar, the man whose job it was to keep watch on the 'political literacy' of the troops. It meant that the Russian army was no longer the slave of the Bolshevik idea and of Bolsevik methods. But there was another army tradition that proved harder to abolish. This was the practice of *dedovshchina* – 'grandfathers' rights' – whereby older conscripts ('grandfathers' in army slang) are allowed to terrorise new recruits. The practice was common in the Soviet army, but was kept in check by strict discipline. In the more lax atmosphere of the post-Soviet army, *dedovshchina* became an epidemic, and alarming numbers of recruits died at the hands of their fellow soldiers. It still goes on.

Raw recruits

What with *dedovshchina* and the war in Chechnya, many young Russians came to see their call-up papers as a death sentence and dessertion numbers grew alarmingly. Moreover, the physical and

Farewell to arms   SS-20 missiles lie ready for dismantling.

Finishing touch   A worker swabs down a MiG 29 on its assembly line.

mental condition of 18-year-old men in Russia has plummeted. So many are unfit for active service that the army remains chronically short of men. In these circumstances, the Russian government has long been considering doing away with conscription and restructuring the army as a professional fighting force, along the lines of the British army. Yeltsin promised to end conscription by 2000, but failed to deliver. President Putin has asked for a new proposal to be ready in 2004, but does not expect it to be fully implemented for ten years after that.

Mourning past glories

In the meantime, the Russian armed forces continue to shrink. In 2001, the defence ministry announced that it was closing bases on Cuba and in Vietnam. This money-saving move pained many high-ranking officers who came up through the Soviet army: it was yet more evidence that the Cold War was lost, and that the army's power and influence had evaporated. Many saw the tragic sinking of the Kursk submarine in 2000 as an indication of the overall state of Russia's armed forces.

In addition, there were more rumblings of discontent in 2001 when American forces attacked Afghanistan

A weapon for all seasons

Mikhail Kalashnikov is by any standard one of the most successful designers in history. Born in 1919, he joined the army as a tank mechanic in 1938. He was wounded in the first days of World War II and while recovering in hospital he heard other soldiers talking about how good the Germans' guns were compared to Soviet issue rifles. From his sickbed he started to design a cheap, reliable gun that would work in the extremes of the Russian climate. By 1947 he had developed a prototype – too late for the war, but in time for the Cold War. It went into production in 1949. Since then 70 million Kalashnikov's have been made. Independence fighters, guerrillas and terrorists around the world admire its sturdiness and low cost. It is powered by gas, has a calibre of 7.62 mm and is considered to be accurate to about 980 ft (300 m). The gun's design, with its characteristic banana-shaped magazine, has been borrowed and adapted by armies around the world. At 50 years old, the AK remains an essential tool of the 21st-century fighter.

Mikhail Kalashnikov.

(using military bases in former Soviet republics, among others). The idea that Americas might win a war in Afghanistan when Russia had not (1979-1989), was disturbing for the veterans of the war who now run the Russian army and are in charge of the defence ministry. Furthermore, the American military build-up in central Asia due to that conflict also caused concern.

Swords into ploughshares

The shrinkage of the army has had a huge effect on the infrastructure which used to supply its hardware. Some sectors of the former military-industrial manufacturers have turned to light industry. Former chemical weapons factories now produce detergents, pesticides and cosmetics. The MiG plant in Moscow has experimented with making microlight planes for sporting purposes. Production lines that once turned out guns and grenades now turn out food mixers and shower units.

The arms industry has also taken to supplying other people's armies. Syria, for example, equipped itself with the latest Russian Sukhoi and MiG fighters in the 1990s. The tradition of light arms, exemplified by the ever popular Kalashnikov rifle, is also still going strong.

Russia also produces mobile artillery pieces. These guns come in calibres ranging from 122 mm to 203 mm, and they can provide devastating firepower over distances from 6 miles (10 km) to 19 miles (30 km).

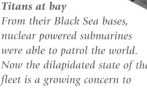

Titans at bay
From their Black Sea bases, nuclear powered submarines were able to patrol the world. Now the dilapidated state of the fleet is a growing concern to neighbouring powers.

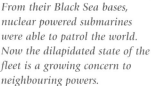

Hope of the future   The Sukhoi 30 made its debut at the Le Bourget airshow in 1999, proof that Russia was still among the best in the world's aerospace industry.

The network in the skies

The USSR was quick to exploit developments in aviation as a means of revolutionising transport across its immense territory. With an eye to the future, Russia is collaborating internationally on supersonic research.

Air transport is a vital means of communication in a country 700 times the size of the United Kingdom. Russia is the world's largest nation – 6.6 million square miles (17 million km²). The greater part of its coastline is ice-bound. Eighty per cent of the population live west of the Ural Mountains, while 80 per cent of the resources are east of them. The remaining 20 per cent of its inhabitants live in isolated towns and communities, many of which are inaccessible by land for part of the year due to the extreme climate.

Growth of Aeroflot

At its peak Aeroflot, the national carrier, was the largest airline in the world and the most highly developed civil aviation operation outside the USA. Having initiated the first continuously operating jet service in 1955, it acquired a massive fleet of 7500 aircraft. In 1990 it had 65 000 pilots supported by half a million employees working in 1000 airports.

Unlike other airlines, Aeroflot owned rather than rented its planes. It was not price accountable and aviation fuel in the USSR was cheaper than mineral water. A ticket from Moscow to Leningrad cost less than a kilo of sausages. While Western Europeans relied on cars, buses and trains for transport, Soviet citizens would hop on an Ilyushin aircraft to travel to the next city.

International links

Aeroflot developed a worldwide network of international routes, too. In return for opening up its air corridors across its territory to foreign carriers, it obtained landing rights in other countries. Its Ilyushin Il-18, Aeroflot's workhorse for 30 years until the late 1980s, became a familiar sight around the world. Places such as the eastern coastal city Vladivostok – gateway to Japan and Korea – became accessible year-round despite being locked in ice for three months at a time.

Aircraft development

Technologically, the Soviet Union kept abreast of other countries in its research. It built its own supersonic airliner – the Tupolev 144 – in parallel with the Anglo-French Concorde. Passenger

Air freight   Aeroflot's new cargo plane, the Ilyushin Il-96 T, has American engines thanks to new US-Russian trade links.

and freight transport were not its only lines of business. It had 16 types of planes and helicopters that were used by other sectors of the economy – in agriculture, prospecting, geological research, fishing and construction. Between 1970 and 1989, the number of planes used in agriculture alone rose every year by 200 to 250.

The empire crashes

The end of the Soviet Union in 1991 meant the end of the Ministry of Civil Aviation, which was, in effect, the Aeroflot head office. In five years, Aeroflot was stripped bare. Countless planes were

Taking the weight   An Aeroflot advertisement. Travelling by plane became second nature to Russians in the Soviet era.

Heavy lifter   The MI-26, the world's most powerful helicopter, can carry loads of up to 20 tons.

mothballed. The newly formed republics requisitioned whatever aircraft were on the ground to form the basis of their fledgling national carriers. Airports such as Murmansk, Kirovsk and Petrozavodsk were left on the brink of closure – and many internal routes had to be abandoned.

The cost of a ticket rose a staggering 180-fold. Capacity, which was 92 per cent in 1990, dropped to 60 per cent.

Meanwhile, private airlines mushroomed. At the end of 1994, there were 300 airlines and related companies in the former Soviet Union, including 80 in the republics of the Commonwealth of Independent States. Ninety per cent of these companies were in deficit, and even those with assets could not find the cash to maintain their fleets, let alone renew them. Although international traffic doubled in the early 1990s, the only beneficiaries were Western companies.

Competition in the skies

Russia's aerospace industry, bolstered by the state through the second half of the 20th century, is now having to compete in a finely tuned international market. It is finding that the intense rivalry between the two aerospace giants, Boeing and the European Airbus Consortium, has imposed limits on its ambitions. In 1998, Boeing had 660 machines, as against the Airbus Consortium's 556. In 1999, the balance had swung the other way. Russia relies heavily on foreign products for its aircraft. Even nationally made planes are routinely supplied with Pratt & Whitney or Rolls-Royce engines, and on Russian airlines these days it is common to come across an A-310-300 or a Boeing 767.

Showing off Crowds throng Moscow's second aerospace show in 1997. In the middle of the row is a supersonic TU-144.

The project turned the Tu-144 into a sophisticated flying laboratory to research the development of a new supersonic passenger plane – which may, perhaps, emerge to fill the gap left by the withdrawal of the Anglo-French Concorde from the skies.

Supersonic research

Russia continues to be a pacesetter in the world of supersonic flight technology. In early 2004, Russia announced that it had successfully tested the prototype of a hypersonic vehicle capable of penetrating the missile shield of any given enemy. Whether this type of technology ever makes its way into the more domestic side of aviation is unknown.

Gas guzzler The supersonic Tu-144, nicknamed Konkordski in the West, proved so fuel-hungry that it was relegated to non-passenger work.

New projects

Despite the chaotic state of Russia's airline industry, technological research has continued with international participation. The end of the 1990s saw the successful completion of the Tu-144LL project, a Russian-American collaboration that found a new use for the Tu-144D supersonic aircraft, relegated to non-passenger work by technical problems.

New stock Tupolev 154 passenger planes near completion in Saratov.

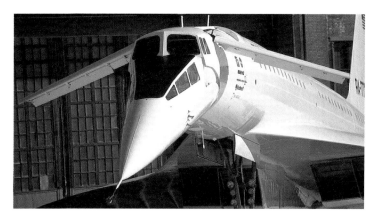

The atom bomb race

During the Cold War, the Bomb was seen as a safeguard against the outbreak of war. But now the former states of the Soviet Union are left with the remnants of an industry that poses a threat to its own people.

Nuclear umbrella *Workers check one of the missiles still in service.*

W hen the Soviets exploded their first atomic bomb in 1949, it signalled the start of a hectic race between the communist and capitalist blocs. In the dangerous game of nuclear deterrence, the rivalry was supposed to achieve a 'balance of terror'.

Decline and fall

To preserve that balance, nuclear weapons became ever more sophisticated. Not only did this place huge demands on the economy, it also strengthened the climate of secrecy and oppression at home and masked the system's inefficiencies.

It did not make any difference that the 'father' of the Soviet hydrogen bomb, Andrei Sakharov, became the most famous of dissidents with his demands for a treaty on the banning of nuclear tests. He was sent into internal exile for his outspokenness.

In 1986, the dangers inherent in nuclear power combined with in-built inefficiencies to produce the catastrophic explosion of the Chernobyl reactor. While 45 people were killed in the accident,

Vital resource *Reactors like this one at Sosnovy Bor produce 10 per cent of Russia's electricity.*

it is thought that several hundred more lost their lives as a result of radiation poisoning, and the consequences for unborn generations are untold; 62 000 sq miles (160 000 km²) were contaminated.

A few months after Chernobyl, Mikhail Gorbachev released Sakharov from his exile in Gorky. Then, on July 22, 1987, Gorbachev announced that he accepted without reservation the advantages of scrapping all nuclear missiles in Europe. In the face of US president Ronald Reagan's commitment to his Star Wars project, Gorbachev in effect recognised that his nation was economically at the end of its tether and could no longer compete in, let alone win, the arms race.

A nuclear rubbish tip

Chernobyl's poisonous legacy is still evident across Ukraine, Belarus and Russia's Bryansk region, where thyroid cancer, particularly among children, is only one of the many consequences of the catastrophe. Across the former USSR, several similar reactors pose an equal threat.

Chernobyl was not the first disaster. In 1957, a release of plutonium at Kyshtym in the Urals irradiated 250 000 people and contaminated a huge stretch of territory along the River Techa. Kazakhs denounced the dire effects on their health of some 500 nuclear tests conducted between 1949 and 1989 in the Semipalatinsk area. Meanwhile, Norway and Sweden look warily at the northerly Kola Peninsula, which housed the world's highest concentration of nuclear material.

In the current poor economic climate, Russia's goodwill on the subject of disarmament can do little to prevent the dangers of an export trade in its nuclear technologies and materials.

Safety threat *Novovoronezhskiy nuclear power station is among those that may one day prove unsafe.*

Dissident voices *Andrei Sakharov (1921-89), helped to develop the Soviet H-bomb, but he and his wife, Elena Bonner, became powerful critics of nuclear deterrence.*

Visionary breakthrough

Forming part of Russia's fine tradition of scientific research, Dr Svyatoslav Fyodorov's work in ophthalmology laid the foundation for a spectacular advance in the treatment of diseases of the eye.

Far-sighted *Svyatoslav Fyodorov.*

When in 1976 the ophthalmologist Svyatoslav Fyodorov claimed to have corrected shortsightedness by making tiny cuts in the cornea, medical practitioners everywhere reacted with incredulity. Up until then, the only solution to the problem had been to use glasses and contact lenses.

The birth of microsurgery

Fyodorov's technique is based on the principle that by making minute incisions in the cornea, the curvature flattens out to correct the myopia. In the 1930s, a similar operation had been tried by a Japanese professor, Sato, but he succeeded only in making his patients' sight worse.

Dr Fyodorov, director of Moscow's Laboratory for Research into Experimental and Clinical Eye Surgery, worked to perfect the operation. In 1980 he founded the Institute for Eye Microsurgery, and from 1984 his technique spread rapidly to the

Taking turns *In microsurgery centres using Fyodorov's techniques, patients from around the world undergo production-line operations to cure their shortsightedness.*

High-tech research

Russia's 4000-plus research organisations in science and technology employ a million or so people. In 1996, government guidelines identified those areas that should be given priority: astronomy and space research, new materials, information technology, chemical products, production technology, electronics, and anything that might offer the possibility of advances in biology or in genetic engineering.

USA and Europe. Numerous studies showed its benefit for mild and medium myopia.

From 1986, Fyodorov practised at his own multidisciplinary Scientific-Technical Enterprise for Eye Microsurgery. The centre combined an eye clinic with two factories for making instruments, a non-specialist clinic and a hotel for patients who had come from farther afield for treatment.

Foreign interest

Subsidiaries opened in many other places at home and abroad. In France, Fyodorov's work attracted particular interest. In 1989, the French industrial and telecommunications giant Bouygues set up a new company, IRIS, capitalised with 43 per cent French finance and 57 per cent Soviet expertise, which built a hotel and medical complex in Moscow under Fyodorov's direction. Subsequently, he organised a surgical tour on a hospital ship to ports in the Black Sea, the Mediterranean and The Gulf. When the Soviet Union came to an end, Fyodorov was 64. He entered politics and used his energy and his wealth to set up his own party. In 1995-6 he ran unsuccessfully for president. He died in 2000.

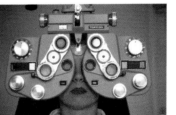

Fast track *Fyodorov's treatment of myopia depends on lasers and high-speed testing techniques.*

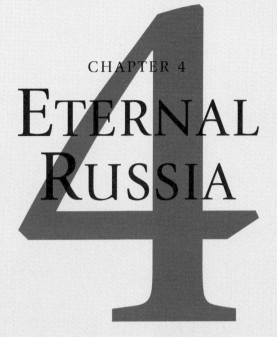

CHAPTER 4

ETERNAL RUSSIA

During the last years of communist rule, Western Sovietologists were all agreed on one thing: that Russia changes very slowly, and always has done. The country was seen as a kind of geopolitical glacier, rendered even more static and immutable by the icy climate of authoritarianism. This is why the world was so shocked by *glasnost* and the eventual collapse of the state – it all seemed so out of character. But at a deeper level, the old idea about slow change is still true. The Russians are as long-suffering, as resourceful, as melancholic and as passive as they ever were. This means they can endure hardship which would crush a weaker people; but it also means that they can shrug off or ignore such outrages as the destruction of their country's natural resources and the slow erosion of their state's democratic gains. Russia is an infuriating and charming country – and that at least will never change.

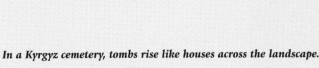

In a Kyrgyz cemetery, tombs rise like houses across the landscape.

Russian women

Women in Russia, it is said, are emancipated but not liberated. They were never chained to the kitchen sink, but they are not storming the citadels of male chauvinism either.

Strike a pose *A self-portrait by Natalya Goncharova (1881-1962).*

There is something deeply matriarchal about Russian society, or at least about the Russian family. Most Russian women work, as well as taking complete responsibility for the home (it is a very rare Russian man who can cook). And since life expectancy for men is short and living space is hard to come by, many families have a widowed grandmother as a permanent member of the household. Many Russian children are brought up primarily by their *babushka*, rather than by their mother and father.

Yet women are not equal. The only equality they have is equality of hardship: no one bats an eyelid to see a woman road-mending or hacking ice from the tramlines with a crowbar. The aims of Western feminism – respect in the workplace, equal pay, non-sexist representation of women in the media – all these things would strike most Russian women as so distant and so trivial as to be laughable. 'We already have the right to be treated the same as men,' one liberal woman journalist has written. 'What we want is the opportunity to be treated like women.'

International women's day

That opportunity does come at least once in the year – on March 8, International Women's Day. This day is still a public holiday, as it was under the Soviet regime. It is like a cross between Mother's Day and St Valentine's Day: women receive gifts, are praised to the skies in elaborate toasts – but probably still have to do the washing-up. In post-communist Russia there are new perils and new opportunities for Russian women. Prostitution is a new and terrible danger. Once practically unknown in Russia outside the big cities, it is now a global criminal industry which feeds on vulnerable young women from all over Eastern

Washerwoman *In an age-old scene, a peasant woman does her laundry.*

Women's work *Many Russian women still take pride in the fact they do tough physical work. In Soviet times it was seen as a mark of social equality.*

Europe. The USSR was a nanny state which protected its citizens from that kind of danger. It was also a nanny state in the literal sense, providing free child care for all women. This boon has now gone.

On the other hand, women can now take a full and equal part in the free economy. Many women have made spectacular successes in business, and 37 per cent of company directors are women. This in a country where, 20 years ago, it was remarkable to see a woman behind the wheel of a car.

Kollontai: for Leninism and free love

Alexandra Kollontai was the only woman in Lenin's government, and the only Bolshevik to link the political revolution to the idea of free love. She was an utterly modern feminist: she used her influence to lobby for women's rights, championing issues such as collective child care and easier divorce. She lived openly by her liberated sexual principles, and this scandalised her prudish male colleagues. She went abroad as an ambassador (the first woman ever to hold that post), and made vital contributions to Soviet wartime policy. She wrote stories, published as *Love of Worker Bees*, which explored themes of feminism and sexuality.

Into the woods

For Russians, the forest is not so much a landscape as a way of life. The forest is where everyone goes to gather mushrooms, pick berries or catch small game. It is the place to get necessities and to track down those little extras – all free, of course – to fill the store cupboard for winter. Everyone knows how to marinate mushrooms, turn berries into jam, or pickle them in alcohol and salt, and how to smoke meat. Tradition dictates that the forest is also a place to fear, the home of wolves and bears. There are the characters of folk tales, such as Baba Yaga the witch, who according to legend lives in a house built on chickens' legs, and eats children for breakfast.

The timeless countryside

Around the hearth After a day's work, Georgians gather by an open fire to cook their evening meal.

Even today the Russian countryside is full of scenes that would not be out of place in a Tolstoy novel: huge haystacks standing beside wooden huts, women washing clothes on river banks, fishermen in little boats, villagers gathered around a well. Little has changed in the last 100 years, except for the coming of electricity.

If 'old Russia' still survives, it is in the unchanging landscapes and the enduring cycle of country life. In Russia, almost every family has a little plot out in the countryside and, come the good weather, that is where they go for weekends and holidays, and where they grow food to bottle and pickle. But for those who live permanently in the country, life is not so simple.

are at the bottom of the garden. However, the countryside is immune to economic upheaval. Far away from the urban centres, the problems of inflation and devaluation are of little concern. People grow what they need, buy the minimum, or do without. As ever, they get around the neighbourhood in winter by horse-drawn sledge; as ever, they help each other out.

Life in the izbas

Almost every corner of rural Russia now has electricity – its supply was one of Lenin's prime aims – but not necessarily running water. Those who live far from the city may have to go to a well for fresh water, digging away the snow and breaking the ice in winter. The *izbas* (peasants' houses) may all have television aerials, but in 30 per cent of rural houses the toilets

Surface charm The chocolate-box prettiness of this izba belies a rural way of life that is far from easy.

The *banya*: relaxing in the steam bath

Russians are fond of taking steam baths, or *banyas*, which they believe are good for both the body and the mind. In towns, the *banya* is a popular meeting-place, where men put the world to rights over a few drinks and women enjoy their beauty treatments; in the countryside, it is a way of life. The *banya* is usually a little wooden cabin divided into two sections: the first is

for undressing, and the second – the steam room – contains heated stones that are sprinkled with water to release clouds of steam. People lash each other lightly with birch twigs and take turns in the steam room. They have breaks for vodkas or cold beers and *zakuski* (snacks). Finally, they roll in the snow or plunge into the invigorating cold waters of a nearby lake.

On the zigzag path of reform

Nobody foresaw the collapse of the USSR, so nobody planned for it. From Gorbachev on, Russian leaders found themselves dealing with one crisis after another. It was the politics of emergency management, and it left the country dazed and exhausted.

Hero worship Many older Russians long for the strong leadership and the ideological certainties of the Stalin era.

Boris Yeltsin, elected president of the Russian Federation in June 1991, declared the Soviet Union defunct on Christmas day that year. Mikhail Gorbachev suddenly found himself president of a country that no longer existed. He went to his office in the Kremlin to clear his desk – only to find Yeltsin sitting in his chair. The Communist Party which brought both men to power had been outlawed in August after an attempted coup against Gorbachev. The Soviet era was over; the era of untrammelled capitalism was about to begin.

Buy and sell

The face of Russia changed in a morning. Now everybody was an entrepreneur. The broad streets of central Moscow became vast marketplaces selling everything from car parts to Mars bars. State controls of prices were abolished. Inflation wiped out lifetime savings in an instant. The rouble became worthless, and the US dollar was the unofficial Russian currency. The country's net worth was calculated and divided among its citizens, all of whom received a 'voucher' to invest as they chose; most chose to sell it for food.

It was hoped by Yeltsin's young team of pro-market ministers that the economy would emerge from this 'shock therapy' with a solid foundation for a Western economy. But Yeltsin, constantly fearful of the political effects of reform, could not resist meddling. He sacked the reformers, provoked his pro-communist parliament into armed rebellion (which he smashed with tanks), and retreated into an alcoholic sulk.

An air of authoritarianism hung over Yeltsin's last years in office, typified by his vicious war in Chechnya and by his choice of a former middle-ranking KGB man, Vladimir Putin, as prime minister. Putin had almost no experience of government, but was nevertheless nominated by Yeltsin as his successor. In 2000 he was duly elected president of Russia on a slogan which only a secret policeman could have dreamed up: 'Democracy is the dictatorship of law.'

The changing face of the mafia

The Russian mafia is the sinister offspring of *glasnost*. The first *mafiozniki* were veteran black marketeers, men used to making their money at the edge of the law. Their big chance came with Gorbachev's 'dry law', a nationwide vodka ban which created a huge and lucrative underground demand for alcohol. In the 1990s the mafia extended its activities into drugs, political intrigue and international prostitution. Vast fortunes were laundered in the West. Like many Communist *apparatchiks*, the top mafia men have now reinvented themselves as legitimate entrepreneurs.

The call of history Gorbachev hoped to take Soviet socialism back to its Leninist roots; President Putin places his rule in an older, imperial tradition.

Voice of the right The rhetoric of Vladimir Zhirinovsky taps into feelings of lost national prestige.

Memories of the gulag

The history of the gulag is still emerging, both from the bitter experiences of those who endured its privations and from newly opened archives.

Remnants of horror *Watchtowers, barbed wire and snow are reminders of a grim past.*

Since the autumn of 1999, Russians have been gripped by an ongoing television series, *The boats have anchored*. The programmes are dedicated to the songs of the gulag, the general term for the hundreds of penal colonies and work camps that proliferated in the USSR from the 1920s to the 1980s.

A history recovered

In 1988 the Memorial Association was founded to document the camps and to commemorate the victims of Stalinism. Everyone who comes has an unhappy story to tell. They remember the time when anyone – anyone at all – could become a *zek* (prisoner of the gulag) for nothing more than stealing a slice of bread, for receiving or copying or passing on *samizdat* (an underground publication), or for being more than 20 minutes late. Every story is like an echo of the tales told by famous *zeks* such as Yevgeniya Ginzburg (*Journey Into the Whirlwind*) and Alexander Solzhenitsyn.

Fifteen million zeks

In his *Gulag Archipelago* (1973), Solzhenitsyn revealed the extent of the Soviet system of concentration camps (gulag is an acronym from the Russian *Glavnoye Upravleniye Lagerei*, Chief Administration of Corrective Labour Camps). Today, some of the gulag archives have been opened, providing

Faceless zeks *Peasants, workers, leftists, rightists and dissidents were all reduced to ciphers in their shabby uniforms and banished to the gulag.*

horrific figures: 2.5 million deaths in 1953 alone; 15 million arrested between 1930 and 1953 and thrown into a universe of brutality, hunger, cold and forced labour. The total number of dead is estimated at some 14.5 million people.

The inhabitants of the gulag were also a slave labour force, used on the huge construction projects of the 1930s. Almost 200 000 prisoners were employed on the building of the Moscow-Volga-Don Canal in the 1930s, and almost that number on the Baikal-Amur Railway.

The martyrs of Kolyma

Siberia was the main location of the gulag, in particular around Kolyma and its gold mines in the far north-east. From Yakutia to Kamchatka, from the Arctic to the Sea of Okhotsk, camp succeeded camp (Solzhenitsyn lists 32 camps in this area). In winter, the temperature drops to –50°C (–58°F). The system remained in operation, though at a lower level, until the collapse of the USSR.

Hardly anything remains of the nightmare today except decaying buildings and the memories of the survivors.

Voice of the damned *Alexander Solzhenitsyn spoke for those who had suffered in the camps. Expelled from the USSR after receiving the Nobel prize for literature in 1970, he returned to Russia 20 years later.*

Forced resettlement

Another type of Siberian gulag was made up of 'special settlers' from areas of ethnic minorities that Stalin considered to be dangerous. Deprived of any civil or political rights, 2.8 million of these people were transported from their homes for no other reason than their ethnic origins. Finns were deported from Leningrad, Poles from Ukraine, Germans from the Volga, Koreans from the Far East, Jews from the west, Tartars from Crimea, along with countless others. Mostly, the deportees were dumped in Siberia and left destitute. It was a policy that lasted from 1932 to 1956, the year in which Nikita Khrushchev denounced Stalin.

Ecology under threat

Soviet administrators wanted to believe that Russia's natural wealth was inexhaustible. They never considered the long-lasting effects of industrial pollution on health, both of the population and the environment. A clean-up operation is long overdue.

At first glance, Dzerzhinsk is much like any other town – grey façades looming up from open countryside, smoking chimneys reflected in the waters of a lake. But when in 1998 Greenpeace linked up with an American photographer, Stanley Greene, they exposed the wretched reality. This quite ordinary city some 218 miles (350 km) east of Moscow is so polluted that it is poisoning its inhabitants. It is not alone. There are many towns in a similar situation.

Oil hazard Oil from a Baku refinery sprays from a decaying tap on to the shore of the Caspian, the world's largest inland sea.

Chemical dumps

In Dzerzhinsk, the doctors see daily testimony to the crimes committed by industries that scorned both people and nature. Nine out of ten women in labour have complications. Numerous babies are born with birth defects. Pollution affecting the air, ground and food has reduced life expectancy to little more than 50 years.

Water birds landing on Dzerzhinsk's lake soon die. The water's clear reflective surface conceals the end products of the chemicals on which the town's inhabitants depended for their livelihood, but which are now hastening their end. Over the years, the lake has become a deadly cocktail of effluents.

In Volgodonsk, 50-years' worth of toxic waste from its chemical plant has turned fields white. Stockpiles of sodium sulphate threaten the entire Rostov region. Using the woefully inadequate reprocessing facilities available it will take 20 years to clear the pollutants. Meanwhile the local population is suffering from lung and eye diseases caused by evaporation from the waste.

Disappearing seas

Since *glasnost* lifted the veil and allowed the formation of ecological groups – more than 60 000 registered in the old Soviet Union in 1998 – the scale of the disaster has gradually become clear.

Lake Baikal, the place they call the 'sacred pearl of Siberia', which holds one-fifth of the world's fresh water, is dangerously polluted by the cellulose factory in Baikalsk. The Volga is at risk of asphyxia from algae fed by run-off from fertilisers and pesticides. Heavy metals have built up in the bottom of reservoirs, upsetting the ecological balance so that fish can no longer get to their spawning grounds. Nationwide, Russia's stocks of sturgeon – once the source of the world's caviar – fell from 42 000 tons in 1980 to 5000 tons in 2000.

The Caspian, an inland sea in which pollution builds inexorably, is dying. The Aral Sea has halved in size (see box, left), and the Sea of Azov faces a similar fate. Fishing yields in the Sea of Azov have declined by 97 per cent since the 1970s, the amount of water flowing into the sea has fallen and its salinity increased.

The death of the Aral Sea

The fishermen began to abandon the shores of the Aral Sea in the mid-1960s. After 1991, the exodus accelerated: 75 000 people are said to have left a lake that has become an ecological catastrophe. Once, the Aral Sea was fed by the water of the Amu-Darya and Syr-Darya rivers, running down from the heights of the Pamirs. Then cotton was introduced, along with massive irrigation systems, which directed water away from the Aral Sea. By the 1960s, 60 per cent of the water was lost en route; now, the inflow is a mere trickle and even this water is polluted with pesticides and defoliants. The Aral is evaporating and its area has halved. Fishing villages lie empty 18 miles (30 km) from the shore, overlooking the hulks of fishing boats. Saline-laden winds spread desolation.

No entry A soldier bars access to one of 1800 communities evacuated after the explosion of the Chernobyl nuclear power station in 1986.

Oil lake *A leak from a pipeline spreads oil through woodland in the Pechora valley, which runs northwards from the northern Urals.*

Measures such as prohibiting fishing and poaching, processing industrial waste and banning gas and oil exploration would provide some respite for the Azov, but there are no resources and little enthusiasm among the population to implement such drastic pro-

posals. Ecological concerns are low on the list of priorities. There is no money to repair leaky oil pipes or to upgrade ageing industrial installations. According to the most reliable figures, a quarter of all tap water in Russia is not fit to drink and 35 million people live in cities where the air is not fit to breathe. Greenpeace estimates that three-quarters of the former USSR is contaminated by dioxins.

State secrets

Despite the accumulating evidence, the extent of the ecological problem remains hidden to the rest of the world. It is still hard to assess the impact of the catastrophe at the Chernobyl nuclear power station in 1986. Officially, the death toll is 'only' 45 – the firemen sent in to fight the inferno in Reactor No 4. What of those who have died, and have yet to die of radiation sickness? The physicist Vassili Nesterenko, director of the Nuclear Energy Institute of Belarus's Academy of Sciences, had his career ruined for trying to find out the truth in his fight to save the children of Chernobyl.

In another case, Alexander Nikitin, an army captain, claims he was arrested in 1996 and accused of high treason for giving Norwegian ecologists information on the pollution from the nuclear waste dumped by the Northern Fleet stationed on the Kola Peninsula and around Arkhangelsk. Nikitin was released in 2000. Nothing has been done to remedy the situation he revealed.

Poison protest *Greenpeace members demonstrate against the building of an incineration plant near Moscow.*

Clearing up *Workers tackle the Pechora oil leak, in the territory of the Komi people.*

From Red Army to Russian army

The Russian Army has a long tradition that harks back as far as the defeat of the Mongol horde at Kulikovo Field. Now it is trying to assimilate the Soviet years into its history, while continuing to function as a fighting force.

The Red Army was born in the chaos of the Russian civil war. It was the metal fist of the Revolution, created to defend the regime from its enemies. That revolutionary spirit became central to the Red Army's mythology and tradition. From the wastes of Siberia to the ruins of Berlin, from the streets of Prague to the mountains of Afghanistan, the Red Army was always a crusading army, fighting with ideology as well as guns.

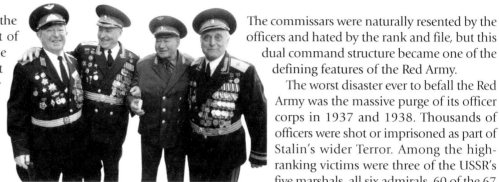
Red Army veterans.

Officers and commissars

So it is strange to note that in the first days, most of the key personnel were former officers of the tsar's imperial armed forces. These 'bourgeois specialists' were recruited because they were the only people who knew how to run an army. To counter any anti-Soviet influence they might have, officers were shadowed by 'political commissars', men drawn from the ranks of the working classes and chosen for their ideological zeal with the power to countermand orders or have serving officers removed.

Recalling glory *Every year on May 9, the Russian army celebrates its victory over Nazi Germany in the Great Patriotic War.*

The commissars were naturally resented by the officers and hated by the rank and file, but this dual command structure became one of the defining features of the Red Army.

The worst disaster ever to befall the Red Army was the massive purge of its officer corps in 1937 and 1938. Thousands of officers were shot or imprisoned as part of Stalin's wider Terror. Among the high-ranking victims were three of the USSR's five marshals, all six admirals, 60 of the 67 corps commanders, 136 of 199 divisional commanders. It has been pointed out that no army has ever suffered such great losses in war as the Soviet Army then suffered in peacetime.

The purges fatally weakened the fighting capability of the armed forces as war loomed. The Red Army was taken completely by surprise when Germany invaded in June 1941. Many units deep inside Soviet territory were overrun in their beds by advancing Panzer units. But after a catastrophic first summer, the Soviet armed forces rallied and even found in their ranks leaders of genius such as Georgi Zhukov. In the later years of the war, the Germans were amazed at the fighting spirit of the Russian soldiers. It was partly

Southern fleet   Although now on Ukrainian territory, Sebastopol still harbours Russian submarines that patrol the Black Sea.

due to that same old ideological spirit – the Russian people generally were driven by an immense righteous anger against the Nazis – but it was also the knowledge that, in Stalin's Russia, death in battle was preferable to failure. With the murderous NKVD (secret police) battalions at their backs, Russian troops pushed on through Europe to Berlin.

The front line of the Cold War

After the war, the role and the image of the Soviet army changed. It was no longer the force that liberated millions from Nazism; it was now the whip hand of communist oppression. There were large Soviet garrisons throughout Eastern Europe, but on more than one occasion – Hungary in 1956, Czechoslovakia in 1968 – it was felt necessary to protect socialism with invading tanks.

At the same time, the arms race transformed the armed forces into a huge industry, no longer reliant on the sheer preponderance of manpower alone. The Cold War Soviet army was technologically sophisticated, massively funded and lavishly equipped.

The bottomless funding dried up when the USSR collapsed. Russian forces were unceremoniously booted out of their bases in Eastern Europe and the 'near abroad', but had no homes to come back to. There was also no money to pay officers or even to maintain

Guard duty   The honour guard at Lenin's tomb is drawn from a unit called the 'Separate Kremlin Regiment', formerly a part of the KGB's interior forces.

The Chechen conflict

The fragmentation of the Soviet Union did not end when the 15 Soviet republics became sovereign states. Within the Russian republic there are smaller regions and republics with separatist ambitions. One of these republics is Chechnya, on the border with the Caucasus. Russian troops were sent there in 1993 to prevent the republic breaking away, and have been involved in a low-level but devastating conflict ever since. The city of Grozny, the Chechen capital, has been utterly destroyed. Like the Afghan war before it (1979-89), Chechnya has been called Russia's Vietnam. There are some points of comparison: the Russian troops are mostly conscripts with no clear idea of their role; the Chechens are skilled guerrilla fighters who use their knowledge of the land to harry the invaders; and the main victims of the fighting are defenceless civilians.

The war, which began again in 1999, shows no sign of ending. Putin made it an election promise to conclude the Chechen conflict, and in 2003, a referendum was conducted, but the Chechens continue to resist. There was international pressure on the Russians to curb their most brutal tactics, but this virtually ceased following the global 'war against terrorism'.

infrastructure such as missile bases. As these problems became critical, the government fiddled with insignia, replacing the hammer-and-sickle cap badge on officers' uniforms with the tsarist double-headed eagle. It was a backward-looking gesture, when forward-looking reforms were long overdue.

By train to the Far East

It is the world's longest train journey. For eight days, the Trans-Siberian rumbles past coloured peasant huts, crosses frozen rivers and endless steppes and penetrates dense forests. Linking Russia's European west to its Far East, the railway passes through seven time zones and 6500 miles (10 500 km) to join Moscow with the Pacific port of Vladivostok. It has proved its worth as a supply route in war and trade route in peace.

East-west link *The Trans-Siberian became a symbol of Russian expansion.*

Hauled by mighty Soviet engines, the Trans-Siberian carries its passengers through such extremes of landscape and over such immense distances, that it induces in them a sense of being in a world apart. The train becomes the traveller's domain. Life revolves around the restaurant car, where those who gather for a drink or a meal, or a game of chess, come from far and wide across the Russian Federation. The traveller's only contact with the outside world is at stations, where crowds of babushkas jostle at the windows selling snacks and drinks.

Engine of Russian colonisation

In the late 19th century Tsar Alexander III decided to open up the remote and sparsely inhabited eastern regions of his empire. He was driven in part by military necessity, for the Americans were moving closer having acquired Alaska from the Russians, and European powers were active in China. His plan was to make these vast areas accessible for settlement as a means of relieving overpopulation in the west. He was also keen to exploit Siberia's immense resources of minerals, wood and metals. To serve the

A barrier crossed *A train skirts Lake Baikal's rugged shores. At one time, passengers had to get out at the lakeside and cross by boat, or in winter by sled. Now 33 tunnels through the hills take the line on towards the Pacific.*

Wilderness highway *Two tracks open Siberia to the east and west. These provide vital links for a landlocked area with a dearth of roads.*

pioneers of the new frontier, the tsar authorised the construction of a railway that would reach right to the limits of his realm at Vladivostok. Work began in 1891. When it was finished in 1905, the railway acquired a second line parallel to the first, and branch lines south to Beijing and Port Arthur (Lüshun). Many towns owed their expansion to the Trans-Siberian, such as Omsk, Krasnoyarsk, Novosibirsk, Chelyabinsk, Khabarovsk.

The BAM: the Trans-Siberian's northern offshoot

Skirting Lake Baikal to the north, the Baikal-Amur Magistral (BAM) acts as an alternative route to the Trans-Siberian proper, which cuts through the mountains south of the great lake. Running between Ust-Kut and Komsomolsk-on-Amur, the BAM totals 2750 miles (4400 km) of track, including branch lines. After countless deferrals, the project was tackled with typical Soviet determination. The challenges it faced were immense – permafrost, earthquake-prone zones, marshes, rivers, mountains and a staggering range of temperatures. The line was finally completed in 1984, and soon proved its value, taking the pressure off the Trans-Siberian and opening up new and remote areas of Siberia.

Pit stop *Food and drink stalls on Irkutsk station do brisk trade as a train makes its 20-minute stop. At most of the 97 stations, the train usually halts for three to five minutes beside station clocks with three hour hands showing local time, Moscow time and Vladivostok time.*

Home for a week *The Russian gauge is 4 in (10 cm) wider than the European gauge and the Trans-Siberian's drab green carriages are consequently more spacious. Passengers have a choice between travelling 'soft' class in a double compartment with two couchettes, and 'hard class' with four, six or eight couchettes to a compartment.*

A vital axis

The Trans-Siberian is one of the most important trade routes in the world and Russia's chief means of transporting goods between its European west and the Pacific coastal ports of Vladivostock and Nakhodka, some 60 miles (100 km) farther east. The frequent daily departures carry mainly minerals and fresh produce. Despite modern-day competition from trans-Asiatic road links farther south, the Trans-Siberian's container trains allow it to remain competitive for commercial freight.

Water on tap *The Trans-Siberian may not be the height of luxury, but it works. Every carriage has a hot water heater, so that passengers can make tea at any time on their eight-day journey.*

The end of the line, almost

Before the line was extended to Nakhodka, the Trans-Siberian came to a halt in Vladivostok, in a station strangely decorated with stuccoes and frescoes, arrows and gargoyles. The odd decor recalls the wealth that poured into the city – its name means 'Ruler of the East' – when it was founded in 1860. The sense of style endures in grand, turn-of-the-century redbrick buildings displaying cupolas and wooden balconies. Barred to foreigners for years, the city is open once more. Possibly its faded charms will be renewed by its growing international links, not only with Europe (along the railway), but also with Japan and China, and – through its natural harbour – with other, more distant sources of finance. When Russia is ready to look beyond its eastern shores, Vladivostok will be its staging post.

The peoples of the North

Herding reindeer, hunting and fishing were the traditional means of survival for the nomadic peoples of the tundra and taiga until the Soviet Union's swingeing policy of 'russification' upset the balance. Many were forcibly settled, but a hardy few continue to live as they have always done.

Those whom the Soviets disparagingly called 'the little peoples of the North' depend on herding, hunting and fishing for their livelihood. In the spring, the tribes leave their winter villages in the taiga and travel in search of new pastures for their reindeer, pausing when the herd finds food. In the autumn, with the chief's sled opening the way and the women bringing up the rear, the community retraces its steps to seek the shelter of the forests.

Reindeer economy

The reindeer is the foundation of this way of life. They provide the main means of transport to pull the sledges (although dogs are sometimes used). Reindeer meat, eaten raw, is the nomads' basic food. When sold to the nearest state farm, it provides the main source of income with which to buy other essentials. Reindeer skin is used to cover the conical tents, called *choums*, and to make clothing. Skin from reindeer feet, when dried in the sun, is made into shoes and runners for skis.

Trading places

More than 20 ethnic groups live in northern Siberia. These minorities are scattered either side of the Arctic Circle, and in the Far East they extend southwards to the Amur, Sakhalin Island and the

Summer quarters *In summer the northern people set up camp in choums (conical tents), to be near their grazing herds of reindeer.*

Snug skins *A Nenets woman and her children from the Arkhangelsk region wear clothing made of reindeer skin – the best protection from the bitter cold.*

Hardy survivors

Among the northern people, the most populous are the Nenets from around Arkhangelsk (35 000), followed by the Evenks of the Krasnoyarsk region (30 000), the Evenis of the Yenisei (17 000) and the Chukchi of north Kamchatka (15 000). The Dolgans of the Taymyr Peninsula number fewer than 7000. Other groups are much smaller: the Nganasans of Taymyr (1300), the Yenets of the lower Yenisei (barely 200), the Yukaghirs of Kolyma (1100), the Inuit of the Bering Strait (1700), the Aleuts of Kamchatka (700), the Nivkhs (4600) and the Oroks of Sakhalin Island (700).

New future A Nenets child prepares for school, which may well spell integration with the dominant Russian culture.

Raw material Reindeer skins are set out to dry, before being turned into tents, clothes and shoes.

Kamchatka Peninsula. Each one has its own language and cultural traditions.

Until the 17th century they lived a generally self-sufficient life in harmony with nature, never taking more than they needed from the land. Trade was brisk between the different groups: Chukchis in north-eastern Siberia would exchange reindeer skins and meat for walrus skins and fish with the coastal people. Then life began to change: Russia started to spread its influence to the east, demanding tributes from the local people and trying to win favour with trade fairs and bribes – the most lethal of which was vodka. Merchants would demand huge prices for goods such as flour, sugar and tobacco, and tribes such as the Nenets of north-western Siberia, their ability to negotiate a fair price fogged by alcohol, soon found themselves in debt. In the 19th century it was not unusual for a Nenets still to be repaying his grandfather's debts. The traders also brought diseases such as smallpox, which began to take their toll on the communities.

Winter refuge In winter, the nomadic peoples take refuge in wooden huts in villages in the taiga. Often there is no running water.

Rampant 'russification'

The coming of the Soviets in the early 20th century added to the plight of the northern people. Many were forcibly settled in collective farms from the 1930s onwards, but not without a struggle. Nenets reindeer breeders attacked the town of Vorkuta, but were soon beaten back by the Russian air force. Separated from their natural way of life, suicide was not uncommon. Children were taken from their families and sent to state boarding schools to learn Russian – and to be indoctrinated in Soviet ideology. Mixed marriages increased, further undermining the languages and cultures of the different groups.

The exploitation of natural resources – gas, oil and minerals – in the 1950s and 1960s was of little benefit locally. Jobs went to the

thousands of imported workers. In Chukotka, where the Soviets extracted 40 per cent of the nation's gold, the Chukchis saw not a rouble in return. With industry came pollution: the bones of reindeer-herding Koryaks from the Kamchatka Peninsula were found to have far higher levels of lead and caesium than those of people who did not eat reindeer meat. Radioactive tests in the 1950s and 1960s had contaminated lichen, the reindeers' staple food.

Hope for the 21st century

All is not lost, however, for the nomadic families. In 1993, the Russian government adopted a charter guaranteeing the protection of civil rights and protecting areas occupied by traditional ethnic groups. It held out the possibility for a return to traditional ways, which could save many nomadic groups from extinction. The desire for more freedom is particularly strong in Sakha (Yakutia), where locals have proposed territorial assemblies that would provide a forum for all native groups. Ethnic Siberians dream of the sort of recognition already achieved by tribal groups in North America.

Ancient and modern The dwelling is traditional, but the food is not. A diet of shop-bought goods has contributed to a decline in health among the people.

Arctic hunter In Soviet times many Inuits were forcibly resettled. Today, they are becoming reunited with their fellow tribespeople in Alaska and the Bering Strait.

Tundra, taiga, steppe: the world of the nomads

For centuries nomadic tribes have migrated between frozen tundra and forested taiga, and across the great open plains of the steppes. They have herded animals and traded goods, and their lives have always been dictated by the seasons.

Loose covers *The choum of the Nenets, traditionally covered with many layers of reindeer hide, is now sometimes made with canvas.*

The few remaining groups of herding and hunting nomads in Siberia and Central Asia depend for their livelihood on being able to follow the rhythm of the seasons. They move regularly with their livestock in search of pastures, or shelter. In desert areas their routes are governed by the whereabouts of water sources.

New patterns of life

Native Siberian groups – that is, those whose cultures predate the coming of the Russians – number a little more than 1.5 million (out of a total Siberian population of about 32 million). Today's 'natives' break down into a score of groups (see page 86), some represented only by a few members. The Buryats, a Mongol people who live in the Lake Baikal area, are the most numerous, with about 400 000 individuals. Buryats were once all nomads who lived by herding and hunting, but they were mostly settled under Soviet rule during the 1940s.

The Yakuts – Turko-Mongol people of north-eastern Siberia – are the second most populous group. They survived mainly by herding horses and reindeer, and lived in huts dug into the ground as a protection against the winter cold. In summer, they migrated with their animals to find good grazing land. They would construct *choums* (yurts) – domed tents similar to those used by nomads right across Central Asia. Now mostly settled, the Yakuts have swapped their traditional living-quarters for more comfortable *izbas* (Russian-style cottages).

Hunting in the taiga

In the taiga, the five months from November to March are the hunting season. Hunting is usually done by reindeer or dog sledge, though snowmobiles are also used, if petrol is available. The most common prey are ermine and sable, but the ambition of every hunter is to kill a wolf or bear. These animals are a menace to the herdsmen as they prey on domestic stock.

A land for each season

Nomad life was – and still is for some – dependent on the three distinctive bands of climate and vegetation that sweep across northern Russia from west to east: the tundra, taiga and steppe.

The tundra is a vast icy region straddling the Arctic Circle, stretching from the Bering Strait to the Kara Sea. This is the domain of the Inuit, Chukchi, Eveni and Nenets. Though most of these people have been absorbed into the Russian mainstream and a settled lifestyle, 200 000 continue their nomadic existence in groups of a few thousand each.

In the tundra, the subsoil remains permanently frozen all year round preventing the growth of trees or any plants with deep roots. There is little or no daylight in winter. For a brief few months in summer – when the land is bathed in light for almost 24 hours a day – the snow melts on the region's southerly fringes, allowing the upper layer of soil to thaw and a carpet of moss and lichen to

Adaptable housing *The Turkmen yurt has a felt-covered hole at the top that can be closed for warmth or opened to let smoke out and light in.*

New camp *Kyrgyz nomads set up a new summer campsite in the mountains. The choice of site depends on a combination of traditional places of settlement and the quality of the surrounding grassland.*

Managing the herds   Most nomads of the taiga and tundra live by rearing reindeer. Herds may number thousands of animals.

flourish. Nomads journey north in search of grazing for their reindeer. Wildlife such as wolves, silver foxes and ermine venture out from the protection of the forests. In winter only bears and seals can cope with such extreme conditions.

The wild woods

Pockets of permafrost exist even in the thick swathe of forest, known as the taiga, that borders the southern tundra. Here spruce trees stand crookedly in what is known as a 'drunken forest', their roots unable to penetrate the frozen subsoil.

The taiga comprises about a third of the world's forested area. Birch, pine and larch provide a dense covering for Russian bear, sable and elk, though illegal logging is depleting their habitats.

All change on the steppes

Moving south, the forest thins and gives way to the wide open grasslands and arid plains of the steppes. This was once a great east-west highway between China, Central Asia and Europe for nomadic herdsmen, traders and Mongol invaders. Sunni Islamic nomads – Kazakhs, Tajiks, Tatars, Uigurs and Turkmens who spoke Turkic and Iranian languages – crisscrossed the steppes on their migratory routes. But their nomadic ways are a thing of the past. The settlement of these tribes was begun, often with great brutality, by imperial armies in the late 19th century and continued by the Soviet regime. Thousands of outsiders were transported to the steppes of Kazakhstan, for instance, in the 1940s. Urban centres developed and the land was transformed by huge irrigation schemes and giant collective farms. The nomads were ordered to work on the farms and conform to a settled way of life.

Only a few Kalmuk herders, Buddhists rather than Muslims, retain their nomadic ways, tending their flocks on the right bank of the lower Volga. A few Kyrgyz – Muslims of Turkish stock – still preserve the tradition of carrying goods along the old silk roads, leading camel caravans across the high Pamirs. But it is not a way of life that can survive competition from trucks for much longer.

Beasts of burden   In Central Asia, two-humped Bactrian camels have been used for centuries to carry goods between east and west.

The Caucasus: a melting-pot of peoples

Circassians and Chechens, Ingush and Ossetians, Avars and Abkhazians: the Caucasus encompasses a multiplicity of ethnic groups. With its legendary heroes and fierce mountain dwellers, it is also a place of impenetrable mystery.

Tribal headgear *An Ingush wearing a traditional hat.*

The Caucasus stands between the Black Sea and the Caspian, between Slav and Muslim. Its rugged mountains are home to a mélange of peoples, languages and cultures. Its 22 million inhabitants consist of about 50 ethnic groups living in ten states or autonomous regions. It was always like this: when the Romans occupied the region they had 80 interpreters; the Arabs called it the 'Mountain of Languages'.

Inhabited from prehistoric times, the Caucasus is 650 miles (1000 km) across and its mountains rise to 18 000 ft (5500 m) high. Always at the mercy of conquerors and migrants, its rough landscapes have seen the arrival, settlement and flight of countless ethnic groups. At the end of the 19th century, imperial Russia moved in, hungry for the region's mines and minerals. Soviet rule imposed on the

The magical table songs of Georgia

There is no music in the world like the haunting plainsong of Georgia. And nowhere in the world is singing so intertwined with the solemn, joyous business of drinking wine and feasting. In Georgia, songs are an integral part of any celebration. It is only the men who sing, improvising

Music maker *Instruments like the Svanetian harp enrich the musical tradition – but music without wine or meat for the table is unthinkable.*

swooping polyphonic harmonies over a droning bass line. The themes are the same as in that other great Georgian art form, the drinking toast. They speak of sorrow and happiness, the love of women, respect for elders and guests, the Georgian land and its myths. These table songs are as resonant and dramatic as the Caucasus itself. With your eyes shut and the red wine in your veins, you could believe that the very mountains were singing.

local herders and farmers an improbable set of administrative borders. In this lay the seeds of future trouble, for when the Soviet Union collapsed in 1991, the area shattered into rival factions.

Hidden life   In remote villages, communities continue to follow their ancient pattern of life, as this marriage in the mountains of Dagestan illustrates.

Deep traditions

Until the 19th century, Caucasian society was organised along feudal lines, sometimes with no formal hierarchies, and private ownership of property was often unknown. Even now, the modern way of life has hardly made an impact on the remote mountain villages. They are a world apart,

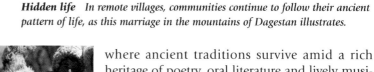

Mix of peoples   Native cultures have been joined by Armenians, Persians, Greeks, Romans, Turks, Mongols and Slavs.

where ancient traditions survive amid a rich heritage of poetry, oral literature and lively musicality, interwoven with their own distinctive architecture and style of handicrafts.

Religious diversity

Three major religions rub shoulders in the Caucasus: Islam, Christianity and Judaism. Islam is represented by the Azeris, who are Shi'ite Muslims, and by Chechens, who are Sunnis. The mountains of Dagestan and Azerbaijan are home for several Tat-speaking Jewish communities. Christians may follow either Orthodox Russian traditions, or those of the Georgian Church, or the Gregorian Church of Armenia. Both local Orthodox and Catholics follow the liturgy of St Gregory the Illuminator, who converted Armenia to Christianity, *c*.300, and made it the 'first Christian nation'.

The Caucasian tinderbox

Since the collapse of the Soviet Union, local tensions in the Caucasus have led to conflicts. Chechnya declared independence from Russia in 1991, which led to fighting between pro-separatist and anti-separatist groups. Russia intervened, in part driven by the

need to ensure the flow of oil from Baku. So far, there is no resolution to this struggle between Russian firepower and ephemeral guerrillas. Since 1992, Azerbaijan and Armenia have been in a separate dispute over Armenian claims to Nagorno-Karabakh, which is in Azerbaijan but populated by Armenians. In Georgia, the Southern Ossetians want union with their northern fellows, which Georgia opposes to keep control of the mountain passes. In the west, the Abkhazians are also fighting for independence from Georgia.

Mourning loss   Chechen women grieve the loss of sons and husbands in Caucasia's cruellest war.

Highland fortress   Watchtowers are typical of the isolated upland villages of the Ingush, a people renowned for their sturdy independence of spirit.

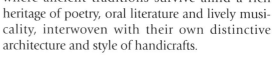

Altaic
- Turk
- Mongol

Caucasian
- North-west
- North-east
- North-centre
- South

Indo-European
- Slav
- Armenian
- Iranian

Country life *Tchaikovsky's house in Klin is a fine 19th-century dacha.*

A room of one's own

Russians are fond of quoting the English proverb 'My home is my castle'. They seem to have a talent as a nation for making a comfortable space out of the most unpromising circumstances. It is a talent they have had plenty of opportunity to hone. Housing has been a chronic problem for successive Russian governments, and the difficulties of finding living room and privacy are not confined to the big urban centres.

Russians love the countryside, and it is the dream of every city-dweller to own a little home in the country, a place to fish, chop wood, swim and grow a few vegetables. This is a country where the word 'peasant' has no negative associations: most Russians know that they are peasants under the skin.

A house of wood

The *izba*, the traditional peasant house, is built of wood chosen both for its practical and aesthetic qualities – pine and fir have a soft yellow glow, while birch has a silvery quality. Usually, the *izba* consists of just one room dominated by the stove that is essential to surviving the rigours of winter. It does not have much furniture: bunks that double as seats built into the walls to save space, a table, a few wooden items of cutlery, and an icon hanging in what is known as the *krasny ugolok*, the 'beautiful corner'. It is only outside that creativity is let loose, on windows framed by wooden traceries, mouldings, pediments and carved, often brightly painted uprights.

Towns underwent rapid change after the 1917 revolution. Many familes moved from the countryside to the city, driven out by war or famine, or else seeking work as the programme of industriali-

Mass living *Suburban apartment blocks provided much-needed housing, but gave industrial cities a bleak uniformity across the former Soviet Union.*

sation got under way. In old cities such as Moscow and Leningrad the large and luxurious homes of the gentry were divided into separate apartments. Whole families would make their home in, say, the dining room of an 18th-century town house, and share the kitchen with the families who lived in all the bedrooms, drawing rooms, dressing rooms and games rooms. The poet Anna Akmatova, for example, lived for years in Leningrad's magnificent Sheremetyev palace, where she shared a poky room with her lover and his ex-wife. This kind of arrangement was the origin of the *kommunalka*, the communal flat

Communal living

The *kommunalka* was a system born of overcrowding and necessity. But some people chose the communal life for ideological reasons. Whole new cities were built by the people who would live and work in them once they were finished; armies of young *komsomoltsy* spent years living in hostels that were little more than army barracks. Many older Russians still look back fondly on the cameraderie and optimism of those years. Certainly the communal life, the process of building socialism with your bare hands, was praised and idealised in countless films throughout the Soviet era.

The Second World War and its aftermath created a new housing crisis. According to official figures, 1710 towns were destroyed, 70 000 villages were burnt and 25 million people were left homeless. The problem was still acute in the 1950s, when Nikita Khrushchev instituted a massive construction programme:

Kizhi: the island-museum

Only 2.3 sq miles (6 km²) in size, the island of Kizhi is a treasure trove of traditional architecture. Set in Lake Onega, 220 miles (350 km) north-east of St Petersburg, Kizhi was turned into a heritage site from the 1950s onwards, as dams raised the lake's waters and threatened low-lying buildings in the area. *Izbas*, windmills, bathhouses and churches were dismantled and rebuilt on Kizhi. The treasures include several churches built without the use of metal. One, the Church of the Transfiguration (1714), has 22 onion domes, each covered with aspen tiles and topped by a Russian cross. The island is a UNESCO world heritage site.

Permanent home *The passion for a settled life spread to many areas, including this group of former nomads in the Seven Lakes region of Tajikistan.*

thousands of five-storey buildings were planted on the edge of cities. Whole suburbs of these identical low-rise homes sprang up. They became known as *khrushchevki* in honour of the man who instigated the policy – or sometimes as *khrushchoby*, a pun on the word *trushchoba*, meaning 'slum'. This slur was unfair: the Khrushchev houses were not luxurious, but they were practical and cosy, and they gave many thousands of families their first experience of living in a self-contained home. They are now seen as infinitely preferable to the high-rises of the Brezhnev era. After the collapse of

Display of wealth *A Kyrgyz carpet maker shows off his wares on the wall of his yurt. Using carpets as wall-hangings is a tradition that is often observed in urban flats.*

communism, the processes that created the *kommunalki* were thrown into reverse. Old buildings became desirable; developers took to offering to rehouse the residents of *kommunalki* in modern blocks with a view to turning their former homes into luxury flats. Many people jumped at the chance.

Driven by the housing needs of foreign businessmen Moscow became a boom town for property speculators. Rates shot up so fast that Moscow became a more expensive place to live than Tokyo. Russia's 'new rich' also played their part: buying up the homes of the pre-revolutionary well-to-do or constructing palatial dachas in the countryside.

The boom is now over, but it has left its mark on the cities, where the gap between rich and poor is fixed in bricks and mortar.

Many cooks *Shared kitchens and bathrooms were common. One of Gorbachev's first promises was to provide every family a home of its own by 2000. Many Soviet* kommunalki *have now gone, but not in the way Gorbachev intended.*

The fun of cooking

It is impossible to generalise about Russian cuisine. In such a vast country countless influences have resulted in as many culinary traditions. About the only thing that unites them is that, however humble a meal may be, it always creates a feeling of conviviality.

Za zdorovye! Zakuski (hors d'oeuvre) and vodka.

The Russians have the Scandinavians to thank for sour cream and smoked meat and fish, and southern cultures for products such as aubergines, grapes and mutton. French cooks, who were first brought to court by Peter the Great in the early 18th century, popularised caviar and created many recipes that are still popular today, such as *salade Olivier* (which we know as Russian salad) or *charlotka* (apple Charlotte). Marital links with the German royal family brought in sauerkraut and the sweet-and-sour sauces that combine meat and fruit in the same dish.

The joy of eating

With a climate that is so demanding, it is only natural to eat a lot, and often. There are no real rules about the times of meals, so if people are eating at 5 pm, it is hard to say whether they are eating a late lunch or early dinner. In the autumn, people love to conserve forest products, such as mushrooms and berries, which are good sources of vitamins for the long winter ahead. Hot soups have a particularly important role in Russian meals – the beetroot-based *borshch*, *shchi* made with pickled cabbage, and *solyanka*, which combines different meats.

One delicacy refuses to be pinned down to season or time of day: ice cream. It is sold everywhere – sellers pass along trains calling 'Morozhenoye!' – and eaten with passion. There is a story that when Winston Churchill visited Russia to co-ordinate the Western wartime alliance in 1942, he was astonished to see a queue of people waiting for ice cream in temperatures of –15°C (5°F) and said, 'Now I see why Hitler will never beat these people.'

Collective markets

Few Russians these days have access to the huge range of products advertised in magazines, because they cannot afford them. But shopping was never easy: the Soviet system was so inefficient that goods were badly distributed and food shortages common. People spent hours queuing on the basis of a rumour of an impending delivery. State enterprises sold mediocre products at fixed prices. Russians were able to find better quality products, and a wider range, in markets where collective farms sold their surpluses – what was produced above the official requirements – at market rates. These markets still exist, offering goods at prices that undercut expensive imports.

Little snacks

No Russian table worthy of the name lacks the traditional appetisers known as *zakuski*, though most visitors find they constitute a meal in themselves. Accompanied by vodka, which is drunk after every eloquent toast, *zakuski* include such delicacies as marinated mushrooms, a selection of canapés, sausages, smoked fish, cheeses, meat pâtés, savoury pastries (*pirozhki*) and caviar. Such an array of hors d'oeuvres constitutes a fine introduction to the Russian love of feasting.

Cold treat *Russians cannot resist ice cream whatever the weather.*

Taking tea *A painting by Boris Kustodiev (1878-1927).*

To your good health

'Za zdorovye!' ('To your health!') – the phrase is everywhere. Vodka occupies a special place on Russian tables and in Russian minds. It comes in many varieties and plays a key role in their fondness for good living. But it is not the only drink they like. Beer, kvas *and tea are all consumed with gusto.*

Vodka was first invented in the 14th century. Three centuries later consumption was being encouraged by the state, which relied on taxes levied on alcohol sales for a third of its budget. Land-owners, too, were all for it, because they produced the wheat and rye from which vodka was distilled, and this, in turn, was used to pay part of the wages of the peasants. The wheels of the Russian economy were oiled by vodka.

Vodka comes in many varieties, either natural or with additives, such as lemon (*Limonnaya*) or pepper (*Pertsovka*). It is traditionally

A look at other drinks

It is not all vodka and tea. Russians may not be known as the world's greatest consumers of mineral water, but they are among its top producers. Most of the mineral water, usually fizzy and powerfully enriched with minerals, comes from the Caucasus (Narzan and Borjomi) and Siberia. Beer and *kvas* are among the most popular alcoholic drinks. The beer, most of which is like lager, is generally locally made. *Kvas* is barley-based or rye-based, and only mildly alcoholic.

Spoiled for choice *Every street corner has a store like this, offering a range of flavoured vodkas.*

Gorbachev versus alcohol

When Gorbachev came to power in 1985, alcoholism was a scourge. In 1960, Russians consumed about 44 pints (25 litres) of alcohol per person per year; by 1980, it had more than doubled. The result was catastrophic: delinquency, disease, absenteeism and premature deaths. Under the slogan 'For a sober leadership and a sober population', Gorbachev passed a 'dry law' that ordered lower production, restricted drinking hours, price rises and punishment for drunkenness. Alcohol vanished from buffets and canteens, drunks from the streets. Serious crime fell by 10 per cent. In 1984, consumption stood at 25.9 billion pints (14.7 billion litres); three years later, it had dropped to 14.4 billion pints (8.2 billion litres). But Gorbachev was up against tradition. As Dostoyevsky wrote in *The House of the Dead*: 'Among Russian people, one always finds a certain sympathy for drunks.' Also, the dry law was disastrous for the economy. Gorbachev backed off, and alcoholism remains, as always, a bearable ill for the Russians.

Mass market *A seller of* kvas, *a sort of mild beer usually made from rye, operates from a tanker.*

drunk as an accompaniment to *zakuski*. Toasting guests is an important Russian ritual and can last for some minutes. For each toast vodka is downed in one gulp from a small glass. There is no respite for visitors who are expected to join in and toast their host, the women at the gathering and the spread of food before them.

Tea is the other grand Russian passion. It dates from the 17th century and always used to be made with hot water from a samovar, a sort of pot-bellied kettle that burns coal to heat water. Today, a strong brew is prepared in a teapot, which is then diluted with hot water. The sweet-toothed add sugar, or a spoonful of jam made from one of the red fruits, such as strawberry, cherry, or redcurrant.

KBAC

Black Sea riviera

All along the Black Sea's sandy and pebbly seashore lies dense woodland dotted with villages as charming as any in the Mediterranean. Blessed with a gentle mixture of sun and soft breezes, the seaside resorts and spas of the Crimea and Caucasus have long been favourite destinations for holidaymakers, tourists and health fanatics.

Russia's popular Black Sea coast stretches from the port of Novorossiysk to Sochi, the greatest of the resorts. Here, in the south-western Caucasus, winters are mild and summers are cooled by sea breezes. The area is rich in lemon and orange groves, tea plantations and tobacco fields, scattered with laurels, yews, cypresses and magnolias. Such a wealth of greenery, fringed with beaches and dotted with hot springs, is a paradise for tourists. Although Russians had begun to favour Turkish and Bulgarian resorts in recent years, many still frequent this attractive region.

A holiday playground

About 20 miles (35 km) south of Novorossiysk, pinewoods give way to the elegant resort of Gelendzhik, which marks the start of this summer playground. Farther south, a safe distance from the oil port of Tuapse, are dozens of little resorts nestling in sub-tropical landscapes.

Sochi is famous for the 30 hot mineral springs that supply the curative waters of Staraya Matsesta. At the beginning of the 20th century, Sochi was no more than a village. Growth started in 1910, when the powers of its mineral waters were discovered. Crammed with sanatoria and tourist complexes, the town has become the nation's prime seaside resort. Some 13 miles (20 km) of coastline are punctuated with white staircases leading down from parks and gardens to sandy beaches. A botanical garden features 1600 plant

Holiday haven   *Sochi, at the foot of the Caucasus mountains, was for decades the resort of choice for the elite of the Soviet* nomenklatura.

Russia's lost beaches

With the collapse of the Soviet Union, Russia lost a number of its famous Black Sea playgrounds to the newly independent nations of Georgia and the Ukraine. Just south of the border with Georgia, the elegant Abkhazian resorts of Pitsunda and Gagra, once favoured by the Soviet elite, have been practically abandoned. Farther north, the beaches of Yalta and Odessa are in Ukrainian hands.

species. Just beyond Sochi, the little spa town of Khosta is surrounded by cork oaks (*Quercus suber*), perhaps introduced from the south of France. With their spongy inner barks, the trees are still a major source of cork. At the southern fringe of the tourist belt, Adler is noted for its exotic plants, and a spectacular mountain gorge.

New image   Sochi has lost its slightly faded charm and undergone a make-over to suit Western European tastes.

Chess: a Russian success story

Tolstoy and Lenin, both chess players, helped to popularise the game; the Soviet regime encouraged it. As a result, in Russia today chess is more of a passion than anywhere else in the world – it is even played on the street.

The history of chess is long on legend, short on fact. The word is thought to come from the Persian *Shah mat*, 'the king is dead'. As for its origins, different historians have favoured numerous individuals – from Adam to the Greek hero Palamedes – and a score of cultures: the Romans, Babylonians, Scythians, Egyptians, Jews, Chinese, and many others, including the Welsh. But all agree that the game is very old. Archaeologists unearthed terracotta chess pieces in Mesopotamia dating back to 6000 BC. The game probably came to Russia either through the Mongols or the Byzantines in the Middle Ages.

Russia's rise to chess stardom started in the mid-19th century, when Mikhail Chigorin challenged the German (and later US) chess star Wilhelm Steinitz. He did not win, but he became an indefatigable promoter of the game in Russia.

National pastime *Whatever the weather (almost), chess players can be seen hunched over boards in Russia's squares and parks.*

Man versus computer

In 1991, no computer could win a game against either Anatoly Karpov or Garry Kasparov (below). Five years later, IBM's Deep Blue took a game off Kasparov, who drew the next two and won the fourth. For each move, Deep Blue worked through 50 to 100 000 million computations. It is only a matter of time before the arrival of the first artificial grand master.

Russia supreme

The true founders of the Russian school were Chigorin's successors, Aaron Nimzovitch and Alexander Alekhin, who moved to France in 1927 and became world champion in 1927-35 and 1937-46. The game appealed to the Soviets because it symbolised the virtues of power, intelligence and discipline. Chess became a compulsory activity in school. Numerous state-sponsored tournaments were held throughout the USSR. People from all levels of society played at home, in the park, in factories and at camp. As a result, Russia produced more champions than any other country. Mikhail Botvinnik, a poor Jew from a Leningrad suburb, was many times world champion in the 1940s and 1950s, and became a national hero.

Other great names succeeded him: Smyslov, Tal and Petrosian, the giant of the 1960s. In the early 1970s, Boris Spassky and Bobby Fischer (USA) duelled like Cold War warriors. Karpov and Kasparov became the heroes of the 1980s and 1990s. In 1984, the two played for a gruelling 48 games before the match was halted on the grounds that both were exhausted. Kasparov did not lose a match between 1985 and 2000 when he was defeated by Vladimir Kramnik.

Passionate player *The novelist Leo Tolstoy (left) plays chess before an admiring audience.*

Divine renaissance

Despite the best efforts of the communist regime, God is not dead in Russia. Religious faith has survived the decades of persecution, the churches are full of the faithful and the curious, and Orthodoxy is once more a power in the land.

Leader of men Patriarch Alexis II is head of Russia's Orthodox Church.

According to long Orthodox tradition, the Russians were converted to Christianity by the Greek brothers Cyril and Methodius. These evangelistic Byzantine monks translated the scriptures into the Slavonic tongue, and for this purpose created the alphabet (now called Cyrillic after its inventor) in which Russian is still written today.

Heart and soul

Russians were then, and still remain, a deeply religious people. Probably no nation on earth makes such casual and frequent reference to its soul – *dusha bolit*, 'my soul hurts', is a perfectly natural way to describe an emotional upset – and ordinary conversation is peppered with profane little references to God, the world beyond and the Devil, especially the Devil. This was true right through the godless years of Soviet rule. Even when the state was bulldozing churches and annihilating priests, it never tried to root out the religion in Russian speech.

Religion of peace Buddhism, the religion of the Kalmyks, Buryats and Tuvans, also has a following among urban Russians.

The communist faith

It has been noted that Soviet communism was a religious creed rather than a political conviction. It is as if the Russians needed to have somehing to believe in, even if it was atheism. Lenin was transformed into a god almost as soon as he died: his every recorded word had the authority of Holy Writ, and it is no exaggeration to say that his cult amounted to a form of worship. The Communist Party was like a kind of secular priesthood, interpreting the teachings of Lenin for ordinary believers. And the earthly paradise of Communism (as opposed to the present reality of developed socialism) was always a little way into the future, just out of reach.

So the collapse of communism was not just a political and economic disaster, it was also a crisis of faith for millions of communist believers. Their world view was destroyed along with their life savings and their standing in society and the world.

What filled this spiritual gap in people's lives? The old religion, Russian Orthodoxy. As the Soviet Union crumbled, people

Called to the priesthood New recruits are coming forward to train.

The shaman's drum

Many Siberian tribes – such as the Koryaks of Kamchatka and the Nenets of the Yamal Peninsula – mark the death of a man with the sacrifice of a reindeer, so that the animal's spirit can accompany the soul to the next world. The Soviets disapproved of animism and persecuted shamans. Now their chants can be heard once again, accompanied by the rattle of the tambourine that induces a trance and allows the shaman to converse with the spirits of earth, ocean and sky.

flocked back to the neglected churches. It became a fashion among young people to be baptised. Churches which had been abandoned, or converted to use as warehouses, recording studios and factories, were restored by eager volunteers.

People came back to services clutching icons which had been pilfered by their parents or grandparents during the mass desecration of churches in the 1930s.

The power of the Church

At the same time the Church and its hierarchy enjoyed a massive surge of prestige. Under President Yeltsin, the Patriarch Alexis became a powerful political figure.

The fact that the Church hierarchy in Russia had meekly collaborated with the communist state, and that it was so deeply infiltrated that many of its priests and leaders were also KGB agents, was politely ignored by the secular authorities and the public in return for the blessing of the patriarch.

The Church used its new political influence to move against the many Christian and pseudo-Christian sects that had begun to proselytise in Russia. It even opposed a new law guaranteeing religious freedom, because it gave free rein to

Facing Mecca   Muslims pray in an Uzbek mosque. Islam was established in the Uzbekistan region in the 16th century. There are more than 62 million Muslims in Central Asia, as well as 11 million in the Russian republic.

groups such as Scientologists, Moonies, Baptists, Catholics, Mormons. All these faiths were seen merely as variants on Western heresies. To the Church they were false creeds leading people away from the truth of Orthodoxy. It would be a sad irony if the Orthodox Church, persecuted throughout the 20th century, became an enemy of religious freedom in the 21st century.

The triumph of faith

But in the end, the Church is bigger than politics, and its true nature is best seen at worship.

Russian churches are twilit places, often illuminated just by oil lamps, or by the candles before every icon. The choir is hidden from view, which somehow makes the glorious music all the more angelic. Priests come and go according to some strange and sacred choreography: they swing silver thuribles of incense, chant prayers, parade icons or great golden crosses. It is all as beautiful as it is ineffable, as if the whole Russian religion were an attempt to draw little pictures of heaven.

Next year in Jerusalem

There are very few practising Jews in Russia, but the fact that the faith has survived at all is little short of miraculous. Jews were persecuted before the Revolution, and in the Soviet era most Jews abandoned religion. Being a Soviet Jew merely meant belonging to an ethnic minority. Some Russian Jews have gone back to the synagogue, but often they have left Russia to do it: more than a million Russian Jews went to Israel in the 1990s. All over Europe, particularly in Germany, there are vibrant new Russian Jewish communities, singing songs in Hebrew and Yiddish, observing the Sabbath, keeping the old faith alive.

Sporting stars

For decades, athletic prowess was encouraged as a way of expressing and contributing to the power of the state.

Sporting hero
Oleg Blokhin, renowned centre forward.

The countless sportsmen and women who won medals at the Olympic Games and world championships testified to the propaganda myth of Soviet superiority and invincibility.

In sporting terms, Soviet investment in sport paid off magnificently. Their athletes' performances raised standards worldwide. High-jumper Valery Brumel, boxer Nikolai Popenchenko, gymnast Vladislav Andrianov, hockey player Vyacheslav Vedenin, weightlifter Yuri Vlasov, ice-skater Irina Rodnina – all these were names that inspired awe around the world. The mighty Vasili Alexeyev held 80 world weightlifting records in his career, and the swimmer Alexander Popov was a long-time world record holder in the 100 m freestyle.

It is not surprising that Soviet sporting heroes and heroines were delighted to accept their role as national symbols – they were rewarded with honours, material goods and foreign travel. Their great performances illustrated a slogan of the Soviet era: 'From mass physical culture to Olympic victories'.

Growing talent *Physical education remains an educational priority.*

Medal-winners

Participation in sport was encouraged from childhood. The system was designed to spot and encourage talent early, organising groups and arranging competitions in an ascending scale of excellence – school, district, city, region, republic. The final stage was the *Spartakiad*, when the different peoples of the Soviet Union competed against each other.

Since 1992, the principles have not changed; Russia continues to encourage the young – especially in winter sports

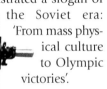

Heavy lifter *Vasili Alexeyev weighed 320 lb (145 kg). His chest measured 60 in (150 cm).*

such as ice-skating and cross-country skiing. Although state sponsorship declined in the mid-1990s – along with Russia's rankings – and top athletes moved abroad, an enthusiastic programme to train youngsters is now in place.

The most popular sports

Ice hockey, closely followed by gymnastics and figure skating, holds pride of place among those sports in which Soviet achievements have been particularly impressive. In the world championships in 1954, Soviet ice hockey players made their stunning debut by winning the gold medal from Canada. A gold medal at the Winter Olympics in Cortina d'Ampezzo in 1956, marked the beginning of

The muscle drain

After the brain drain came the muscle drain. Having seen their status, role, income and often their facilities vanish along with the economy itself, many top Soviet athletes took whatever offers came their way. Emigration was their only hope of a decent life. Their income in post-Soviet Russia was derisory; even the coaches of national teams could expect no more than US$300 a month. If it was hard on the athletes (particularly in track and field), it was even worse for the trainers and scouts. To survive they scattered worldwide. According to the Olympic Committee, 300 handball players and coaches, 100 skaters and 400 ice hockey players fled overseas. Without trainers and scouts, what hope is there of finding a new generation of stars?

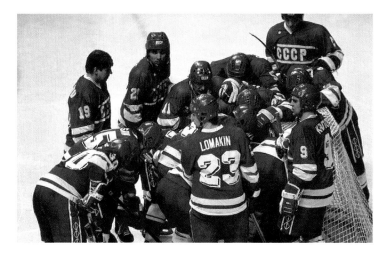

Teamwork *The USSR's ice hockey team dominated the sport from the 1950s to the 1970s, and its players became national heroes.*

a 20-year reign at the top of the sport. In the 1960s, the nation had some 250 000 registered competition players, 3 million younger players, and thousands of teams. Today, the situation is very different. Many of the best players have taken up offers to play professionally in Canada and the USA.

Football has suffered a similar decline. When the national team marched beneath the flag of the USSR, it carried off trophy after trophy: the Olympic gold (1956) in the final against Yugoslavia in

Sprint champion *Alexander Popov, 100 m record holder from 1994, finally admitted defeat at the Sydney Olympics in 2000.*

the first European championships (Paris, 1960), the bronze medal in England in 1966, gold in the Seoul Olympics in 1988. Lev Yashin, the goalkeeper for Moscow Dynamo, was considered the best of all time. But in 1997, in FIFA's world listing of national teams, Russia had dropped to eighth place. A poor showing in the 2002 World Cup led Romantsev, the head coach of the Russian team, and other coaches to resign.

Magic on ice

Ice-skater Irina Rodnina inspired a whole generation. Despite, or perhaps because of, her rigorous training in Moscow, Rodnina displayed astonishing creativity. When her first partner Alexei Ulanov married another skater, Lyudmila Smironova, a nationwide search found a replacement, Alexander Zaitsev. With Zaitsev (they married in 1975), she won three Olympic titles (1972, 1976, 1980) and ten world championships. No one could forget their performance in the world championships in Bratislava in 1973. Despite a sudden and astonishing silence in the music due to a technical problem, the couple did not miss a beat. They danced on without music, to complete their sequence of jumps and turns to perfection. Russia still dominates ice-skating: Ilia Kulik won a gold medal at the 1998 Nagano Olympics.

New goals

Russia is determined to regain its place as the top of the sporting league. It has even begun to broaden its repertoire: in 2001, two Russians were among the world's top 50 junior golfers, just seven years after the opening of the country's first golf course; and the first open equestrian competition was held.

Legendary goalie *Lev Yashin of Moscow Dynamos was nicknamed 'the Black Spider' for his agility and skill in defence.*

101

CHAPTER 5

LIFE IN THE CITY

Russians will still tell you that their country has two capitals: St Petersburg, the proudly Western, coldly classical 'Venice of the North'; and Moscow, the chaotic, medieval fortress city which stands guard against Asia. St Petersburg, say Muscovites, is Russia's biggest museum; Moscow, say Petersburgers, is Russia's biggest village. But these two rivals are not the only cities with rich and glorious histories. There is Novgorod, the even more ancient capital of the Russian state. In Central Asia, there are the cities of the Silk Road to which Victorian adventurers came to watch the trade in the slave markets. And to Russia's south, past the ragged crags of the Caucasus, the noisy, commercial cities of Armenia, Georgia and Azerbaijan straddle the land corridor between Russia and the Near East.

The cathedral of Vladivostok: onion domes are a familiar sight in Russian cities.

The Golden Ring

To the north and east of Moscow lie a number of medieval towns that make up what has become known as the Golden Ring. The name reflects the countless golden cupolas on the churches scattered across the landscape. This part of provincial Russia was once the heart of the ancient principality of Muscovy.

Work of art *Suzdal's Nativity of the Virgin Cathedral, built in 1225.*

Vladimir, Suzdal, Yaroslavl and Sergiyev Posad are among the dozen or so towns in the Golden Ring. They date back to the 12th, 13th and 14th centuries when they were founded on rivers and lakes as outposts of Kievan Rus. Each one has a kremlin, the central citadel that served both as fortress and church, around which markets and other churches arose.

Sergiyev Posad: centre of Russian Orthodoxy

Just an hour's drive north of Moscow, the little town of Sergiyev Posad ('Sergei's Settlement') has a special status as the former residence of the Orthodox patriarch and site of a theological university and seminary. It has been a place of pilgrimage for 500 years. The Bolsheviks declared it a museum town and renamed it Zagorsk after a Communist Party member was assassinated in 1919. Now it has reclaimed its original name, which honours its founder,

the 14th-century St Sergius of Radonezh. Built on a hill, the Trinity monastery is a *lavra*, a monastery of the highest rank. Its thick walls, with their 11 towers, withstood a 16-month siege when the Poles occupied Moscow in the 1600s. The monastery acquired vast wealth from tsars and nobles eager for its blessing. To decorate the cathedral, the 15th-century artist Andrei Rublev painted his most famous icon, the *Old Testament Trinity*, now in the Tretiakov Gallery, Moscow (the icon in the cathedral is a copy). The patriarch and his administrators moved back to Moscow in 1988, but the monastery is, in the eyes of many, Russia's greatest.

Pereslavl Zalesskiy and Rostov Veliky

In Pereslavl Zalesskiy (Zalesskiy means 'beyond the woods'), water is a constant presence. Built on the River Trubezh and Lake Pleshcheyevo in the 12th century, the town is often called Russia's Venice. Its roots long predate its official foundation. Finno-Ugrian tribesmen were supposedly drawn here in the 7th century by a mysterious blue rock they worshipped. The kremlin

Ivanovo's textile trade

Compared to others in the Golden Ring, Ivanovo is a relative newcomer, celebrating its centenary in 1971. Its industrial drabness conceals a 16th-century castle, but it is mainly famous for its textile industry, which started in the 18th century and once supplied one-third of Russia's cotton. The town had an excess population of women textile-workers, who became a byword for man-grabbing assertiveness. The first revolutionary soviet was formed here in 1917.

Enduring glory *Vladimir's 12th-century Golden Gate, once the city's main entrance, is of particular interest since similar models in Istanbul and Kiev have not survived.*

Church fortress *Rostov's kremlin is one of the finest in Russia. It contains six churches and five palaces.*

rivals Moscow's in size (70 acres/28 ha), but its 15 mile (23 km) rampart is now a grassy ring around the central town.

Rostov Veliky (Rostov the Great, so-called to distinguish it from its namesake on the River Don), is one of Russia's oldest towns, first mentioned in the 9th century. It stands on Lake Nero, on the shores of which lemon trees grow in profusion, making Rostov an important area for market gardening. The town was largely destroyed during the Mongol invasions in the 13th century; the centre of Rostov dates from the 17th century.

Yaroslavl and Kostroma

The towns of Yaroslavl and Kostroma at the northern end of the Ring of Gold, 155 miles (250 km) and 190 miles (300 km) respectively north-east of Moscow, were independent city-states until they fell under Moscow's influence in the 15th century. Yaroslavl, named after its founder Yaroslav the Wise in 1010, was Russia's second largest city until the 18th century. Its brick buildings, decorated with colourful glazed tiles, recall its former wealth. Kostroma has a different feel: in 1773 it was destroyed by fire and rebuilt in a formal classical style. But one building survived the inferno – Kostroma's pride – the St Ipaty Monastery, founded in 1332 by Boris Godunov. It was here that the Romanov dynasty was born in 1613 when Mikhail Romanov accepted the crown.

Vladimir and Suzdal

Vladimir was the foremost city of Russia until the 14th century, with Suzdal nearby as its subsidiary. Together, the two formed a centre of artistic, religious and intellectual excellence. In Vladimir, there is little sign of its roots except for two 12th-century treasures, the Assumption Cathedral and St Dmitry's, both with remarkable stone carvings.

Suzdal, by contrast, has a mass of religious buildings. Here, the 11th-century kremlin, and 33 churches and five monasteries from the 13th to the 19th centuries have survived the ravages of time so well that the town has the feel of a living museum.

St Sergius of Radonezh

St Sergius was born around 1313 as Bartholomew Kirillovich, the son of noble parents who had fallen on hard times and moved to the village of Radonezh, north of Moscow. With Russia in Tartar hands, he lived as a hermit in the woods before becoming a monk. He was made head of a monastery in Troitse, the town later named after him as Sergiyev Posad. Sergius refused an offer to become patriarch, but his reputation was such that leaders would come to him for blessing. Among them was Grand Prince Dmitri Donskoi, who came to him in 1380 before leading his army to victory over the Tartars at Kulikovo. Sergius is thus credited with uniting the Russians and reviving the national spirit. He died in 1392 and was canonised 30 years later.

Painted glory *The Church of Elijah the Prophet, 1647-50, built by a rich Yaroslavl merchant, has a superb collection of religious and secular frescoes and paintings.*

Holy ritual *The commemoration of Sergius's death in October is one of many elaborate celebrations held at the Trinity Monastery of St Sergius in Sergiyev Posad.*

Lenin's tomb There is now no long queue to view the city's most famous corpse, which lies in the red granite mausoleum against the Kremlin's wall. No one is sure how long the corpse will endure, and some favour reburial. Nearby, in the wall itself, lie other national heroes, such as the cosmonaut Yuri Gagarin.

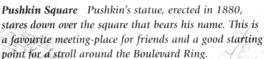

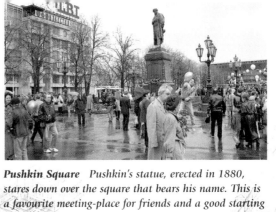

Pushkin Square Pushkin's statue, erected in 1880, stares down over the square that bears his name. This is a favourite meeting-place for friends and a good starting point for a stroll around the Boulevard Ring.

1. **Patriarch Ponds**
2. **Gorky's House**
3. **Pushkin Square**
4. **Statue of Yuri Dolgoruky**
5. **Tverskaya Street**
6. **Bolshoi Theatre**
7. **Theatre Square**
8. **Hotel Metropol**
9. **Lubyanka Square**
10. **Polytechnical Museum**
11. **Church of the Trinity in Nikitniki**
12. **St Basil's Cathedral**
13. **GUM**
14. **Lenin Mausoleum**
15. **State Historical Museum**
16. **Manège Square**
17. **Kremlin**
18. **Russian State Library/ Pashkov House**
19. **House of Friendship**
20. **The Arbat**
21. **Pushkin House Museum**
22. **Ministry of Foreign Affairs**
23. **Pushkin Museum of Fine Art**
24. **Cathedral of Christ the Saviour**
25. **Tretyakov Gallery**
26. **New Tretyakov**

Underground With 144 stations, 155 miles (250 km) of track and 8 million journeys taken daily, the Moscow metro is considered one of the best in the world. Constructed at the height of the Stalinist era in the 1930s, it was built using slave labour. In a euphemistic phrase of the time, it 'mobilised the whole country'. The result is astonishing. The marbled, gilded, frescoed stations, designed by top artists, were meant to double as air-raid shelters. Several stations are tourist attractions, among them Kievskaya, Komsomolskaya, Mayakovskaya and Revolution Square.

GUM Built in the 19th century, the shopping centre was nationalised in 1921 and turned into the State Universal Store (GUM). The biggest shop in the world, it was also a byword for poor quality. Now it has been transformed into a well-stocked place full of imported products.

The many faces of Moscow

Moscow stands at the crossroads between West and East, old and new. Gilded onion domes and ancient palaces butt up against the soaring grey structures of the Soviet era. The streets throng with a multitude of different faces from across Russia and the new republics. Though the capital of the Soviet Union, Moscow was for two centuries eclipsed by its northern rival, St Petersburg. Nowadays, St Petersburg looks like a country cousin by comparison. It is Moscow that is the political, economic, cultural and religious centre of the nation. Its 10.1 million inhabitants were always regarded as privileged because wages were higher and shortages of everyday goods were less common. Even today the average monthly income of a Muscovite is US$293 compared to US$68 for a Siberian. Gradually the city is adapting to its new-found freedoms and taking on the garish trappings of commercialism. It is doing its best to remake itself in the image of a Western European capital, yet Moscow still retains its essentially Russian atmosphere.

Heart of the Kremlin   *Four remarkable churches are situated on Cathedral Square in the centre of the Kremlin: Archangel Cathedral (1508) in the south-eastern corner, Annunciation Cathedral (1489), the Church of the Twelve Apostles (1656) and Assumption Cathedral (1479).*

Gorky's last house   *This superb example of Russian art nouveau, with its stained glass and its wood carvings, was built by Fyodor Shekhtel in 1900. The novelist Maxim Gorky lived here from 1928 until his death in 1936. It is now a museum.*

Labour Day   *The great May Day festival in Moscow has changed its tone somewhat since the bombastic military parades of the Soviet era.*

St Basil's   *Moscow's magnificent cathedral is as much an image of Red Square as the Kremlin's wall. With its embossed and twisted onion domes and its nine chapels, it is a treasure of Russian architecture. Legend has it that Ivan the Terrible, who ordered its construction in the 16th century, had the architect blinded so that he would never be able to build its like again.*

Manège Square   *The area north-west of the Kremlin was completely revamped as part of the major refurbishments leading up to the 850th anniversary of Moscow's foundation in 1997. With the luxurious Okhotny Ryad underground shopping mall, it is now a popular place to wander.*

Moscow

1 Gorky Park, the capital's most famous and popular park, flanks the River Moscow and covers about 290 acres (120 ha). Winter and summer, Muscovites come here to canoe, take rollercoaster rides, skate, wander, snack and flirt.

2 Lomonosov Moscow State University is the tallest of the city's seven Stalinist skyscrapers. It was built between 1949 and 1953, 250 ft (75 m) above the River Moscow on Sparrow Hills (formerly known as Lenin Hills). It offers the best view of the city.

3 Novodevichy (The New Convent of the Virgin) was founded by Grand Prince Vasili in 1514 to celebrate the taking of Smolensk from Lithuania. Rebuilt in the 17th century, it was often used as a prison for troublesome women, such as Peter the Great's half-sister Sophia.

4 Kolomenskoye Museum-Reserve was the summer residence for the tsars in the 16th century, located in the south of the city on a bend of the River Moscow. Today it is an architectural museum.

5 The All-Russian Exhibition Centre (VVTs) was built in the 1950s and 1960s to glorify the achievements of socialism. It is now a commercial centre.

6 Komsomol (Young Communist League) Square is also known as Three Stations Square. It is the main entry point into the capital for travellers arriving from the north-west (Leningrad Station), the Urals (Kazan Station) and Siberia and the Far East (Yaroslavl Station).

4

5

6

Stark contrast The 16th-century Church of the Conception of St Anne, in the ancient Kitay-Gorod quarter. This historic building makes a typically Muscovite contrast with the vast Hotel Rossiya (back left), one of the massive building projects of the 1960s.

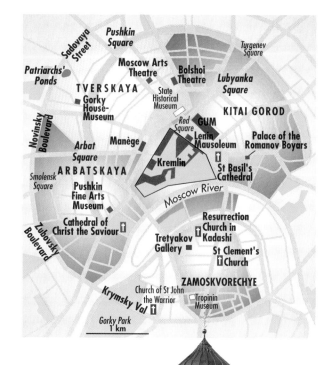

The Pushkin Museum of Fine Art Founded in 1898, the Pushkin Museum was intended to contain copies of Classical sculptures for the benefit of students. But its main claim to fame today is its fine collection of Impressionists and Post-impressionists, among them works by Claude Monet, Paul Gauguin and Pablo Picasso.

A church reborn The Cathedral of Christ the Saviour is a reconstruction of a former church built between 1839 and 1883. The original building was dynamited on Stalin's orders in 1931. Its replacement is a hastily reconstructed copy of the original. It is the brainchild of Moscow's mayor, Yuri Luzhkov, who raised the funds to complete it for Moscow's 850th anniversary in 1997.

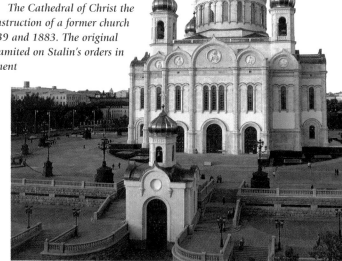

Tourist heartland The Arbat, Moscow's equivalent of Oxford Street with touches of Soho, was much changed in the 1960s when bulldozers flattened a square, a monastery and several churches. It has been pedestrianised and once again is full of life, with portrait painters and buskers touting for custom outside cafés and antiques shops.

Bolshoi Theatre The theatre was built in 1780, destroyed twice by fire (1805 and 1853), then finally rebuilt in 1856. Initially overshadowed by St Petersburg's Mariinsky Theatre, its corps de ballet won international acclaim in the 1950s and has remained a symbol of excellence. Still revered around the world, it faces financial difficulties at home. Its name means 'Big', in contrast to the Maly ('Little') Theatre next door.

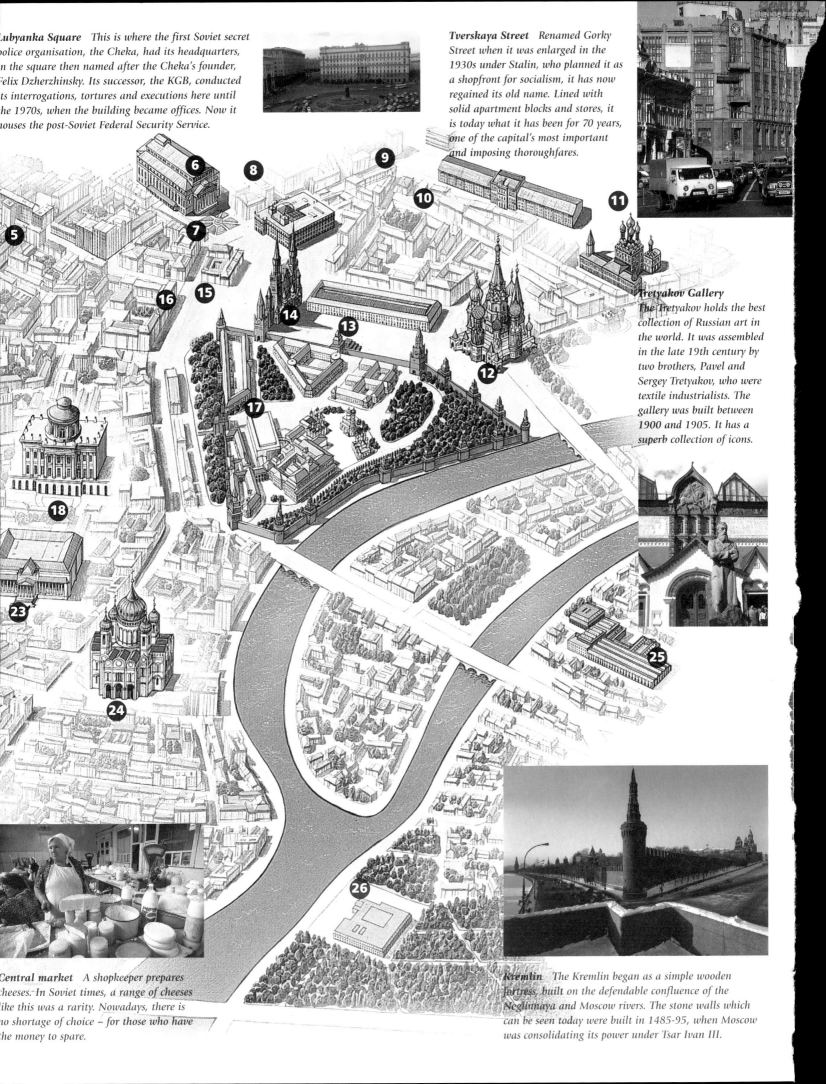

Lubyanka Square This is where the first Soviet secret police organisation, the Cheka, had its headquarters, in the square then named after the Cheka's founder, Felix Dzherzhinsky. Its successor, the KGB, conducted its interrogations, tortures and executions here until the 1970s, when the building became offices. Now it houses the post-Soviet Federal Security Service.

Tverskaya Street Renamed Gorky Street when it was enlarged in the 1930s under Stalin, who planned it as a shopfront for socialism, it has now regained its old name. Lined with solid apartment blocks and stores, it is today what it has been for 70 years, one of the capital's most important and imposing thoroughfares.

Tretyakov Gallery The Tretyakov holds the best collection of Russian art in the world. It was assembled in the late 19th century by two brothers, Pavel and Sergey Tretyakov, who were textile industrialists. The gallery was built between 1900 and 1905. It has a superb collection of icons.

Central market A shopkeeper prepares cheeses. In Soviet times, a range of cheeses like this was a rarity. Nowadays, there is no shortage of choice – for those who have the money to spare.

Kremlin The Kremlin began as a simple wooden fortress, built on the defendable confluence of the Neglinnaya and Moscow rivers. The stone walls which can be seen today were built in 1485-95, when Moscow was consolidating its power under Tsar Ivan III.

St Petersburg, the city-museum

St Petersburg's special qualities derive from its extraordinary history, architectural elegance and glorious riverside setting. Springing from nowhere in the 18th century at the behest of its creator, Peter the Great, it was his 'window on the West,' the only Russian city with access to Europe from the Baltic. It was the nation's capital between 1703 and 1918.

St Petersburg was created entirely by the drive of Peter the Great, who wanted to secure the north of the country against Sweden and to match Europe in every respect. It would provide Russia with access to the Baltic at a time when power was based on sea-faring, for which Peter had a passion. The marshy land at the mouth of the River Neva was to be his chosen base. With vision, drive and expertise Peter made himself the nation's spearhead, founding his new capital in 1703.

The triumph of the will

Peter was ruthless when it came to achieving his ends. By decree, he gathered an army of peasants from his nobles. He set them to work on this unpromising site, digging canals to drain it and driving piles into the marshland to act as foundations for his stone buildings. The nobles were ordered to construct their own

Historic core St Petersburg's founding building, the Peter and Paul Fortress, has stood on the banks of the Neva since 1703. Peter the Great built it as a defence against the Swedes. Until 1917 it held political prisoners.

buildings. Stone was restricted to the centre, while suburbs were to be of wood. Everything was worked out in detail – the height of the buildings, the dimensions of the windows and the size of the bridges. According to some estimates around 100 000 people died during the construction, inspiring the proverbial description of Peter's creation as 'the city built upon bones'. In 1712, ten years after building started, the empire had a new capital, supposedly named by Peter not after himself, as many believe, but after his patron saint, St Peter.

Construction continued at a frantic pace, with architects and artists brought in from all over Europe. By the time of Peter's death in 1725, the population had risen to 40 000, and 90 per cent of Russia's foreign trade passed through the new port.

City under siege

In September 1941, ten weeks after Nazi Germany invaded the Soviet Union, the Wehrmacht cut Leningrad (St Petersburg) off from the rest of the country. Only some 500 000 of the 3.5 million inhabitants had time to flee. Those who remained entered a nightmare: on top of a growing shortage of food and ammunition, and constant bombardment by enemy artillery, they suffered the hardest winter in living memory. They were reduced to eating the cats and dogs, and when these were gone (according to rumours) some resorted to cannibalism. Estimates of the dead range from 700 000 to 1 million. The siege ended only when the Germans retreated on January 27, 1944. It had lasted 872 days, rounded up to the legendary 900.

A name that went full circle

Peter's immediate successors returned to the familiarity of Moscow, but in 1730 his niece, Anna Ivanovna inherited the crown and set up a European-style court in St Petersburg. There followed a century of new growth under Anna, Empress Elizabeth, Catherine the Great

Master horseman The statue depicts Peter the Great trampling the serpent of treachery underfoot. By the French sculptor Etienne Falconet (1716-91), it was immortalised in Alexander Pushkin's poem, The Bronze Horseman.

Guardian beacon *The Rostral Column, with its ships' prows and guardian goddess, is one of two beacons on Vasilevsky Island.*

St Isaac's Cathedral *Designed by the French architect Auguste Montferrand, St Isaac's is the world's third largest church in area: 43 000 sq ft (4000 m²). Its lavish interior includes columns made of malachite and lapis lazuli, marble and semiprecious stones.*

and Alexander I. Fine new palaces, government buildings, academic institutions and churches were built.

By the mid-19th century, St Petersburg was one of Europe's greatest capitals. It became a focal point for Russia's early industries, but there was an undercurrent of discontent. Working conditions were appalling; there was a massive gulf between rich and poor; and the people's demands for constitutional reforms went unheeded. In 1825, a group of democratically minded officers led an abortive coup against the newly proclaimed tsar, Nicholas I. It was bloodily suppressed. Eighty years later, on what became known as Bloody Sunday, Nicholas II's troops opened fire on workers attempting to deliver a petition to the tsar, sparking the revolution of 1905.

The outbreak of war against Germany in 1914 was accompanied by a wave of patriotism during which the city's German name was Russianised to

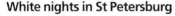

White nights in St Petersburg

Although St Petersburg does not experience the midnight sun, it is far enough north, at a latitude of 60°, for late June to bring 'white nights' of twilit beauty. For a few days either side of the summer solstice (June 21), when the sun sinks just below the horizon, the city is bathed in a soft, magical light. It seems that on these nights, in particular the last ten days of June, no one sleeps. The quaysides come alive with people admiring the palaces reflected in the Neva's broad waters and watching the eight movable bridges opening to allow ships to pass through. A White Nights Dance Festival mounts a programme of special events from folk to ballet, and an International Film Festival has daily screenings and parties.

Rare domes *The onion domes of the Resurrection Church, modelled on St Basil's in Moscow, are an unusual sight in the city of spires. The church marks the spot where Alexander II was assassinated in 1881, hence its other name, the 'Church of the Saviour of the Spilled Blood'.*

Victory column *Conceived by Carlo Rossi, Palace Place is flanked by the Winter Palace. The granite column, erected in 1834, commemorates Alexander I's victory over Napoleon in 1812.*

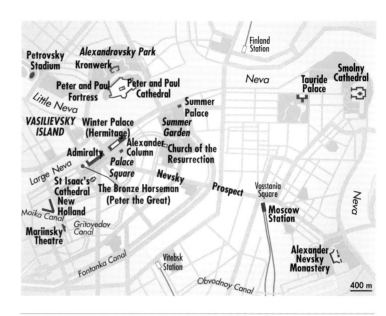

'Petrograd'. In February 1917, at the height of the war, a new revolution broke out. This time Tsar Nicholas II was overthrown and within a few months the Bolsheviks, led by Lenin, had seized power. Moscow became the nation's capital, and so it remained. But after Lenin's death in 1924 the city which was the 'cradle of the revolution' was renamed in his honour: Petrograd became Leningrad.

As Leningrad, it endured unimaginable horrors during the 872-day siege by the invading Germans (see box on page 113). After the war the city was rebuilt and restored, and as the Soviet era came to an end, there was much public debate about its 'true' name. In 1991, by popular demand, Leningrad reverted to St Petersburg, the name it was given by it founding genius nearly 200 years before.

'Venice of the north'
Originally, St Petersburg grew up on 100 or so little islands drained by canals, many of which have now been covered over. Although often compared to Venice, it was in fact inspired by Amsterdam, which Peter knew well. Peter and his French architect, Jean-Baptiste Leblond, avoided Russian models: the churches would not have onion domes, but spires visible from afar. There would be charming canals, avenues, palaces and gardens.

The grandest avenue
'Nothing is more beautiful than the Nevsky Prospect, at least in St Petersburg; it is everything to the city. Is anything lacking in the splendour of this avenue, our capital's

Nevsky Prospect *Today and 100 years ago.*

beauty queen?' So begins the 1835 novella by Nikolai Gogol, *Nevsky Prospect*. It remains the city's best-known street, its 2.5 miles (4 km) leading from the Admiralty, with its golden spire, past a swirl of restaurants, shops and galleries, to the Alexander Nevsky Lavra (monastery).

The city has a unity of architectural style, because so much of it was planned and built over a short period. But within that framework there is an astonishing variety: Dutch and German severity in façades and stairways that typify the fashion of the time; Baroque exuberance introduced by the Italian Bartolomeo Rastrelli; and the Neoclassical restraint favoured by Catherine the Great and Alexander I in colonnaded squares designed by Carlo Rossi. Into this historic mix, a few eclectic late 19th-century additions

A short history of the world's biggest museum

The Hermitage, ranging along the banks of the Neva, consists of five buildings of which the largest, the Winter Palace, has 1057 rooms. Catherine the Great started this vast project in 1754, and to adorn her new creation began to extend Peter the Great's art collection. In 1764, she bought 225 canvases originally intended for Frederick II of Prussia. In 1770, she purchased a French collection of 400 pictures, including 12 Rubens, seven Van Dycks, five Poussins and three Watteaus. At her death in 1796, the collection comprised more than 4000 pictures, 10 000 drawings and as many carvings. Nationalised after the 1917 revolution, it was further enriched by confiscations. The number of items now in the collection totals 3 million, including works by

Monet, Degas, Renoir, Cézanne, Picasso and Matisse. It is displayed in 400 rooms in the Winter Palace, the Small and Large Hermitage.

and even some art nouveau creations from the early 20th century fit happily. The dour contributions of Soviet architecture were consigned to the city's outskirts.

Intellect and culture
Old capital versus new capital, Moscow versus St Petersburg: the two have constantly vied for supremacy. Today, Moscow is dominant in terms of universities and cultural institutions, but it owes its rise to St Petersburg's innovations. Here was the country's first museum, Peter the Great's Cabinet of Curiosities, and its first university. If Moscow became the place for administration, St Petersburg remained the leading centre for intellectuals and artists. Once again it is the 'window on the West' of Peter the Great's imagination.

Late addition *A fine Art Nouveau building in a St Petersburg suburb.*

114

Palatial wonders

The Winter Palace was the royal family's city residence. In summer, they took to the country. Every sovereign had a favourite palace, or created something new in order to leave an enduring mark on history. To the south of the city is Tsarskoye Selo (Tsar's Village), where Elizabeth, daughter of Peter the Great, had Rastrelli build her a Baroque palace in 1752, which she named Catherine Palace after her mother. It was remodelled in Neoclassical style by Catherine the Great, only to be devastated by the Germans in the Second World War. Much has since been restored, or recreated, including the Amber Room. The room was covered with engraved amber panels given by Frederick-William, king of Prussia, to Peter the Great. These

Victory fountain The figure of Samson forcing open a lion's mouth, from which spurts a 66 ft (20 m) fountain, is a symbol of Russia's victory over Sweden in 1709. It is the centrepiece of the Grand Cascade in Petrodvorets.

Regal wealth The 990 ft (300 m) façade of the Catherine Palace in Pushkin, 15 miles (25 km) south of St Petersburg, includes Atlas figures originally coated in gold leaf.

Netherlands art The Picture Hall in the Catherine Palace contains a fine collection of Dutch and Flemish masterpieces.

vanished in the war and their whereabouts are a constant source of rumours. The 'village' was renamed Pushkin in 1937 in honour of the poet, who was at school there, and both names are in use. A few miles south is Pavlovsk, a classical gem built for Catherine's son Paul I. Its English garden is a famous beauty spot, beloved by locals and tourists alike.

On the Gulf of Finland is Petrodvorets (Peter's Palace), where Peter the Great lived while overseeing the creation of his nearby naval base, Kronstadt. Its original heart, a single villa named Monplaisir, spawned a series of palaces and sets of cascades and fountains. This, the 'Russian Versailles', later became the favourite retreat of Nicholas II and his family.

St Petersburg's secret island

Kotlin Island, 18 miles (30 km) west in the Gulf of Finland, is better known by the name of its fortress, Kronstadt. Founded by Peter the Great to protect his new city, it has been a naval base ever since, closed to outsiders. The base's sailors were notoriously rebellious, first threatening the tsar's authority in the uprisings of 1905-6, then being some of the first troops to rally to the Bolshevik cause in 1917, and finally revolting against the Bolsheviks in early 1921. Hungry and desperate, they seized the fortress and two ironclads, and set up a Provisional Revolutionary Committee of their own. In March, after a bombardment, 50 000 Soviet troops advanced across the frozen sea and massacred the rebellious sailors. The island was opened in 1996, allowing tourists to admire the Byzantine-style Naval Cathedral (left), now a sailors' club and museum.

Novgorod, the great city of Rus

Though Kiev is commonly described as the mother of Russian cities, Novgorod 'the Great' prides itself on being the more ancient. Both date back to the 9th century, when the Varangian Norsemen established what would later become the heart of the Russian state. With its diverse range of architecture, Novgorod is virtually an open-air museum.

According to tradition, Novgorod was founded by the Varangian Rurik. Its establishment by Rurik is seen as the starting point of Russian history. In fact, it was in existence before the Varangians arrived. They named their prize Holmgarth, 'island enclosure'. Later, it acquired its present name, 'new town'.

By the 12th century, when Moscow was no more than a village, Novgorod had grown to rival southerly Kiev as one of the two great cities of the Rus. Its position on the River Volkhov allowed it to dominate the 'River Roads' that the Varangians took from the Baltic down to the Black Sea. In 1136, the town, made wealthy by its trade in furs, had its own government with princely rulers that owed their power to citizens' assemblies. As an independent state, it gave itself the name of 'Lord Novgorod the Great', with buildings to match its claim.

Under constant threat from Swedish invasions, the city lost ground to Moscow and entered into a slow decline. By the end of the 15th century, Moscow emerged as the dominant power in the increasingly centralised Russian state. A century later, Ivan the Terrible sacked Novgorod. In the 18th century, the foundation of St Petersburg further eclipsed Novgorod's status.

Ancient keep Novgorod's kremlin's 1500 ft (450 m) stone walls were built in the 14th century. The walls, with their nine towers, enclose many medieval buildings.

The Novgorod school

Byzantium's influence on Russia is most evident in its icons. They were always created according to precise rules, but there are certain traits that allow experts to distinguish different schools. In Novgorod, surrounded by the marshes that protected it from the Mongol invasions, artists were able to preserve the Byzantine tradition. This was given a new impetus by the arrival in 1378 of Theophanes the Greek from the city of Constantinople.

He gave Russian iconic art a distinctive form – graceful, bright, less austere, with elongated proportions and delicacy of detail. This, the so-called Palaeologus Renaissance, was to define the Novgorod school for the next century. His portraits, notable for their soulful expressions, are still visible in the Church of the Transfiguration and in frescoes in Our Saviour-in-Ilino.

A 16th-century icon in Byzantine style.

It suffered a final catastrophe under German occupation between 1941 and 1944, but such is its historical eminence that the Soviets worked hard to restore its kremlin. Further restoration now allows tourists to take a walk through time. The kremlin's tortuous lanes are medieval in design, while across the river the old commercial area round Yaroslav's Court retains the chequerboard street plan beloved by Catherine the Great. Its churches, in various stages of restoration, have frescoes from the 12th century.

Glistening domes In the marshlands to the south of the city stands the 12th-century Yurev Monastery. Its cathedral, St George's, has well-restored onion domes studded with stars.

The good life in Tbilisi

Perched like a vulture on the edge of a ravine above the River Kura, Tbilisi is one of the most head-spinning cities in the world. The old town is a tangle of colourful houses each with a hanging balcony. The distinctive geometry of Tbilisi's churches helps to give the city its special look: each squat little edifice is topped with a perfectly conical spire.

Georgians tell this story about their country: when God was distributing land to the peoples of the Earth the last two nations in the queue were the Armenians and the Georgians. But there was only one parcel of land left, and it was a rocky, barren and inhospitable place. The two peoples drew lots for this last remaining homeland, and the Armenians won. 'But where shall we live?' the Georgians asked God. 'There is no room left on the Earth for us.' 'Don't worry,' whispered God, so the Armenians would not hear. 'You can have a little corner of Paradise.'

Georgia is indeed a beautiful country. Many Western visitors compare it to Italy because of its warm, Mediterranean atmosphere and because of the sunny disposition of its people. Georgians make

Hot springs   *Old Tbilisi spread out from the ruins of the ancient fortress of Narikala. The city owes its name to its hot sulphur-rich springs – tbili is Georgian for 'hot'.*

a religion of hospitality, but they are also known for their business acumen: they practically ran the black market in the USSR, and they were the first to exploit the free market when it came.

They have an ancient culture which they cherish. Their language is unique, and it is written in a wonderfully beautiful script consisting of 38 elegant and sinuous letters. There is also a long literary tradition, in which the best-known Georgian work is *The Man in the Panther's Skin* by the 12th-century poet Shota Rustaveli.

Georgia suffered much hardship in the 1990s. There was a bloody civil war with Abkhazia, economic collapse, political chaos – and for a time life was pretty bleak even in Tbilisi. But now, at last, the country is recovering its traditional, indestructible *joie de vivre*.

Guardian church   *Clinging to one of Tbilisi's hills, the church of Metekhi was built around the tomb of a local saint. It dominates the rocky gorge of the River Kura.*

Georgian variety   *In Tbilisi's market, stall-holders sell an enticing range of spices and fresh herbs to flavour the rich and pungent Georgian cuisine.*

The Christians of Mtskheta

About 10 miles (16 km) to the north-west of Tbilisi lies a little town, Mtskheta, that was the capital of Georgia from the 2nd to 5th centuries. As the area's ancient religious centre, it preserves many masterpieces of early Christian art and architecture. Perched on top of a hill, the church of Dzhvari testifies to the ingenuity of its 6th to 7th-century builders. The 4th-century cathedral of Sveti-Tskhoveli was for centuries the place of coronation and burial for Georgia's monarchs.

Past glories of Samarkand

Samarkand, Uzbekistan's fabled second city, lies on the frontier between Persian culture and that of the Central Asian nomads, straddling the old trade routes that funnelled tea and silk to the West. Its glorious architecture testifies to its historical significance as a one-time capital of a princely state.

Seized and then relinquished by Genghis Khan, this oasis on the River Zerevshan finally became an imperial capital under Tamerlane in the 14th century. That was its high point. The conqueror poured his wealth – amassed on his blood-curdling campaigns – into glorious mosques and institutes of learning, gardens and parks. By the 16th century Samarkand was in decline. In the late 19th century, the medieval city was swamped by Soviet apartment blocks, office buildings and industrial complexes (mainly devoted to textiles, metallurgy, food processing and chemicals).

The city's most splendid attributes are its mosques. Hemmed in by intricately decorated *madrasahs* (Koranic schools), the amphitheatre of the Registan, one of Central Asia's most awe-inspiring sights, was once bustling with teachers and pupils, traders and craftsmen. The Bibi Khanym mosque, finished just before Tamerlane's death in 1404, is a memorial to the emperor's favourite wife. This massive structure – the main gate is 115 ft (35 m) high – was ruined by earthquakes and is undergoing restoration. There is an observatory on a hilltop, built by Tamerlane's grandson Ulugh Bek in the 15th century, from where the scientist prince and astronomer made astonishingly accurate observations. Compared to these wonders, the Shahr-i-Zindah necropolis and the Guri Amir Mausoleum, Tamerlane's tomb, are understated reminders of Samarkand's days of glory.

Seeking Allah *In Uzbekistan, 80 per cent of the population is Muslim. Children begin their Koranic study at a young age.*

Registan glory *The 17th-century Sher Dor ('Lion Bearing') madrasah is covered with tiles and glazed bricks to create a kaleidoscope of colour.*

Trompe l'oeil *In the 17th-century Tilla Kari ('Golden') mosque, the flat ceiling is made to seem dome-like by an intricate pattern of tiles.*

Tamerlane, Uzbekistan's tyrannical hero

Following in the footsteps of Genghis Khan, another fearsome empire-builder, Tamerlane (Timur 'the Lame'), terrorised 14th-century Asia from the shores of the Black Sea to northern India. His butchery knew no bounds: 90 000 massacred in Baghdad, 5 million dead in India.

Between expeditions, Tamerlane would return to his beloved Samarkand laden with the fruits of his plunder, including scholars and craftsmen. His architects transformed the city, building elaborately decorated mosques and academies. In 1404 he died while on a campaign to China.

Bukhara, a tapestry of cultures

Walls once encircled the ancient oasis city of Bukhara, protecting the erudite outpost of Persian culture from invaders. But the walls were breached and successive rulers have left their architectural mark – in minarets, mosques and madrasahs – on Uzbekistan's third city.

The dome of Mir-i-Arab

Bukhara lies on the Zerevshan downstream from Samarkand. It has had varied fortunes in its 2000-year history: as the capital of the Samanid state in the 9th and 10th centuries, it became famous for its scholars and artists. Its khans were noted patrons of art, architecture and science. Bukharans included some of Islam's most eminent mathematicians, geographers and poets.

After suffering under both the Mongols and Tamerlane, Bukhara emerged in the 16th century as an independent khanate, with numerous bazaars and 10 000 students in 100 madrasahs. Its empire, which included Uzbekistan, Turkmenistan and Tadjikistan, fell into the Russian orbit in the 19th century. The region makes its living from textiles, handicrafts, herding and agriculture.

Living history

Still largely intact, the original fortified area of Bukhara encircles the 16th-century Ark, as the citadel is known, beside which winding streets of blank-walled brick and adobe buildings link the old commercial areas. Grander buildings are decorated with frescoes and carved panels. Under the arcades of the old bazaars run traders' galleries punctuated with domes. Mosques give way to merchants' tents, madrasahs to mausoleums. Many of these are gems of Islamic architecture from Samanid times.

Prized products *Bukhara's famous carpets are distinguished by their reds and their geometric motifs.*

Towering landmark *The Kalon Minaret was Central Asia's tallest building (155 ft/47 m) when it was constructed in the 12th century.*

Bukhara's Aristotle

One of the greatest medieval philsophers was ibn Sina, better known by the Spanish version of his name, Avicenna (980–1037). As a teenager he cured the sultan, who gave him the run of his library. Driven from Bukhara to Isfahan by war, he wrote more than 200 books, displaying such vast knowledge that he was known as 'Aristotle of the East'. His *Canon of Medicine* became a valuable source of reference.

New capitals

Once the administrative centres of the Soviet Union's far-flung outposts, the capital cities of the new republics are looking to the future in their latest roles as national seats of government, while cherishing their historical roots.

When the Russians arrived in the 19th century, many of the towns destined to become the capitals of the new republics more than 100 years later were mere villages.

Baku, city of 'black gold'

At the end of the 19th century, the Azerbaijani capital of Baku was a small, insignificant town surrounding a 9th-century fortress on the shores of the Caspian Sea. This all changed in the 1870s when it became a major centre for Russian oil production. The town expanded rapidly to its present population of 1.7 million, about half of whom are Azeri; the remainder include Russians and Armenians. More than 13 000 Armenians fled the city following clashes with the Azeris in 1990. Today, the Maiden's Tower (a castle keep) guards the winding streets of the old town, as it has done since the 13th century. At its feet stand monuments, mosques and other masterpieces of medieval Islamic architecture, including the palace of the Shirvan shahs, which dates back to the 11th century.

Yerevan's ancient roots

The Armenian capital is the oldest town in the Caucasus. A fortress stood on its site, on the banks of the River Razdan, in the 8th century BC. It came under Turkish then Persian control before being ceded to Russia in 1828. Though now a working capital with thriving industries, Yerevan remains proud of its history, recalled in its many museums. The greatest is the Materanadan, whose ancient Armenian manuscripts include the 9th-century Lazarus Gospel.

Tashkent, Central Asia's greatest city

Dominating the old Silk Road from China, the Uzbek capital was once an ungainly mix of traditional and Russian colonial architecture. Many of the old buildings were shattered by an earthquake in 1966. As a new city, it has become a centre for

Imperial splendour Kazakhstan's Central State Museum occupies Almaty's former cathedral.

Local colour The Barakat, Dushanbe's covered market.

transport, scientific research, culture and industry. It has the only metro system in Central Asia. Tashkent has 2 million inhabitants, making it the fourth largest city in the former USSR, after Moscow, St Petersburg and Kiev.

Bishkek – new town, old ways

In the early 19th century, an Uzbek khan built a fort to guard his caravan routes through the Tien Shan. The Russians built a city around it, calling it Frunze. In 1991, when Kyrgyzstan became independent, the city was renamed Bishkek ('place below the mountains'). Although a modern industrial centre, the 619 000 inhabitants still enjoy traditional activities such as horse-racing. In Bishkek's theatres minstrels sing epics from Kyrgyz literature.

Dushanbe, Tajikistan's unruly ruler

Old Tajiks still remember their capital, Dushanbe, as a village, before Soviet-era construction created a city of 562 000 people. The setting is attractive, with a backdrop of mountains and tree-lined avenues, but it is a hotbed of unrest. Refugees and Islamic militants sparked civil war in the early 1990s. Despite the occasional shoot-out, Dushanbe lives in an uneasy peace. It is the industrial and cultural hub of the republic.

Old and new In Tashkent, vestiges of the past, such as the 16th-century Kukeldash madrasah, contrast with modern buildings.

Offspring of communism and Islam

The capitals of the Central Asian republics evolved as modern industrial cities in the 20th century. Their main historical legacy lies in their Islamic architecture, of which the Soviet authorities disapproved yet maintained to placate local feeling. Today the cities are taking on characters of their own as the showcases of national culture.

Luxury palace   In Ashgabat the presidential palace combines Classical and Islamic styles.

Imperial legacy   Baku's parliament building reflects the religious and cultural influence of the Persians, who ruled the region for centuries.

Ashgabat, a desert city

Turkmenistan's capital, Ashgabat ('city of love'), in the Kara Kum desert, was just a village when the Russians arrived in 1881. It grew to become the capital of the Turkmenanian Republic, but was flattened by an earthquake in 1948 that killed 100 000 people. Rebuilt, it is now the showplace of Turkmen nationalism. A 900 mile (1500 km) canal from the border with Afghanistan feeds the city's lake.

Study in pink   Yerevan's buildings of rose-tinted tuff and grey basalt hem shady squares and extensive parks. In a region where earthquakes are common, buildings higher than two or three storeys are rare.

Almaty, a capital ex-capital

The 1 million Kazakhs, Russians, Chinese, Uzbeks and Mongols of the mountain city of Almaty (as it is now called) are benefiting from a boom in banks, restaurants and hotels. As Alma-Ata, the city was Soviet Kazakhstan's capital, but in 1997, a new capital, Astana, was decreed on the steppes 600 miles (1000 km) north. It has had little impact on Almaty. Institutions have been loath to move, and it will take many years for Astana to live up to its elevated status.

CHAPTER 6

CULTURE AND FOLKLORE

A nyone wishing to understand the soul of Russia has no lack of material. Russian writers, playwrights, poets, composers, choreographers, dancers, painters and film-makers have all created masterpieces that form part of our worldwide cultural heritage. Their roots can be found in strong folkloric traditions and Orthodoxy. Russians have never ceased to be innovative, but the parameters keep shifting. The written word, censored for 70 years, is enjoying a greater degree of freedom. Art has escaped the shackles of socialist realism. New forms of creativity have emerged. Yet for artists, freedom from state control has also meant freedom from state support and a loss of prestige. And there is the danger that an influx of Western mass-market material will threaten high artistic standards.

A Buryat Mongol woman of the Lake Baikal area in local costume.

A musical heritage

Russian music has its roots in Slavic folk songs and the chants of the Orthodox Church. The strength of the vocal tradition has been carried through to the popular operas of today. In terms of the classical repertoire, it all began with Mikhail Glinka in the 1800s, who chose purely Russian themes for his works and set the tone for future composers.

The composer Mikhail Glinka (1804-57) is generally acknowledged as the founder of the Russian national school, and thus the 'father' of modern Russian music. He was educated in St Petersburg, and grew to musical maturity in Italy and Germany. His ground-breaking operas *A Life for the Tsar* (1836) and *Ruslan and Lyudmila* (1842), based on a poem by Alexander Pushkin, successfully harmonised the Russian folk-song tradition with European music.

Pagan and religious influences

Popular songs, the foundation of the nation's music, were passed down from pre-Christian Slav traditions. The Slavs practised the cult-worship of the sun and the earth; their songs were lively and cheerful. Only later, under the 'Tartar yoke' in the 13th-15th centuries, did they start to compose in a nostalgic and mournful vein, singing of maidens weeping over the loss of a fiancé, inconsolable mothers and peas-

Musical genius Sergei Rachmaninov (1873-1943), composer and pianist, was the last of the Russian romantics.

Resonant singer Feodor Chaliapin (1873-1938) was the archetypal Russian bass singer. He had a terrific stage presence and became the incarnation of all the great operatic bass parts, notably Mussorgsky's Boris Godunov.

ants mourning the destruction of their lands. 'From the meanest cabby to the greatest of poets,' wrote Alexander Pushkin, 'our songs are ones of melancholy.'

Another significant influence was the Orthodox chant. The Graeco-Syrian roots of the chant were much modified by its slow transmission across Bulgaria, and then, once established in Kiev and Novgorod, modified again by the influence of folk songs. The chants were sung *a capella* (without accompaniment), for the faithful believed their voices would reach God's ears only if they were unsullied by the sound of instruments considered to be derived from pagan roots – a view that endured until the 17th century.

Modern Russian music

From the time of Peter the Great (1672-1725), the tsars invited foreign artists to perform to the exclusion of local talent. Following Glinka's example, however, a number of Russian composers

The Group of Five

To counter the increasing influence of Western European works, in the 1860s five composers set about developing a national school of Russian music. Their mentor was Mili Balakirev (1837-1910), who had been inspired by Glinka. The group included Mussorgsky, Cui, Borodin and Rimsky-Korsakov. In 1862, Balakirev founded the Free School of Music, where he introduced new music by the Five at its concerts.

The Five Makovsky's humorous portrayal of the Group of Five.

Musical trio *Shostakovich sits between Aram Khachaturian (1903-78) and Prokofiev (right).*

Cellist abroad *Mstislav Rostropovich, an outspoken defender of human rights, was stripped of his Soviet citizenship in 1978. He has since led a brilliant international career both as a cellist and conductor.*

The ups and downs of Shostakovich

The genius of Dmitri Shostakovich (1906-75), one of the greatest composers of the 20th century, evolved both despite and because of Soviet approval. He came to prominence as a brilliant student in St Petersburg (then Petrograd) and began a love-hate relationship with Soviet officals. As an approved composer, he was commissioned to write a symphony to honour the October Revolution (No.2, 1927). But his opera *Lady Macbeth of Mtsensk* (1934) was denounced as a counter-revolutionary 'muddle'. His 7th, *Leningrad*, written during the siege in 1941, reconfirmed his status at home and abroad. His 15 symphonies and numerous smaller creations range from the succinct and witty to the monumental works so beloved by the state.

richness, particularly in choral works.

Igor Stravinsky (1882-1971) and Sergei Prokofiev (1891-1953) were among the most innovative of the 20th century composers. Stravinsky achieved worldwide acclaim for his work for Diaghilev and the Ballets Russes, including *The Firebird* (1910). His ultra-

modern *Rite of Spring* (1913) shocked traditionalists and heralded his position as leader of the musical avant-garde. Prokofiev studied with Rimsky-Korsakov at the St Petersburg Conservatoire and made his name with ambitious operas such as *War and Peace* (1941) and film scores for such epics as *Alexander Nevsky*.

Rising star *Yevgeni Kissin (born in 1971) is one of Russia's most promising young pianists.*

developed a genuinely Russian school. They included the Group of Five (see box, left), Pyotr Ilyich Tchaikovsky (1840-93) and Alexander Glazunov (1865-1936). Their inspiration came from great historical events (as did Glinka's in *Life for the Tsar* and Borodin's in *Prince Igor*), folklore (Rimsky-Korsakov's *Sadko*) and literary masterpieces (Tchaikovsky's adaptations of Pushkin's verse-novel *Eugene Onegin* and his short story, *The Queen of Spades*). These composers tended to focus on opera. Russian music is defined by its vocal

A passion for opera

In Russia, opera has universal appeal. The richness of the repertoires and the beauty of theatres such as the Bolshoi in Moscow and the Mariinsky in St Petersburg may well have something to do with its popularity. But that does not explain why in Russia opera, far from being the preserve of an élite as in the West, is an entertainment for the masses. One reason is that all operas, whatever their origins, are sung

in Russian, which makes them more accessible. Another reason is that under Soviet rule entertainment of any kind was limited, and opera, considered to be the least subversive of art forms, had official backing. Today, deprived of state funding, companies have had to slim down their productions, but stalwarts such as Prokofiev's *Love of Three Oranges* and Tchaikovsky's *Eugene Onegin* still have their place in the repertoires.

Avant-garde *Prokofiev's ballet The Buffoon (1921) was commissioned by Sergei Diaghilev for his dance company.*

Popular culture *Tchaikovsky's Eugene Onegin, written in 1878, is the most widely performed of all operas.*

Art, ancient and modern

'Russian art is above all art that comes from the heart. That is the fire that burns in our artists' works.' Maxim Gorky's words provide the key to understanding the artists of Russia, their passion for realism and the avant-garde, and their respect for iconography.

Symbolic fantasy Influenced by the Impressionists, Mikhail Vrubel (1856-1910) developed an original style of symbolism, combining the fantastic and the folkloric, as in his painting, The Swan Princess (1900).

Over the centuries, the commitment to truthfulness in Russian art has never prevented artists from reassessing the aesthetic foundations of their work and experimenting with radically new approaches. Yet Russian painting has always been firmly rooted in iconography, even when exploring modernism.

The glory of the icon

In ancient Russia, Byzantine traditions infused every aspect of art. Icons imported from Byzantium played an important role in the teaching of Orthodoxy from its 11th-century beginnings until the start of the 14th century. In the 15th and 16th centuries, following the growth of a centralised state ruled from Moscow, schools of art were established, such as those in Pskov, Novgorod and Tver, 30 miles (50 km) north-west of Moscow. Tver was capital of a state that was Moscow's rival until its demise in 1485.

Although at this time the icon was regarded as a religious object acting as a bridge to God rather than a work of art in its own right, traditional representations of the saints became progressively more personal. Compositions acquired livelier colours, which allowed for greater complexity.

The flowering of a Russian style

During the 13th century, the evolution of non-religious genres – began to undermine iconographic traditions. Artists started to use oil paints on cloth and began to experiment with perspective.

In 1758, the foundation of the Academy of Fine Arts in St Petersburg attracted foreign artists. Under their influence, Russian artists began to paint historical subjects in a classical style, exploring current events in Russia in the guise of themes based on classical mythology. Portraiture and landscape painting also achieved widespread success at the hands of artists such as Fedor Rokotov (1735-1808) and Vladimir Borovikovsky (1757-1825).

Heights of realism Vasily Polenov (1844-1927) excelled in both historical scenes and landscapes, as in this one, A Backyard in Moscow (1878).

Andrei Rublev: master icon painter

Andrei Rublev is the finest Russian icon painter, and *The Trinity* is his greatest work. The image is full of symbolism: taken together, the figures of the three angels describe a circle, a shape with no beginning or end. This represents the unity and eternal nature of the Godhead. The central angel represents Christ, and he is blessing the chalice, which stands for his acceptance of suffering. His head is inclined to the figure of God the Father on the left, who blesses his Son. Unrealistic devices such as the 'flatness' of the image enhance the symbolism: icons are not pictures, they have no connection with the material world; an icon is meant to be a fleeting glimpse of the divine, a little prayer in paint.

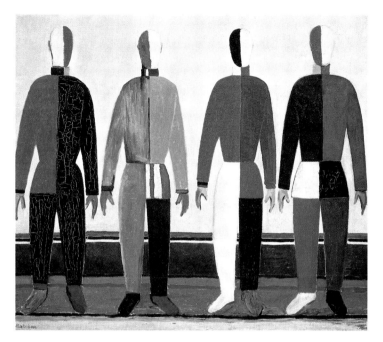

Sporting life   Kazimir Malevich painted The Sportsmen *in 1928-32 as part of a series representing peasants and workers.*

The dawn of realism

Little by little, Russian art acquired characteristics of its own, particularly in the work of the Romantic artists, who portrayed both their human subjects and the world of nature in a lyrical style. Historical themes were explored in a totally new way by two great reformers within the academic establishment, Karl Bryullov (1799-1852) and Alexander Ivanov (1806-58), in whose works historical and religious subjects were portrayed as comments on current events.

Artists became interested in contemporary life, including the lives of the underprivileged. Paul Fedotov (1815-52), who portrayed nature with a sharp eye for social problems, presaged the development of Realism. With a mordant irony he revealed the underside of Russian life. This shift to a more realistic view reached its peak with the group known as the Itinerants (see box, above).

Avant-garde revolutionaries

Moving away from social issues, a number of young painters took up the challenge of Modernism in the early 20th century. They chose to work with geometric shapes and concrete materials. Between 1910 and 1920, countless artistic associations sprang up, eager to explore new avenues, thrusting Russia into the forefront of the avant-garde for that turbulent decade of war and revolution. 'The World of Art', 'The Blue Rose' and 'The Knave of Diamonds' were just some of the groups which set out to rival the Italian Futurists and French Cubists. Rejecting all the norms of Realism, they found their inspiration in the search for something utterly fundamental, in Russian primitivism or 'pure form'. In 1915, Kazimir Malevich (1878-1935) staged a remarkable exhibition in Petrograd. Entitled '*0.10*,' it consisted of 29 black rectangular shapes on white backgrounds, hung at random. Not only was it ridiculed, it also provoked a fight between Malevich and an enraged critic of what the artist called 'Suprematism' – the pursuit of forms alien to nature, and thus owing everything to the artist's creativity. Officially spurned, Malevich died in obscurity in 1935.

Other avant-garde movements such as Constructivism (using glass, wire and sheet metal to produce abstract reliefs) and Rayonism (a Russian offshoot of Cubism) were equally radical. But, by exploring simple forms, they influenced all the visual arts both at home and abroad.

Still life   Aristarkh Lentulov (1882-1943) *painted this picture,* Samovar, *in 1913. Influenced by Cézanne, Lentulov was a leader of the Knave of Diamonds group, which included Marc Chagall and Wassily Kandinsky.*

The literature of resistance

The story of Russian literature, like the story of the nation, is one of shocking reversals. Until the late 20th century, it was subject to the whims of the tsars and the Soviet censors. Dissenting writers were banished to the gulag or forced into exile. But for all that, Russia has retained a strong literary tradition.

In literature, the reign of Peter the Great (1682-1725) brought an end to the literary isolation imposed by Russia's remoteness from Western Europe and by its exclusively religious writing. Peter's determination to open Russia to the West led to the introduction of the printing press, the setting up of academies and the arrival of foreign artists and writers – all factors that marked a break with the past and paved the way for literary enlightenment.

The classical renaissance

The dominant figure in the upsurge of literary creativity was Mikhail Lomonosov (1711-65), one of the most brilliant minds of his time. Lomonosov was a polymath: scientist, poet, grammarian and linguistic reformer. He wrote the first Russian grammar, propounded the theory of three literary styles (high, medium and low) and laid down the rules that governed the development of Russian verse. He helped to found Moscow University, and as Alexander Pushkin said, he 'is himself a university'. Pushkin (see box) was the first to free himself of foreign influences, setting an example for all those who came after him, notably Nikolay Gogol (1809–52), Ivan Turgenev (1818-83), Fyodor Dostoyevsky (1821-81) and Leo Tolstoy (1828-1910), who were to become the giants of a golden age of novels.

Going to extremes Fyodor Dostoyevsky wrote: 'Throughout my life, I have pressed to the limits, doing what you have dared only half to do.'

A village for writers

In a pine and birch forest on Moscow's south-western outskirts lies the village of Peredelkino, created in 1930 as a colony for those writers in favour with the authorities. But the writers lived insecure lives, liable to disgrace at random. Several residents, such as Boris Pilnyak (1894-1937) and the short-story writer Isaac Babel (1894-1941) died in Stalin's purges. Boris Pasternak lived there for many years, until his death in 1960. His grave in a pine grove near the railway station is now venerated, and his dacha (below) where he finished *Dr Zhivago* is now a museum.

Literary lion Leo Tolstoy, the author of War and Peace *(1869) and* Anna Karenina *(1877), is the acknowledged giant of Russian prose.*

Pushkin: poet and novelist

Alexandr Pushkin (1799-1837) is a national treasure – the greatest Russian poet and the founder of modern Russian literature. Every educated Russian can quote him. He was schooled in the French classical tradition typical of the time, but from his peasant nanny he received a strong grounding in Russian folklore. Pushkin revealed his prodigious talent for poetry as a teenager. He entered government service in St Petersburg at the age of 18. In 1820 he wrote his romantic poem *Ruslan and Lyudmila*. Now a classic, it flouted all poetic rules and, in conjunction with some offensive satires, resulted in Pushkin being banished to the Caucasus for four years. Here he wrote *The Prisoner of the Caucasus* in 1922. Drawing heavily on Russian history and folklore, Pushkin wrote for the people, notably in his tragic verse drama *Boris Godunov* (the basis for Mussorgsky's opera). His verse novel *Eugene Onegin* is a work of genius (and the source of Tchaikovsky's opera). Pushkin was forever at odds with the tsar's censor, and was ill at ease at court. He was killed at the age of 38 in a duel in defence of his wife's honour.

Expelled writer Vasili Aksyonov, author of many comic anti-Soviet works, was expelled from the country in 1981.

Broken idealist Vladimir Mayakovsky (1893-1930) exemplified the hopes and despair of his times. A passionate supporter of the Revolution as a poet and artist, he fell into disfavour and committed suicide in 1930.

Communist oppression

At the dawn of the 20th century there was an explosion of poetry. Never before or since have so many first-rank poets arisen in one country at the same time: Alexander Blok, Anna Akhmatova, Boris Pasternak, Marina Tsvetaeva, Nikolai Gumilev, Vladimir Mayakovsky. The 1917 Revolution released a flood of creativity. But the outpouring was gradually curtailed by the heavy hand of the the state. The all-powerful Writers' Union, founded in 1932, allowed Soviet authors little room for manoeuvre. Among the million condemned to the gulag were many writers who paid with their lives for their determination to express themselves. Boris Pasternak's *Doctor Zhivago* was banned on the grounds that 'it represented the

October Revolution in a libellous manner'. It was published in Italy in 1957, translated into 18 languages, and won its author the Nobel prize for literature in 1958, which he was forced to refuse. There was a brief thaw under Khrushchev in the 1960s, but only in 1985, under Gorbachev, did things begin to improve.

New insights The Cherry Orchard (1904) by Anton Chekhov (1860-1904) is among those plays which, like his earlier production, The Three Sisters (1901), brought new depths of psychological insight to the stage. Chekhov is the most widely performed of all Russian playwrights.

Writers abroad Nina Berberova's poetry was one of many works created by expatriate Russians. Between 1917 and 1922, Russia's intelligentsia left the country in large numbers. Other emigrant writers included Vladimir Nabokov (1899-1977), author of Lolita (1959).

Dissident exile Alexandr Solzhenitsyn received the Nobel prize for literature in 1970. He was expelled in 1974. In the USA, he completed The Gulag Archipelago, before returning home in the 1990s.

Georgia's long literary tradition

Georgia was to Russian poets of the 19th century what Italy was to Western European poets in the 18th. In its seductive landscape and exotic culture, many found inspiration, such as the poets Alexandr Pushkin and Mikhail Lermontov (1814-41) and the dramatist Alexandr Griboedov (1795-1829). For this little country, with its strange and complex language and its mixture of East and West, has an ancient and distinctive literary tradition of its own. As an early convert to Christianity, it had an extensive religious literature. Then in the reign of Queen Thamar (1184-1212), a golden age for Georgia, an epic poem emerged that became the foundation of a national literature: *The Man in the Panther's Skin* by Shot'a Rustaveli. The Persian influence remained strong until the end of the 18th century, when Georgian national feeling underwent a revival. The Russian occupation brought Georgia into the orbit of European intellectual life. The realistic novel thrived with works by Ilia Tchavtchavadze (1837-1907) and the poetry of Akaki Tsereteli (1840-1915), both distinguished patriots. Contemporary Georgian writers such as Otar Tsiladze strive to preserve the spirit of their traditions.

Masters of dance

Russians are superb dancers and take justifiable pride in their excellence, whether leaping high with traditional Cossack-style aplomb or performing classical ballet with grace and finesse.

Classic steps Bolshoi dancers, led by Yekaterina Maksimova and Vladimir Vasiliev, perform The Nutcracker *in 1994.*

In 1909, the Ballets Russes, under the brilliant direction of Sergei Diaghilev, toured Western Europe to universal acclaim. Diaghilev employed the greatest stage artists of the time – the dancer Vaslav Nijinsky, choreographers George Balanchine and Michel Fokine, composers Sergei Prokofiev and Igor Stravinsky, designers Léon Bakst and Alexander Benois.

On just one occasion Diaghilev fell foul of the critics. Stravinsky's *The Rite of Spring* (1913), with its Baroque staging, audacious costumes and dissonant music, reduced the audience to shrieking, hissing outrage, matched only by their astonished admiration at Nijinsky's gravity-defying leaps.

On the death of the founder in 1929, the Ballets Russes dissolved. But almost a century later, Russian dance has lost nothing of its prestige.

The Bolshoi, Russia's pride

Russian ballet has remained supreme among the performing arts. Ever since its foundation in 1776, the Bolshoi *corps de ballet* has relentlessly upheld its tradition of seeking perfection of technique and dazzling staging. It was at the Bolshoi that the prima ballerina Maya Plisetskaya started her career in 1945. The evocative power of her dancing and the sheer poetry of her positions won her an inter-

Russian star A 1915 Ballets Russes programme shows Nijinsky in L'Après-midi d'un Faune.

national reputation. Her repertoire included such classics as Aurore in *Sleeping Beauty* and Odette in *Swan Lake*, which she danced more than 1000 times in four decades.

Another Russian star, Galina Ulanova, was 47 when she made her London debut in 1956, and nearing 50 when she opened in the United States, winning accolades for her roles in *Giselle* and *Romeo and Juliet.*

St Petersburg, cradle of dance

The Imperial School in St Petersburg trained many of the greatest dancers, including the legendary Vaslav Nijinsky – who appeared as Petrouchka in the first performance of Stravinsky's ballet in 1911 – Anna Pavlova, Maya Plisetskaya and Rudolf Nureyev. But it was the French choreographer and dancer Marius Petipa (1819-1910) who deserves the credit for fusing Italian, Russian and French styles and leading the dancers of St Petersburg's Mariinsky Theatre to worldwide acclaim. Petipa worked at the Imperial Theatre for more than 60 years. His productions of *Sleeping Beauty* (1890) and *Swan Lake* (1895) set the standard for the classical repertoire throughout the 20th century – a tradition that is continued by the Mariinsky today.

Backstage One of the Bolshoi's corps de ballet works at her arabesques in a grimy back room.

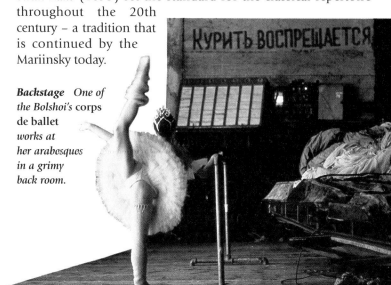

Folklore: a living tradition

Russians know how to preserve their traditional folklore, as dance performances readily show.

Most famous are the displays of *kazachok*, or Cossack dancing. The dance is done to a repetitive musical phrase played at a steady accelerando. Dancers in national costume (braided shirts and trousers tucked into black boots) perform acrobatic manoeuvres, rivalling each other in their straight-legged, toe-touching leaps and their knees-bent kicks.

Film-making: the art of the people

Russian cinema does not begin and end with Eisenstein. More than a decade after the fall of communism, Russian film-makers still dominate international film festivals.

Mournful heroine
Tatiana Samoilova plays the unhappy heroine mourning her soldier lover in Mikhail Kalatozov's film, The Cranes Are Flying, *which won the Palme d'Or in Cannes in 1958.*

In 1922 Lenin pronounced that 'of all the arts, film is the most important for us'. He based his judgment on a film made by 21-year-old Lev Kulechov (1899-1970), who combined documentary sequences with scenes played by actors. This form of montage reflected the revolutionary view that history progressed from scene to contrasting scene.

The star director

The greatest exponent of this view was Sergei Eisenstein (1898-1948). 'America focuses on narrative,' said Eisenstein of American cinema, dismissively. By contrast, Eisenstein intended to show not only stories, but also ideas and evolving thoughts by original cross-cutting camerawork and by the overall structure of his films. He succeeded brilliantly in *The Strike* (1924), *The Battleship Potemkin* (1925) and *October* (1927).

Flourishing talents

Eisenstein was not the only influential film-maker. The two decades after the Revolution produced a range of great silent films. Among them were Vsevolod Pudovkin's *Mother* (1926), based on a novel by Maxim Gorky, and Alexander Dovzhenko's *Earth* (1930), both of which were close to Eisenstein in their use of montage. Boris Barnet's *Okraina* (1933) is one of the most beautiful Soviet films, made before the heavy hand of Stalinist censorship killed the creativity of Russian film-makers.

Taxi Blues *A film directed by Pavel Lungin in 1990.*

The industry found its way again in the 1960s, after the thaw initiated by Khrushchev. Directors such as Andrei Tarkovsky (*Andrei Rublev*, 1966) – though Tarkovsky later moved to the United States – Andrei Konchalovsky (*Asya's Happiness*, 1967) and his half-brother Nikita Mikhalkov (*Urga*, 1991) attracted considerable international acclaim. Today, Alexander Sokurov (*Mother and Son*, 1997; *Moloch*, 1999) and Pavel Lunguin (*Taxi Blues*, 1990) are greatly admired by film enthusiasts.

Modern classic The Barber of Siberia, *a portrait of pre-Revolutionary Russia, directed by Nikita Mikhalkov, 1998.*

Epic cinema *Sergei Eisenstein's* Ivan the Terrible *(1944) was acclaimed as a masterpiece.*

Tortured genius

Sergei Paradjanov (1924-90), an Armenian film-maker, won fame with his lyrical *Shadows of Our Forgotten Ancestors* (1964). His 1967 masterpiece, *The Colour of Pomegranates*, about the Armenian minstrel Sayat Nova, abandoned traditional narrative for a flow of iconic images. The state disapproved, and jailed him for five years. Under *perestroika*, he worked again, but died in Paris. A museum in Yerevan honours him.

Once upon a time…

Most Russians are only a generation or two removed from their peasant roots, and the old songs, stories, dances, traditions and superstitions are still very much part of life, even in the cities and among the educated middle classes.

Dazzling show *An Uzbek dancer performs wearing a traditional costume woven from multi-coloured threads.*

Russians love to tell stories. There is an established oral tradition that goes back 1000 years to the *byliny*, warlike poetic sagas of Slavonic princes and their battles. It is not the least bit unusual for a grandmother to recite Pushkin's fairy tales to her grandchildren – hundreds of lines, word-perfect. At another extreme, the national passion for storytelling manifests itself in the Russian love of jokes, especially, in Soviet times, jokes that poked fun at the system: 'What is the difference between capitalism and socialism?' ran one old favourite. 'Capitalism is the exploitation of man by man, and socialism is the exact opposite.'

Stories for children

Russia also has a rich stock of home-grown fairy tales, and they are strong meat compared to the sweet and harmless stories of Western Europe. Every Russian child knows about Baba Yaga, the shape-shifting witch who rides in a mortar propelled by a pestle, and who lures babies by imitating their mother's voice and eats them roasted. Then there is the demon Vii, whose great drooping eyelids trail on the ground as he drifts through the forest.

The glory of Easter

Orthodox believers greet each other on Easter Day with the words 'Christ is risen!' To which the response is: 'He is risen indeed!' The phrase is repeated again and again at the height of the midnight service on Easter Saturday, as the congregation processes around the outside of the church carrying candles. On Easter Day Russians eat *kulich*, a kind of sweet bread, which they spread with *paskha*, a curd cheese enriched with sugar, nuts and raisins. Many people like to have their *kulich* blessed beforehand.

Superstitions are tightly intertwined with the everyday rituals of life. There are hundreds of these little fossils of Slavonic paganism, which neither Christianity nor communist materialism have been able to eradicate. If you sit on the corner of the table you will not marry for seven years; you must never make a gift of a knife; if you tread on someone's toe, you will argue with that person unless they tread on yours in return; it is even bad luck to wish a person good luck: rather, wish them bad luck, to which they reply 'Go to the devil'.

And when someone sets out on a journey, the whole household must sit together in silence for a moment before leaving. This last custom – '*posidim na dorozhku*', 'Let's sit for the road' – can be infuriating if you are already late for a plane, but it is always faithfully observed.

Greeting guests

Naturally enough, there are many traditions connected with celebrations. An honoured

Intricate headgear *At a festival in Bashkortostan, in the lower Volga region, local women don traditional Turkic costumes.*

Nested dolls *Matryoshkas have become a cipher for Russia, a cliché for use by cartoonists and newspaper columnists. These wooden dolls must clearly have started out as a kind of talisman of fertility, but now you are just as likely to find them painted with the faces of Russian leaders from Putin back to Peter.*

The roots of the Russian choral tradition

One feature of Russian folkloric traditions is the powerful female voice, which is the product of an astonishing vocal technique. Female polyphonic choirs have deep historical roots in the pagan rites of the eastern Slavs. When Christianity spread eastwards from Byzantium in the first centuries of the last millennium, it soon acquired distinctively Russian traits, expressed in its choral traditions. Further musical development had to await the emergence of the Russian school in the 18th century, and the work of operatic composers such as Vasily Pashkevich, Evstignei Fomin and Alexei Vertovsky. At that point, Russian choirs assumed a style of performance, both on the concert platform and in opera, that delights audiences today.

Happy occasion A professional dancer performs at a Tajik celebration. Well-off Tajiks often employ professionals at marriages and birthdays.

one day die out. But generally folkloric tradition in Russia is alive and well because it is not seen as folklore at all. The songs, old sayings, folk beliefs – these things are not museum pieces but genuine expressions of that most cherished of cultural artefacts, the wild and wayward, the grand and generous Russian soul.

The balalaika: symbol of popular music

Three strings and a triangular wooden body – a simple combination that has given the balalaika a special place in Russian music. It is usually strummed rapidly with one finger. Probably invented in the 18th century, the balalaika became a favourite with travelling entertainers. It was popularised by the musician and impresario Vasili Andreyev, whose band of balalaika players made their first appearance in 1888.

Today, the instrument comes in six sizes, from piccolo to double bass.

guest is always met at the threshold with the *khleb-sol*, a fresh loaf with a little pot of salt. The guest must break off a piece of bread, dip it in the salt and eat before entering the home. At the height of a party, someone might sing some *chastushki*, little four-line limericks with a witty or bawdy punchline. Real masters of the art will improvise new-minted *chastushki* for the occasion.

Some traditions are strictly local. In Samara, for example, it has been the custom for boys to tumble girls in the snow on Christmas day, perhaps an old folk memory of enforced winter baptisms of the heathen Slavs. Possibly some of these local practices will

MAPS, FACTS AND FIGURES

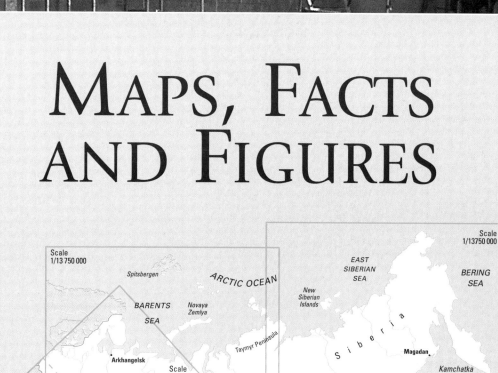

Scale
1/13 750 000

Scale
1/13750 000

Spitsbergen

ARCTIC OCEAN

*BARENTS
SEA*

*Novaya
Zemlya*

*EAST
SIBERIAN
SEA*

*New
Siberian
Islands*

*BERING
SEA*

•Arkhangelsk

Scale
1/7 875 000

Taymyr Peninsula

S i b e r i a

•Magadan

*Kamchatka
Peninsula*

•KYIV
(KIEV)

•MOSCOW

p. 136-137

RUSSIA

p. 144-145

UKRAINE

*BLACK
SEA*

p. 142-143

•Habarovsk

Scale
1/2 550 000

•ASTANA

KAZAKHSTAN

p. 140-141

Scale
1/6 000 000

JAPAN

*SEA
OF JAPAN*

**p. 138-
139**

UZBEKISTAN

Ulan Bator

MONGOLIA

NORTH
KOREA

•PYONGYANG

ASHGABAT •TASHKENT •BISHKEK

KYRGYZSTAN

BEIJING•

SEOUL•
SOUTH
KOREA

TURKMENISTAN

•DUSHANBE
TAJIKISTAN

KABUL•

CHINA

*EAST
CHINA
SEA*

AFGHANISTAN •ISLAMABAD

Shanghai •

PAKISTAN INDIA

•NEW DELHI

Key to maps

Place names

■ **CAPITAL**   ● City

● Major city   • Town

Borders

——— International border

------- Maritime national
border

Topography

▲ Mt Narodnaya
1895 m   Peak

URAL MTS   Mountain range

Elevation tints

Metres

5000
4000
3000
2000
1000
500
200
0
- 200

Depth tints

Metres

- 200
- 500
- 1000
- 2000
- 4000
- 6000

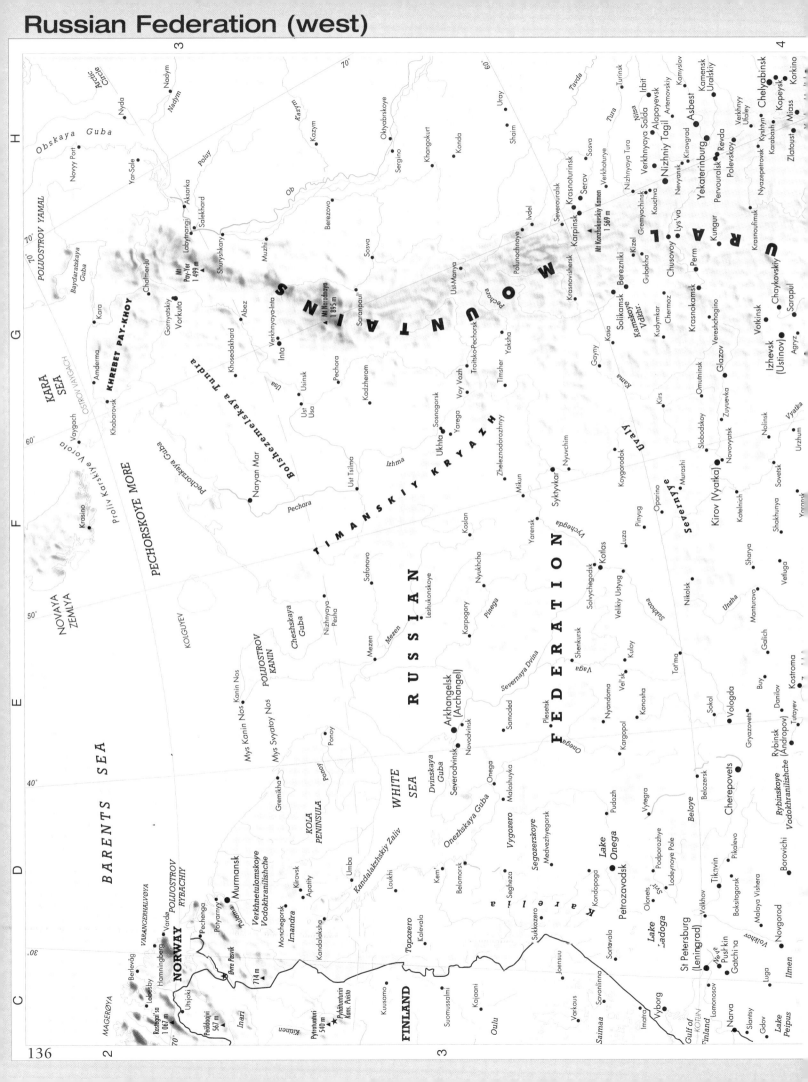

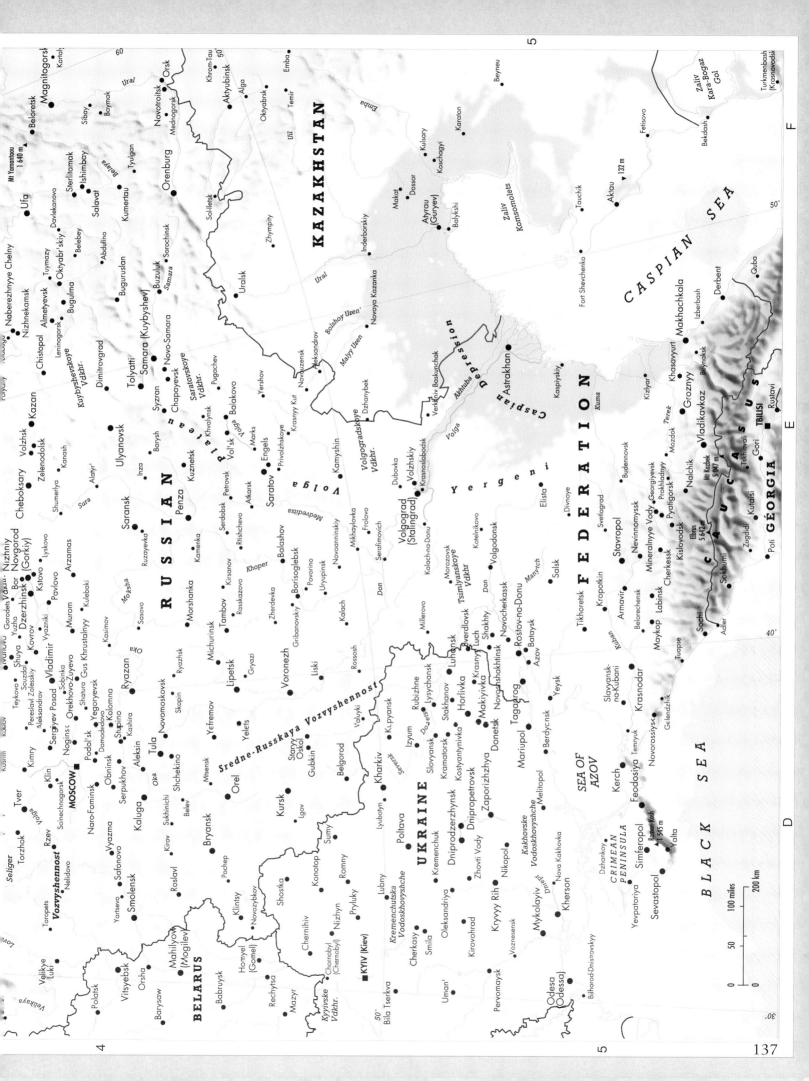

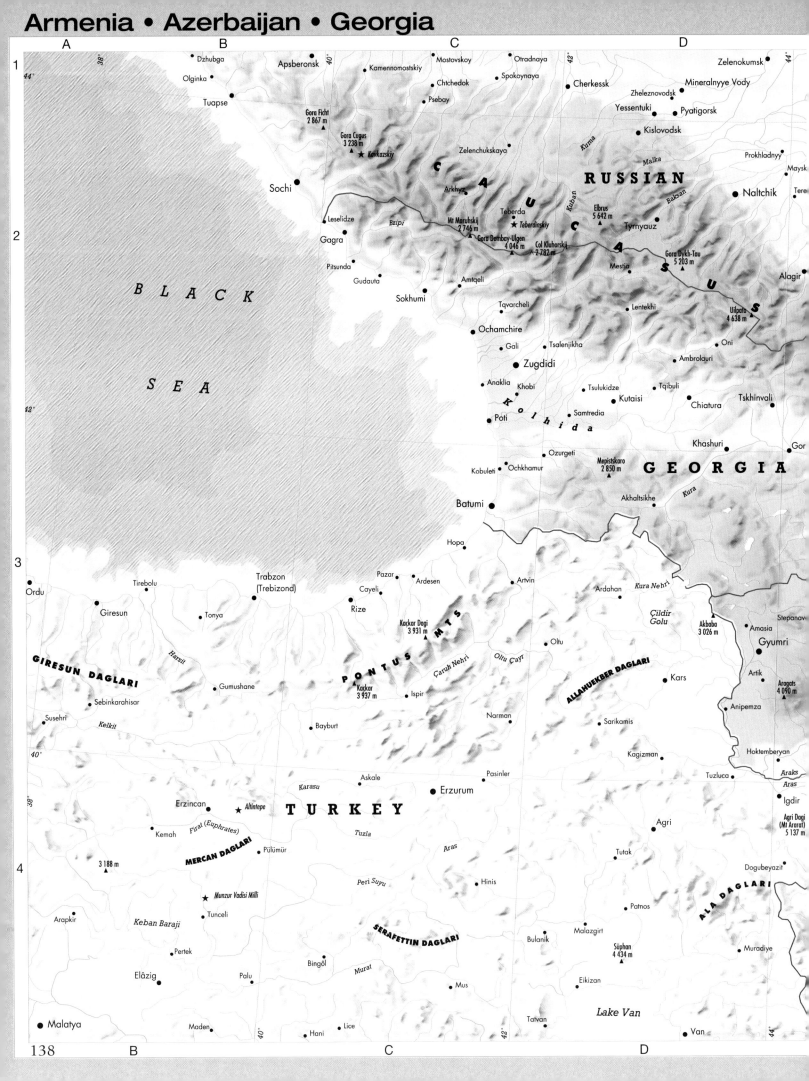

A   B   C   D

1

44°

38°

40°

42°

44°

Dzhubga

Olginka

Apsberonsk

Kamennomostskiy

Mostovskoy

Otradnaya

Zelenokumsk

Tuapse

Chtchedok

Spokoynaya

Cherkessk

Zheleznovodsk

Mineralnyye Vody

Psebay

Yessentuki

Pyatigorsk

Gora Ficht
2 867 m

Gora Cugus
3 238 m

Kislovodsk

Prokhladnyy

★ Kavkazskiy

Zelenchukskaya

C

A

RUSSIAN

Maysk

Naltchik

Tere

Sochi

Arkhyz

U

Kuban

Elbrus
5 642 m

Baksan

Leselidze

Mt Maruhskij
2 746 m

Teberda

Kuma

Malka

★ Teberdinskiy

C

Tyrnyauz

2

42°

Bzipi

Gagra

Gora Dombay-Ulgen
4 046 m

Col Kluhorskij
2 782 m

A

Gora Dykh-Tau
5 203 m

Mestia

S

Alagir

Pitsunda

Gudauta

Amtqeli

Lentekhi

Uilpata
4 638 m

Oni

Sokhumi

Tqvarcheli

U

S

BLACK

Ochamchire

Gali

Tsalenjikha

Ambrolauri

SEA

Zugdidi

Tsulukidze

Tqibuli

Chiatura

Tskhinvali

Anaklia

Khobi

Kutaisi

Poti

Kolhida

Samtredia

Khashuri

Gor

Ozurgeti

Mepistskaro
2 850 m

GEORGIA

Kobuleti

Ochkhamur

Akhaltsikhe

Kura

Batumi

3

40°

Hopa

Ordu

Tirebolu

Trabzon
(Trebizond)

Pazar

Ardesen

Artvin

Ardahan

Kura Nehri

Stepanav

Giresun

Tonya

Cayeli

Rize

Kackar Dagi
3 931 m

Çildir
Golu

Akbaba
3 026 m

Amasia

Gyumri

GIRESUN DAGLARI

Harsit

PONTUS MTS

Oltu

Kars

Artik

Aragats
4 090 m

Sebinkarahisar

Gumushane

Kackar
3 937 m

Çaruh Nehri

Oltu Çayr

ALLAHUEKBER DAGLARI

Anipemza

Susehri

Ispir

Narman

Sarikamis

Kelkit

Bayburt

Kagizman

Hoktemberyan

40°

Askale

Pasinler

Tuzluca

Araks

4

38°

Erzurum

Aras

Igdir

Karasu

Erzincan

★ Altintepe

TURKEY

Agri

Agri Dagi
(Mt Ararat)
5 137 m

Kemah

Firat (Euphrates)

Tuzla

Aras

Tutak

Dogubeyazit

3 188 m

MERCAN DAGLARI

Pülümür

Peri Suyu

Hinis

Patnos

ALA DAGLARI

★ Munzur Vadisi Milli

Tunceli

Malazgirt

Arapkir

Keban Baraji

Bulanik

Süphan
4 434 m

Muradiye

Pertek

Bingöl

SERAFETTIN DAGLARI

Murat

Eikizan

Elâzig

Palu

Mus

Lake Van

Malatya

Maden

Hani

Lice

Tatvan

Van

B   C   D

E   F   G   H

1

44°

Stepnoye

Kochubey

Terekli-Mekteb

CHECHEN

Mozdok

Kraynovka

Kizlyar

Lopatin

Malgobek

CHECHNYA

Chervlennaya

Gudermes

Sulak

Karabulak

Groznyy

Khasavyurt

2

Nazran

Urus-Martan

Shali

C A S P I A N

Beslan

Vladikavkaz

Makhachkala

Kaspiysk

FEDERATION

Buynaksk

S E A

Kazbek
5 047 m

Qazbegi

Teboulosmta
4 494 m

Karabudakhkent

Barisakho

Diklosmta
4 285 m

Botlikh

Izberbash

42°

Pasanauri

Gunib

Tianeti

Tsurib

Kumukh

Dagestanskiye Ogni

Akhmeta

Bezhta

Vachi

Derbent

Telavi

G

Qvareli

Dyoultydag
4 127 m

DAGESTAN

Mtskheta

Guton
3 646 m

Khuchni

Belidzhi

TBILISI

Lagodekhi

Tpig

Yalama

Gurdzhaani

Zaqatala

Kurakh

Müqtädir

Rustavi

Tsnori

Qax

Xaçmaz

Bolnisi

Ivri

Zegani

Chalbouzdag
4 142 m

Quba

3

Ayrum

Kür

Bazar Dyuzi
4 466 m

Däväçi

anadzor

Agstafa

Siyäzän

Sevan

Tovuz

*Mingechaur
Reservoir*

Hrazdan

Samkir

Ismayilli

Altiagat

Kamo

Mingäçevir

Göyçay

Samaxi

*Apsheron
Peninsula*

Gäncä

Yevlax

Agsu

Sumgayit

Mastaga

Artyom

Lake Sevan

Ucar

A Z E R B A I J A N

ÇILOV

YEREVAN

Barda

Kürdämir

BAKI (Baku)

A R M E N I A

Kür

Danizkanari

Lökbatan

40°

Artashat

3 724 m

NAGORNO

Qazimämmad

Ararat

Yeghegnadzor

KARABAKH

Agdam

Imisli

Saatli

Äli Bayramli

Älät

Xankandi
(Stepanakert)

Kür

Goris

Fuzuli

Salyan

Sahbuz

Cabrayil

Bilasuvar

Neftçala

NAKHICHEVAN

Kapan

Aras

Cälilabad

Göytäpä

KÜR DILI

4

Mäkü

AZERBAIJAN

Garmi

Masalli

*Qizilagac
Korfazi*

Naxçivan

Safarabad

Port Ilich

Zurabad

Culfa

Qareh Sü

Lerik

Lankaran

Jolfä

T

Avrora

tur

Khvoy

I R A N

Kijaba

Astara

Marand

Ahar

Ahar

Lari

Namin

Khiyav

0   50   100 miles

0   50   100   150 km

46°   48°   50°

E   F   G

LESSER CAUCASUS

GREAT CAUCASUS

TALIS DAGLARI

A   B   C   D   E   F

1

Caspian
Depression

Kulagino
Karabau
Dmitrievsky
Emba
Sagiz
Makhambet
Zharkamys
Berchogur
Sazdy
Novobogatinskoye
Dossor
Makat
Zhanterek
Atyrau
(Guryev)
Balykshi
Chelkar
Toguz
Baykonur

CASPIAN
SEA

Kulsary
Koschagyl
Aktumsyk
Saksaulskiy
Aralsk
Sarybasat

Fort Shevchenko
Novokazalinsk
Baykonur
(Leninsk)

ARAL
SEA

Prorva
Syr Darya
Dzhusaly

Tauchik
Beyneu
Matay

Zharmysh
Kzyl-Orda

Aktau
(Shevchenko)

Zhetybay
Muynak

Kuryk
(Yeraliyev)
Novyy Uzen
Kungrad
Chimbay

Kyzylkum
Desert

Ustyurt
Plateau

3

Nukus

Bekdash
Zaliv
Kara-Bogaz
Gol

UZBEKISTAN

Sarykamyshkoye
Ozero
Dashkhovuz
Beruni
Urgench

Krasnovodskoye
Plato
Khiva
Gaz-Achak

Kuuli-Mayak
Chagyl

Turkmenbashi
(Krasnovodsk)
Dzhanga

Krasnovodskiy
Zaliv
Oglanly
Darvaza

Amu Darya
Nurata

Cheleken
▲ Khrebet Bolshoy Balkhan
1 880 m
Navoi

Nebit-Dag
Karakum
Gazandzhyk
Bukhara
Aktash

O. OGURCHINSKI
Gumdag

TURKMENISTAN

1 005 m Gyzylarbat
Kazy
Karakul
Samarka

Garrygala
Archman
Seydi

Okarem
Nokhur
Bakharden
Chardzhev

Desert
Kit

4

Gora Tagarav
2 246 m
Karshi

Atrek
Moraveh
Tappeh
Sumbar
Byuzmeyin

Esenguly
Atrak
Gifan
ASHGABAT
(ASHKHABAD)
Uch-Adzhi
Amu Darya

Babol
Gonbad-
e-Qabus
Bojnurd
Kirovsk
Ravnina
Karamet-Niyaz
Kerki

Sari
Behshahr
Gorgan
Shirvan
Darreh Gaz
Kaka
Tedzhen
Mary
Bayramaly
Kara Kum Canal

Gorgan
Jajarm
Quchan
Dushak
Yeloten
Amu Darya

Qareh Su
Hokmabad
Murgab
Aqchah
Andkhvoy

Emamrud
Chanaran
Imeni Chapayeva
Sandykachi
Sheberghan

Dämghän
Davarzan
Sabzevar
Neyshabur
MASHHAD
Shirin

Semnan
IRAN
Gora Karakyr
784 m
Tagtabazar
JOWZJAN BALKH

5

Torud
Rivash
2 119 m ▲
Kala I-Mor
Bala Morghab
Meymaneh

Dasht-e Kavir
Bardeskan
Kashmar
Torbat-e Heydariyeh
Guchgy
(Kushka)
BAND-I-TURKESTAN

KAVIR-I-NAMAK
Roshkhvar
Townahondi

G   H   I   J   K   L

1

69°   72°   75°   78°   82°   48°

Kazakh

Atasu

Agadyr

Karazhal

Akchatau

Ayagoz

Oz. Zaysan

Priozernyy

KHR. TARBAGATAY

atpayev

Zhezkazgan

Aktogay

Urdzhar

Makanchi

Tacheng

Kounradskiy

Sayak

Balkhash

Lepsy

Ucharal

Yumin

KAZAKHSTAN

Steppes

Saryshagan

Mynaral

Matay

Sarkand

Ushtobe

Taldy Korgan

Balpyk Bi

Tekeli

Oz. Alakol

Dostyk

Ebi Nor Hu

CHINA

2

K a z a k h

Chiganak

Zharkent

Yining

44

U p l a n d s

Shu Valley

Khantau

Birlik

Ili

iili

Suzak

Shu

Talgar

Kentau

KHR.

Zhanatas

Karatau

BISHKEK
(FRUNZE)

Tokmak

ALMATY (Alma-Ata)

Karakol (Prjevalsk)

Turkestan

KARA-TAU

Bayzhansay

Taraz
(Dzhambul)

Lugovoy

Kara-Balta

Balykchy

Ysyk-Kol

3

Arys

Talas

KIRGHIZ MTS

Aksu

Shymkent

*Toktogul
Vdkhr.*

KYRGYZSTAN

Chaek

Naryn

hardarinskoye
Vdkhr.

Kara-Kol

Naryn

TASHKENT

Chirchik

Bachu

UZBEKISTAN

Angren

Namangan

Dzhalal Abad

KOKSHAAL TAU

40

Almalyk

Andizhan

Gulistan

Syr Darya

Kokand

Osh

T

Kashi
(Kashgar)

Kaxgar

Dzhizak

Fergana

I

Yarkant

T a r i m   B a s i n

Bekabad

E

Panjakent

ALAI MTS

N

Lenin Peak
7 134 m

Kongur Shan
7 719 m

Shache
(Yarkand)

T a k l i m a k a n   D e s e r t

Zeravshan

Pic Qullai Germo
(Communism' Peak)
7 495 m

S

4

ZERAVSHAN RANGE

P

H

TAJIKISTAN

A

A

CHINA

DUSHANBE

M

N

Vakhsh

I

Murghob

Taxkorgan

Dangara

R

Chaymak

82

Qurghonteppa

Kulob

S

Musishan
7 282 m

Kolkhozabad

3 633 m

Khorugh

Khunjerab Pass
4 709 m

36

Termez

Panj

Amu Darya

Pyandzh
Panj
4 179 m

Misgar

Mazar-e-Sharif

Kondoz

Taloqan

Kowkcheh

Feyzabad

Vrang

KUSH

KARAKORAM

0   50   100 miles

Kondoz

Khanabad

Zebak

Nowshak
7 485 m

Yasin

Gilgit

Rakaposhi
7 788 m

Nagir

K2 (Godwin Austen)
8 611 m

Kashmir

0   50   100   150 km

MANGAN

Aybak

Baghlan

5 092 m

KHWAJA MOHAMMAD MTS

Tirich Mir
7 690 m

PAKISTAN

Gilgit

Masherbrum
7 821 m

Rondu

LADAKH

Pol-e-Khomri

HINDU

6 248 m

Chitral

Jammu

Chilas

DEOSAI MTS

Skardu

Shoyk

Dowshi

Barikot

Konar

Kalam

Nanga Parbat
8 126 m

MTS

Indus

FGHANISTAN

Indus

G   H   I   J   K   141

5

Russian Federation (central)

ARCTIC OCEAN

SEVERAYA ZEMLYA
Mys Arkticheskiy
Krasnoy Armii
Proliv
Pr. Shokal'skogo
O. Shokalskogo
OSTROV KOMSOMOLETS
OSTROV PIONNIER
OSTROV OKTYABR'SKOY REVOLYUTSU
OSTROVA SERGEYA KIROVA
O. BOLSHEVIK
P. VIL'KITSKOGO
O RUSSKIY
OSTROV GREEMBELL
OSTROV RUDOLFA
O. VIZE

C D E F G H I J K L M
130° 120° 110° 100° 90° 80° 60° 50° 40° 30° 20°

FRANZ JOSEF LAND
TERRE NORDAUSTLANDET
ZEMLYA ALEKSANDRY
ZEMLYA GEORGA
OSTROV VILCHEKA

Mys Zhelaniya
OSTROVA ARKTICHESKOGO INSTITUTA
Russkaya Gavan
NOVAYA ZEMLYA
1 547 m
Krestovaya Guba
Pik Sedova 1 115 m
Matochkin Shar
Malye Karmakuly
Krasino
Krasina
O. BELYY
O SIBIRYAKOVA
O. OLENIY

KARA SEA

L. Taymyr
Gora Byrranga Gory
Mys Vkhodnoy
Pyasina Tareya
Agapa
Pyasinskiy Zaliv
Dikson
Yeniseyskiy Zaliv
Volochanka
Ayan
Gora Kamen 1 701 m
Putorana Gory
Oz. Keta
Oz. Lama
Oz. Khantayskoye
Khantayskoye Vdkhr.
Norilsk
Dudinka
Golchikha
Karaul
Igarka
Turukhansk
Nizh. Tunguska
Verkhneimbatsk

Northern Siberian Plain

Kochechum
Tembenchi
Vivi
Kuzmovka
Podkamennaya Tunguska
Bakhta
Boykit
Severo Yeniseyskiy
Gora Yenashimskiy Polkan 1 104 m
Yeniseyskiy
Yeloguy
Yenisey

West Siberian
RUSSIAN FEDERATION

Tombey
Yamal Peninsula
Napalkovo
Gyda
Gydanskiy Poluostrov
Gydan Zal.
Yamburg
Tazovskiy
Tarko-Sale
Pur
Novyy Port
Yaptiksale
Taz Guba
Nadym
Nyda
Pyakupur
Laryok
Vakh
Aleksandrovskoye

Baydaratskaya Guba
Khrebet Pay-Khoy
Amderma
Chalmer-Ju
Gora Poyyer 1 499 m
Vorkuta
Salekhard
Labytnangi
Aksarka
Berezovo
Oktyabr'skoye
Sergino
Severnaya Sos'
Khanty-Mansiysk
Irtysh
Uray
Pim
Lyamin
Surgut
Ob
Nizhnevartovsk
Vasyugan
Demyanka

Pik
Pechorskaya Guba
Usa
Inta
Gora Narodnaya 1 895 m
Usinsk
Usa
Pechora
Kadzherom
Pechora
Sosnogorsk
Voy Vozh
Ukhta
Troitsko-Pechorsk
Berezniki
Gora Konzhakovskiy Kamen 1 569 m
Solikamsk
Ivdel
Krasnoturinsk
Serov
Tavda
Tavda
Tura
Tobolsk
Tyumen
Tavda

Bol'shezemelskaya Tundra
Naryan Mar
Ust Tsilma
Timanskiy Kryazh

PECHORSKOYE MORE
KOLGUYEV
Mys Kanin Nos
Poluostrov Kanin
Cheshskaya Guba
Nizhnyaya Pesha
Leshukonskoye
Nyukhcha
Mezen
Koslan
Mikun
Syktyvkar
Koygorodok
Glazov
Kamskoye Vdkhr.
Kungur
Perm
Izhevsk
Ustinov
Yekaterinburg
Kamensk
Nizhniy-Tagil
Nitsa
Kama

BARENTS SEA
SVALBARD (NORWAY)
SPITSBERGEN
BARENTSØYA
EDGEØYA

Varangerhalvøya
SØRØYA
Hammerfest
Severomorsk
Murmansk
Monchegorsk
Kirovsk
Apatity
Kandalaksha
Umba
Kola Peninsula
Gremikha
Ponoy
WHITE SEA
Mezen
Pinega
Arkhangelsk
Severodvinsk
Novodvinsk
Onega
Pinega
Nyukhcha
Shenkursk
Kotlas
Solvychegodsk
Veliky Ustyug
Nikolsk
Yoshkar-Ola
Kirov (Vyatka)
Severnyye Uvaly
Glazov
Naberezhnye Chelny
Oktyabr'skiy
Ufa

NORWEGIAN SEA
Tromsø
Harstad
Narvik
Kiruna
Vestfjorden
LOFOTEN ISLANDS
Alta
Ivalo
Inari
Lappland
Karelia
Kem
Belomorsk
Segheza
Medvezhyegorsk
Petrozavodsk
Podporozhye
Vytegra
L. Onega
Beloye
Vologda
Sharya
Murashi
Kostroma
Yaroslavl
Ivanovo
Nizhniy Novgorod
Sura
Cheboksary
Kazan
Dimitrovgrad
Ulyanovsk
Tolyatti
Samara

Arctic Circle
NORWAY
SWEDEN
FINLAND
Trondheim
Östersund
Hanösund
Örnsköldsvik
Luleå
Tornio
Oulu
Kalevala
Loukhi
Kuusamo
Joensuu
Iisalmi
Kajaani
L. Ladoga
Sortavala
Vyborg
Tikhvin
Cherepovets
Rybinsk
Rybinskoye Vdkhr.
Gorkovskoye Vdkhr.
Kostroma
Vladimir
Sergiyev Posad
Vladimir
Murom
Arzamas
Moksha
Saransk
Penza
Chapayevsk
Saratov
Volga Plateau

Pori
Tampere
HELSINKI
G. of Finland
St Petersburg (Leningrad)
Puskin
Novgorod
Staraya Russa
Bologoye
Lovat
Valdayskaya Vozvyshennost
Tver
Bezhetsk
Sergiyev Posad
MOSCOW
Oka
Tula
Novomoskovsk
Ryazan
Lipetsk
Tambov
Balashov
Volgogradskoye Vdkhr.
Khoper

Trondheim
Narvik
Kiruna
Örnsköldsvik
Vaasa
Kokkola
Vaasa
Turku
Gulf of Bothnia
80 miles
200 km
300 km
100
200
100
0
0

142

Russian Federation (east)

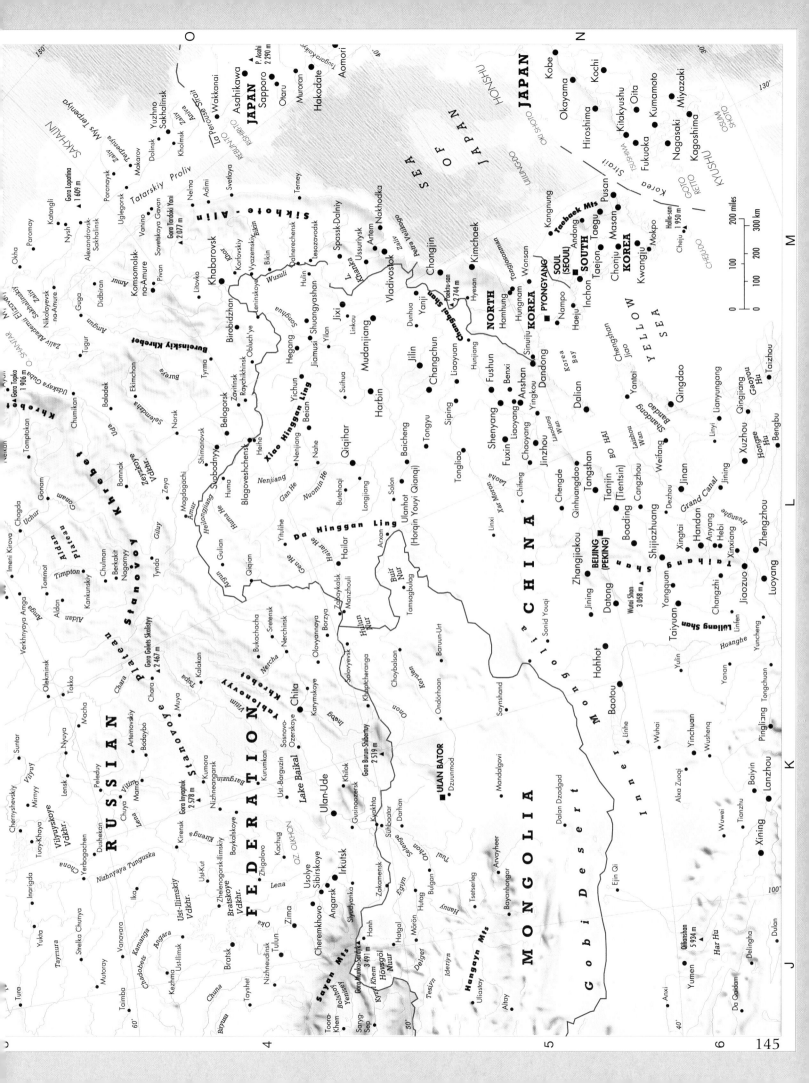

Nine nations of Eurasia: the statistics

The nine states in this statistical profile are linked by a joint history in the Soviet empire and by membership of its loose successor, the 12-nation Commonwealth of Independent States (CIS). The nine form a region of astonishing complexity in which numerous minorities are demanding a greater say in their own affairs.

ARMENIA

Official name: Republic of Armenia
Capital: Yerevan
Area: 11 580 sq miles (30 000 km²)
Population: 3.07 million
Density: 265 per sq mile (102 per km²)
Most significant minorities:
Kurds: 1.7 %, Russians : 1.1%, Azeris : 0.2%
Religion: Armenian Orthodox.
Currency: Dram
HDI (Human Development Index): 0.754
GDP (per person p.a.): $749
Language: Armenian
Government: republic with a parliament

UZBEKISTAN

Official name: Republic of Uzbekistan
Capital: Tashkent
Area: 172,740 sq miles (447 400 km²)
Population: 25.37 million
Density: 146 per sq mile (56 per km²)
Most significant minorities:
Russians: 6.0%, Tajiks: 4.8%, Kazakhs: 4.1%
Religions : Islam
Currency : Sum
HDI (Human Development Index): 0.727
GDP (per person p.a.): $310
Language: Uzbek
Government: republic with a parliament

KYRGYZSTAN

Official name : Kyrgyz Republic
Capital: Bishkek
Area: 76 620 sq miles (198 500 km²)
Population: 4.92 million
Density: 65 per sq mile (25 per km²)
Most significant minorities: Russians 15.3 %, Uzbeks 14.3%, Ukrainians : 1.6 %, Germans : 0.4 %

Religions: Islam, 75%; Russian Orthodox, 20%
Currency: Som
HDI (Human Development Index): 0.712
GDP (per person p.a.): $301
Languages: Kyrgyz, Russian
Government: republic with two parliamentary chambers and an executive presidency

AZERBAIJAN

Official name: Republic of Azerbaijan
Capital: Baku
Area: 33 580 sq miles (87 000 km²)
Population: 8.14 million
Density: 242 per sq mile (93 per km²)

Most significant minorities: Russians, 4.1%; Armenians, 3.2%
Religions: Islam, 93.4%; Russian Orthodox, 2.5%
Currency: Azerbaijan manat
HDI (Human Development Index): 0.623
GDP (per person p.a.): $751
Languages: Azeri, Russian
Government: republic with a parliament

KAZAKHSTAN

Official name: Republic of Kazakhstan
Capital: Astana
Area: 1 049 150 sq miles (2 717 300 km²)
Population : 15.47 million
Density : 14.7 per sq mile (5.6 per km²)
Most significant minorities: Russians, 34.1%; Ukrainians, 4.9%
Religions : Islam, 47%; Russian Orthodox, 44%, Protestants 2%
Currency: Tenge
HDI (Human Development Index): 0.750
GDP (per person p.a.): $1600
Languages: Kazakh, Russian
Government: a presidential republic with two parliamentary chambers

GEORGIA

Official name: Republic of Georgia
Capital: Tbilisi
Area: 26 905 sq miles (69 700 km²)
Population: 5.18 million
Density: 192 per sq mile (74 per km²)
Most significant minorities: Armenians, 8.1%; Russians, 6.3%; Azeris, 5.7%

Religions: Russian Orthodox, 75%; Islam, 11%; Armenian Orthodox, 8%
Currency: Lari
HDI (Human Development Index): 0.748
GDP (per person p.a.): $637
Languages: Georgian, Abkhazian
Government: presidential republic with a parliament

RUSSIA

Official name: Russian Federation
Capital: Moscow
Area: 6 592 850 sq miles (17 075 400 km²)
Population: 145.29 million
Density: 20.7 per sq mile (8 per km²) (Moscow region: 830 per sq mile/ 320 per km²)
Most significant minorities: over 100 minorities including Tatars, 3.8 %; Ukrainians, 2.3 %;

Chuvash, 1.2 %; Bashkirs, 0.9 %
Religions: Russian Orthodox, Islam
Currency: Rouble
HDI (Human Development Index): 0.769
GDP (per person p.a.): $2381
Language: Russian
Government: presidential system with a parliament (Federal Assembly) consisting of the Federation Council and Duma. There are 7 administrative federal districts containing the country's 89 republics and regions.

TAJIKISTAN

Official name: Republic of Tajikistan
Capital: Dushanbe
Area: 55 232 sq miles (143 100 km²)
Population: 6.43 million
Density: 116 per sq mile (44.9 per km²)
Most significant minorities: Uzbeks, 24.9%; Russians 3%
Religions: Islam, 85%
Currency: Somoni
HDI (Human Development Index): 0.667
GDP (per person p.a.): $170
Language : Tajik
Government: republic with one chamber (National Assembly)

TURKMENISTAN

Official name: Turkmenistan
Capital: Ashgabat
Area: 188 405 sq miles (488 100 km²)
Population: 4.83 million
Density: 25.6 per sq mile (9.8 per km²)
Most significant minorities: Uzbeks, 9.2%; Russians, 6.7%

Religions: Islam, 89%; Orthodox, 9%
Currency: Turkmen manat
HDI (Human Development Index): 0.741
GDP (per person p.a.): $1510
Language: Turkmen
Government: republic with two chambers (Assembly and Council of the People)

Climate, relief and vegetation

Covering more than 8 million sq miles (21 million km²), the territory that includes Russia, the Caucasus and Central Asia is a vast region of forests, steppes, deserts and lakes, extending from the Baltic Sea in the west to the Pacific Ocean in the east, from the ice-covered Arctic Ocean in the north to the sunny Caucasian uplands in the south.

The region comprising Russia, the Caucasus and Central Asia makes up one-sixth of the world's landmass. It stretches across 6200 miles (10 000 km) from west to east, and 3100 miles (5000 km) from north to south, abutting western Europe, Mongolia, China and the fringes of Japan. In the east, only the Bering Strait separates it from Alaska and the North American continent. In total, it covers 5.7 million sq miles (15 million km²).

In relief and structure, this region comprises a vast platform surrounded by high mountains. In the centre are the immense plains of Siberia and Russia, separated by the low mountains of the Urals, which rise to 6600 ft (2000 m). In the north lie the frozen wastes of the Arctic.

To the east, the Siberian plateau is bordered by great parallel arcs of mountains that extend to the shores of the Pacific Ocean. The mountains rise to heights of between 8250 ft (2500 m) and 14 850 ft (4500 m), and are linked to the volcanic chain that runs along the Kamchatka Peninsula.

In Russia's south-west, the Caucasian countries, between the Caspian and the Black seas, form an isthmus some 620 miles (1000 km) across, which links Europe to Asia. Broad and bulky, the Caucasian chain, which reaches its highest point at Mt Elbrus (18 510 ft/5642 m), makes a formidable barrier.

To the south of Kazakhstan, southern Central Asia extends into a region of steppes and deserts that surround the Caspian and the Aral seas. Farther east, on the borders of Iran, the Indian sub-continent and China, rear the mighty Tien Shan and Altai ranges, dominated by two peaks known as Communism Peak (24 600 ft/7495 m) and Lenin Peak (23 400 ft/ 7134 m), which are both in Tajikistan.

Mighty waterways

Russia's rivers, of which five are longer than 2500 miles (4000 km), have played a major role in the country's history and commercial development. They run from south to north in the west and central regions, and from north to south in Asiatic Russia. A number are frozen for about six months of the year. With the spring thaw they become formidable, fast-flowing waterways. The Volga is the most celebrated of the great rivers. Nicknamed 'little mother' by Russians, it links central Russia to the Caucasus, the Caspian Sea and the Urals.

RIVERS
(length in miles/km)

Ob-Irtysh	3460/5570
Yenisei-Angara	3450/5550
Amur	2744/4416
Lena	2730/4400
Volga	2290/3685
Syr-Darya	1913/3078
Amu-Darya	1630/2620
Don	1162/1870

Frontier river The Amur marks the border between Russia and China for much of its length.

A blast of cold air

Three-quarters of the region lies to the north of the 50th parallel, in close contact with the Arctic Ocean. Exposed to the polar winds and situated far from the moderating influence of the oceans, Russia has the world's most extreme continental climate. Summers are hot and winters are bitterly cold.

In eastern Siberia, Verkhoyansk has recorded temperatures ranging from 32°C (89°F) in summer to a winter low of –69°C (–92°F).

Everywhere, winters are long with an average 120 days of frost each year. It is an intense, dry cold. Three-quarters of the region is snow-covered in winter – it would be possible to travel by sleigh from the White Sea, near St Petersburg, south to the Caspian Sea.

In the north, the ground is permanently frozen to a depth of several metres. This is known as the *vechnaya merzlota*, or permafrost.

The other seasons are short. Spring comes with a thaw of astonishing speed. The snow vanishes, rivers surge and in April and May the ground turns to mud. This is known as the *rasputitsa*. Summer comes fast, with intense heat and torrential downpours. Moscow, on the same latitude

Climates

▮ hot and humid	▯ tundra
▯ semi-arid	▯ sub-Arctic
▯ arid	▯ continental

◀ **CLIMATE**

AVERAGE TEMPERATURES

	January	July
Ashgabat	2°C (36°F)	31°C (88°F)
Astana	–17°C (1°F)	22°C (71°F)
Baku	3.5°C (39°F)	25°C (77°F)
Dushanbe	1.5°C (35°F)	28°C (82°F)
Moscow	–10°C(14°F)	19°C (66°F)
Tashkent	–1.5°C (29°F)	25°C (77°F)
Tbilisi	3 °C (37°F)	25°C (77°F)
Verkhoyansk	–49°C (–56°F)	15°C (59°F)
Yerevan	–6 °C (21°F)	25°C (77°F)

Still waters *The waters of Lake Baikal in Siberia are frozen for six months of the year.*

Baikal's record depth

It may look on a map small against the vastness of Siberia, but Lake Baikal is actually as long as the Adriatic Sea and covers a larger area than Holland. With a depth of down to 5709 ft (1740 m), it is the deepest lake in the world. The next is Lake Tanganyika in Africa, 4708 ft (1435 m) deep. It contains more water than the Baltic Sea – almost 6000 cu miles (23 km³).

Relief
height in metres

5000
1500
500
200
0

ARCTIC OCEAN

▲ RELIEF

as Copenhagen, has an average July temperature of 19°C (66°F).

Autumn lasts just a few weeks then winter strikes. Siberia's rivers start to freeze in September, and Russia's first snowfalls come in October.

The southern fringes of the CIS escape the worst of the climatic excesses. Caucasian

countries, protected from the cooling effects of polar airflows by mountains, enjoy an almost Mediterranean climate. Farther east, Central Asian countries endure desert and semidesert conditions, with annual rainfall measuring a scanty 4-12 in (100-300 mm).

Tundra, taiga, steppe

Running in rough strips from the Arctic coast, the zones of vegetation correspond to the climatic conditions. In the north tundra prevails wherever the subsoil remains frozen in summer. Across almost 770 000 sq miles (2 million km²) of tundra little grows other than dwarf birches, lichens, mosses and a few hardy bulbous plants – all of it forming one extensive reindeer pasture.

Farther south, the taiga, one of the world's greatest forested areas, covers some 2.7 million sq

miles (7 million km²). The taiga is composed mainly of fir, pine, spruce and birch trees. On its eastern and western fringes it merges with mixed woodlands of broad-leafed trees and conifers. Travelling south into more arid areas, the forest becomes thinner and finally gives way to the steppe. Like the North American prairies, the steppe is covered with grasses and scattered with colourful wild flowers in summer. Over the millennia, the plants have decayed to form a dark humus, the famous 'black earth' (*chernozem*), which favours agriculture.

Farther south still, in Uzbekistan and Turkmenistan, Central Asia's semideserts and deserts cover an area of more than 1.15 million sq miles (3 million km²).

▼ A SELECTION OF PEAKS
(feet/metres)

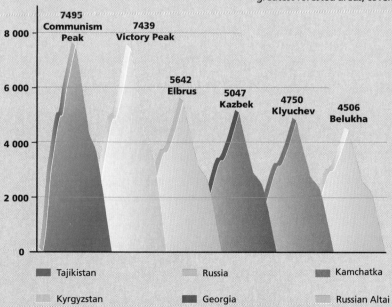

7495 Communism Peak
7439 Victory Peak
5642 Elbrus
5047 Kazbek
4750 Klyuchev
4506 Belukha

8 000
6 000
4 000
2 000
0

■ Tajikistan ■ Russia ■ Kamchatka
■ Kyrgyzstan ■ Georgia ■ Russian Altai

ANNUAL RAINFALL
(in/mm)

Ashgabat	8.6/218
Astana	12.5/317
Baku	9.5/241
Dushanbe	23.9/608
Moscow	21.6/549
Tashkent	16.4/417
Tbilisi	18/457
Verkhoyansk	6.2/157
Yerevan	12/305

Blooming topsoil *The tundra's subsoil remains frozen, but in summer its surface is a mass of mosses and flowers.*

Population, economy and society

The 220 million inhabitants of Russia and Central Asia comprise a multitude of cultural and ethnic groups. Social, religious, economic and political differences have become more marked since the break-up of the Soviet Union in the early 1990s. Economies are making slow progress as they adapt to capitalism and a population imbalance is developing between an ageing north and more youthful south.

A scattered population, unequally distributed

The population of Russia and Central Asia is, for the most part, thinly scattered across the region, with the exception of the west and south where the density is greater. On average, there are fewer than 25 inhabitants per sq mile (10 per km²).

Russia's polar regions, the taiga, deserts and mountains are inhabited by only a few million people, mostly minorities well adapted to the harsh environment. Three-quarters of the popu-

Ethnic symbol A baby, bound to its cradle in the traditional fashion. Dagestan alone has 13 different ethnic groups.

▼ POPULATION
(in millions)

145.3

25.3

15.5

8.1

6.4

5.1

4.9

4.8

3.0

- Russia
- Azerbaijan
- Turkmenistan
- Uzbekistan
- Tajikistan
- Kyrgyzstan
- Kazakhstan
- Georgia
- Armenia

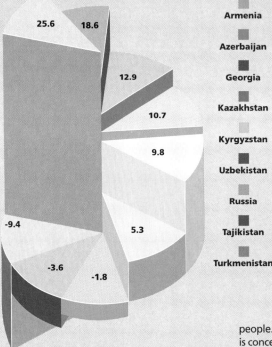

25.6 18.6

12.9

10.7

9.8

-9.4

5.3

-3.6

-1.8

- Armenia
- Azerbaijan
- Georgia
- Kazakhstan
- Kyrgyzstan
- Uzbekistan
- Russia
- Tajikistan
- Turkmenistan

◀ POPULATION GROWTH
(percentage change from 1991-20

INFANT MORTALITY *(per 1000)*	
Turkmenistan	54.8
Tajikistan	56.6
Kyrgyzstan	23.0
Kazakhstan	20.8
Uzbekistan	17.9
Armenia	15.8
Georgia	14.9
Russia	14.6
Azerbaijan	12.7

lation live in the area bordering western Europe, between the Baltic and the Black Sea.

The population density in the Russian Federation is on average 22 per sq mile (8.6 per km²), which rises to 828 per sq mile (320 per km²) in the Moscow area. Almost three out of every four Russians live in a city or town.

The valleys of the Caucasus, with their milder climate, are also densely populated. Covering an area of less than 71 000 sq miles (185 000 km²), the Caucasian republics of Georgia, Azerbaijan and Armenia are home for some 17 million

people. In Siberia and the Far East, the population is concentrated within a band that runs along the Trans-Siberian Railway.

A widening age gap

There is an increasing demographic gap between Russia's ageing population and that of the five fast-growing Central Asian republics. As a direct consequence of its lower birthrate and high male mortality rate (life expectancy is 58 years compared to 73 for American men), the population of

Old survivor This Uzbek has exceeded the average life expectancy of 65 years for a male.

LIFE EXPECTANCY		
	Men	*Women*
Armenia	69	75
Azerbaijan	67	74
Georgia	68.7	76.1
Kazakhstan	58	70.2
Kyrgyzstan	62.6	71.4
Russia	58	72
Tajikistan	64	70
Turkmenistan	62	68
Uzbekistan	65	71

▼ URBAN POPULATION *(percentage)*

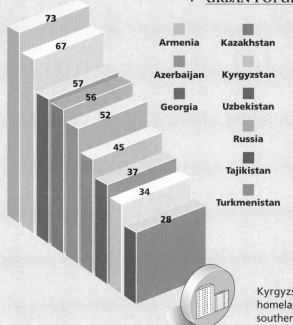

73
67
57
56
52
45
37
34
28

■ Armenia	■ Kazakhstan
■ Azerbaijan	■ Kyrgyzstan
■ Georgia	■ Uzbekistan
	■ Russia
	■ Tajikistan
	■ Turkmenistan

MAIN URBAN CENTRES	
Moscow	10 103 000
St Petersburg	4 669 000
Tashkent	2 143 000
Baku	1 786 000
Novosibirsk	1 426 000
Nizhny Novgorod	1 311 000
Tbilisi	1 310 000
Yekaterinburg	1 293 000
Yerevan	1 250 000
Almaty	1 129 000
Bishkek	619 000

Tiny community A handful of Yakugirs remain along the River Kolyma in Russia's Far East.

the Russian Federation is shrinking. An ageing population could have serious implications for the country's future. Less than 25 per cent of the inhabitants are under 15, while 20 per cent are 60-year-olds – and the proportion is rising year by year.

In the Muslim republics of southern Central Asia the situation is very different. The birth-rate is up, life expectancy is lengthening and the populations are increasing.

In the last 20 years, the population of Uzbekistan, Kyrgyzstan, Tajikistan and Turkmenistan has topped 40 million.

The multi-cultural society

The countries of Russia, Caucasia and Central Asia include nine nationalities of more than a million members and more than 100 ethnic minorities or national groups.

Russians of Slav origin form more than 80 per cent of the population of the Russian Federation. They are also well represented in Kazakhstan and

Kyrgyzstan. The Caucasian mountains are a homeland for numerous ethnic minorities. In the southern Caucasus, Georgians, Azerbaijanis and Armenians are in the majority, while to the north of the mountains live numerous minorities, such as the Dagestanis and the Chechens.

In the five central Asian republics, people of Turko-Mongol origins are in the majority. They also have minority status in some of the autonomous areas of the Volga region, such as

Computer literate In Russia, 24 million children are educated in 72 000 primary and secondary schools.

Chuvashia and Bashkortostan. Only a few hardy individuals occupy the forests and treeless wastes of the northern part of Russia. Chukchis, Ostyaks, Maris, Komis, Buryats and Yakuts are the most numerous, but they are than a tiny fraction of the total population.

Speaking with many tongues

Before the revolution of 1917, more than 200 languages were in evidence in the Russian empire. Today, about 20 different tongues are spoken by more than a million people each. In addition, there are numerous local dialects, often with very small variations.

Until the coming of *perestroika* in the 1980s, the ability to speak Russian was considered crucial for advancement. But after the break up of the Soviet Union in the early 1990's, each of the republics decreed that its national tongue was to be the new state's official language.

In equally rapid moves, small autonomous regions seized the chance to assert their own linguistic rights.

Russian is the mother tongue of 150 million people. In second place come the Turkic languages – principally Uzbek, Kazakh and

ILLITERACY *(percentage)*
▼

3
1.4
1.0
0.6
0.5
0.4

■ Kyrgyzstan
■ Kazakhstan
■ Tajikistan
■ Russia
■ Armenia
■ Georgia

Kyrgyz – spoken by the Central Asian and Caucasian republics. Tajik is spoken by 6 million people in and around Tajikistan.

In the Caucasian mountains, about 70 languages and dialects form a linguistic kaleidoscope in an area more than twice the size of the United Kingdom.

Of the Caucasus's 8 million inhabitants, about 4 million speak Georgian. Otherwise, the most widely spoken language is Chechen (900 000), then Avar (450 000), Kabardian (or Circassian), Adyghe, Lezghian and Dargwa (all around 250 000 or more).

In the more northerly and Arctic regions, dozens of languages – including Inuit, Chukchi and Koryak – are spoken by a relatively small number of people.

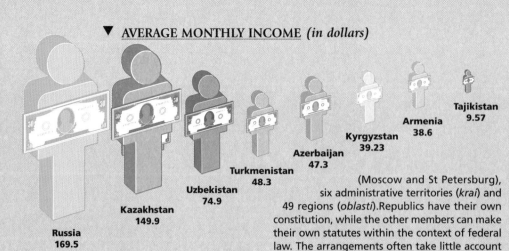

▼ AVERAGE MONTHLY INCOME *(in dollars)*

Russia 169.5
Kazakhstan 149.9
Uzbekistan 74.9
Turkmenistan 48.3
Azerbaijan 47.3
Kyrgyzstan 39.23
Armenia 38.6
Tajikistan 9.57

(Moscow and St Petersburg), six administrative territories (*krai*) and 49 regions (*oblasti*).Republics have their own constitution, while the other members can make their own statutes within the context of federal law. The arrangements often take little account of those ethnic groups that are minorities in their own areas. Chechnya and Tatarstan have declared independence, but have not yet ratified the new constitution.

An economy at risk, a society in crisis

By 1980 the Soviet Union had the second most powerful economy in the world. A series of ambitious Five Year Plans instigated by Joseph Stalin in 1928 had established a heavy industrial base under centralised control to exploit Russia's natural resources, in particular its coal, oil and gas.

Germany's attack in 1941, followed by postwar rivalry with the West, stimulated a vast programme of development.

In agriculture, land was divided into huge collectivised units known as *kolkhozy* (collective farms) and *sovkhozy* (state farms). But with some 780 000 sq miles (2 million km²) under cultivation,

The Russian Federation: republics and other territories

Adygei: 2935 sq miles/7600 km²; 444 900
Alania (ex-Northern Ossetia): 3090 sq miles/ 8000 km²; 678 200 inhabitants
Altai: 35 750 sq miles/92 600 km²; 204 900
Bashkortostan: 55 445 sq miles/143 600 km²; 4 090 600
Buryatiya: 135 635 sq miles/351 300 km²; 1 019 400
Chechnya: 6410 sq miles/16 600 km²; 624 600
Chuvashia: 7065 sq miles/18 300 km²; 1 346 300
Dagestan: 19 420 sq miles/50 300 km²; 2 179 500
Ingushetiya: 1040 sq miles/2700 km²; 466 300
Kabardino-Balkariya: 4825 sq miles/12 500 km²; 782 000
Kalmykiya: 29 380 sq miles/76 100 km²; 305 600
Karachayevo-Cherkesiya: 5445 sq miles/ 14 100km²; 428 600
Karelia: 66 565 sq miles/172 400 km²; 756 400
Khakassia: 23 900 sq miles/61 900km²; 575,400
Komi: 160 580 sq miles/415 900 km²; 1 117 200
Mari: 8960 sq miles/23 200 km²; 750 300
Mordovia: 10 115 sq miles/26 200 km²; 910 000
Sakha (formerly Yakutia): 1 198 145 sq miles/ 3 103 200 km²; 982 900

Tatarstan: 26 255 sq miles/68 000 km²; 3 7638 200
Tuva: 65 830 sq miles/170 500 km²; 310 300
Udmurtia: 16 255 sq miles/42 100km²; 1 639 000

Autonomous regions
Jewish Autonomous Region (Birobidzhan) 13 900 sq miles/36 000 km²; 208 000

Autonomous territories
Aginskaya Buryatia: 7335 sq miles/19 000 km²; 78 400
Chukchi: 284 940 sq miles/738 000 km²; 90 000
Evenki: 296 525 sq miles/768 000 km²; 20 000
Khanty-Mansisk: 201 930 sq miles/523 000 km²; 1 336 000
Komi-Permyaki: 11 585 sq miles/30 000 km²; 160 000
Koryaki: 116 600 sq miles/302 000 km²; 32 000
Nentsy: 68 725 sq miles/178 000 km²; 46 600
Taymyr (Dolgan-Nenets): 332 820 sq miles/ 862 000 km²; 54 000
Ust-Ordinskaya Buryatia: 7720 sq miles/20 000 km²; 145 000
Yamalo-Nentsy: 289 575 sq miles/ 750 000 km²; 600 000

291
416
474
645

1570
1826
2646
2724
4169

Armenia
Azerbaijan   Russia
Georgia   Tajikistan
Kazakhstan   Turkmenistan
Kyrgyzstan   Uzbekistan

The Federation: a land of many parts

After the collapse of the Soviet Union, the Russian Federation inherited a divided and complex administration. In 1993, following the virtual seizure of independence by many of the Russian minorities, Yeltsin adopted a new constitution accepting 89 'Federal subjects' – 21 republics, 11 autonomous regions (*okrugi*), two federal cities

◀ ENERGY CONSUMPTION *(in 1b/kg of oil per person)*

Last-minute checks Scientists at the Baikonur Cosmodrome in Kazakhstan, prepare to launch Soyuz TM 30 to link up with the Mir space station.

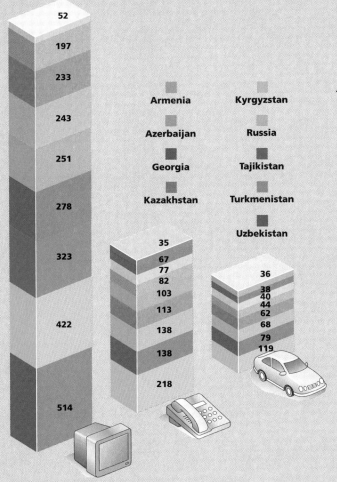

52	
197	
233	Armenia Kyrgyzstan
243	Azerbaijan Russia
251	Georgia Tajikistan
278	Kazakhstan Turkmenistan
	Uzbekistan
323	35
	67
	77
422	82 36
	103 38
	113 40
	138 44
	62
514	138 68
	79
	218 119

◀ CONSUMER GOODS: TELEVISIONS, TELEPHONES, CARS
(per 1000 people)

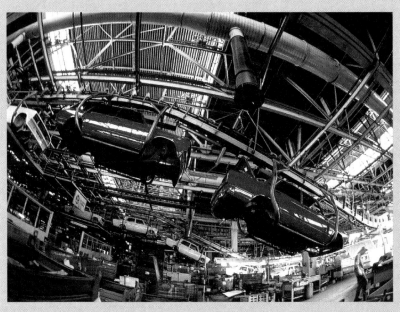

Lada origins *Built at the end of the 1960s, the immense Togliatti car factory, 690 miles (1100 km) south-east of Moscow, produces the Lada. It employs around 110 000 people.*

the inferior soil and low harvests meant that Soviet agriculture always remained the poor relation of the economy compared to industry.

Between 1928 and 1933 Russia's already pitiful standard of living dropped by as much as one-third. Forced collectivisation severed the peasantry – about 80 per cent of the population – from its roots. Millions were deported to the gulag for not complying with collectivisation, and millions more died of famine. Even in the best years, agricultural production never amounted to more than 20 per cent of GDP.

In 1992, after the collapse of the Soviet Union, the government of the Russian Federation introduced a series of radical measures to transform the economy from one that was centrally planned by the state to one that was based on free enterprise and responsive to the marketplace. Its main aim was to privatise the giant state enterprises by creating commercial and industrial companies financed by Russian or foreign investment.

In the countryside, farmers were able to acquire titles to property to allow them to go into business on their own account.

How good intentions faltered: the problems of privatisation

The process of privatisation in both agriculture and industry took some time to get under way. Those sectors that were the most readily viable – such as the oil and gas industries – were rapidly taken up by private companies that have since become extremely wealthy, while some heavy industrial enterprises never found anyone willing to take them on. In a few years, these measures helped to undermine the conditions under which

ordinary people lived. Liberalisation of prices meant inexorable price increases and soaring inflation. The value of the rouble nosedived and the real incomes of both Russians and the inhabitants of their neighbouring states steadily dropped.

At the same time, the rate of unemployment went up and agricultural and industrial production went down. The shortages of everyday goods – even of the most basic food supplies in the cities – fuelled a wide-ranging black market.

In addition, Russia and the other republics now have to endure the full effects of environmental pollution resulting from the all-out industrialisation and large-scale agricultural schemes of the Soviet era. The explosion of Chernobyl's nuclear reactor in the Ukraine in 1986, which exposed thousands of people to the effects of radiation, was one example. Another is the steady disap-

pearance of the Aral Sea due to chemical pollution and the misguided agricultural use of the rivers that feed it. The southern and eastern shorelines have retreated some 50 miles (80 km) in the last 40 years and this once vast inland sea has become two smaller seas. By 2005, the southern sea is expected to divide again. It is estimated that the total surface area will be about 2700 sq miles (7000 km²), one-tenth of its original size.

Russia's investments: decline and collapse

After the catastrophic economic crisis that struck Russia in 1998, investments from both Russian and foreign sources quickly evaporated. Total investment plunged from £3.2 billion in 1997, to £2 billion in 1998, and to less than £700 million in 1999 – hardly more than a fifth of the amount generated two years previously. At present

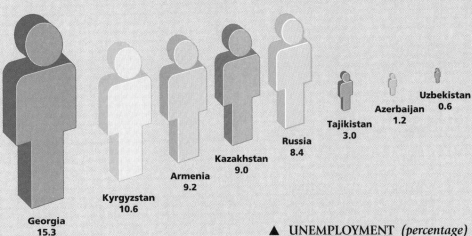

Georgia 15.3 Kyrgyzstan 10.6 Armenia 9.2 Kazakhstan 9.0 Russia 8.4 Tajikistan 3.0 Azerbaijan 1.2 Uzbekistan 0.6

▲ UNEMPLOYMENT *(percentage)*

foreign companies cannot see any benefits in investing in Russia, and capital is being siphoned out of the country.

The press: from censorship to *glasnost*

The role of the press in the Soviet Union have no comparison to the function of newspapers in the West. All Soviet newpapers were official organs of government: *Pravda* was the voice of the Communist Party, *Izvestiya* was the organ of the Supreme Soviet, and so on. In practice, this meant that newspapers were practically indistinguishable from each other: they all followed the same editorial line – the state's line – and they even printed the same articles, reproducing the speeches of Party leaders in full.

Given this situation, it is nothing short of astonishing that a tradition of radical, crusading journalism emerged almost instantly when Gorbachev abolished central censorship of the

News display *Russians in Pushkin Square, Moscow, catch up on news. Papers are usually on view at the most important public places in all major cities.*

many readers simply lost their appetite for news. Some publications survived because they were bought up by super-rich entrepreneurs, most of whom had no interest in journalism, but saw newspaper ownership as a means of promoting their other business interests. This has inevitably had a detrimental effect, as have the intolerant and repressive instincts of the present government.

The Russian press is now again subject to censorship. It is more subtle than the leaden hand of communism, but it is all the more insidious and dangerous for that.

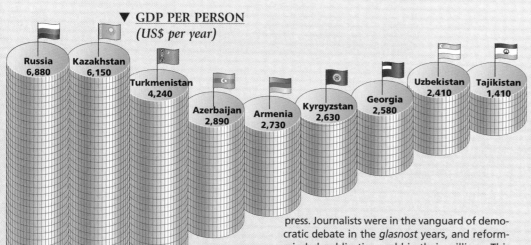

▼ GDP PER PERSON
(US$ per year)

Russia 6,880
Kazakhstan 6,150
Turkmenistan 4,240
Azerbaijan 2,890
Armenia 2,730
Kyrgyzstan 2,630
Georgia 2,580
Uzbekistan 2,410
Tajikistan 1,410

press. Journalists were in the vanguard of democratic debate in the *glasnost* years, and reform-minded publications sold in their millions. This was the brief golden age of journalism in Russia: there was much truth to be told, and there was the freedom to tell it.

The press fared less well once the Russian economy began to slide in the early 1990s. Newsprint became prohibitively expensive, the subscription system collapsed, and

Seeking to exploit the Caspian's oil

The world's oil companies have their eyes fixed on the reserves of oil and gas that lie beneath the Caspian region. More than 20 international oil companies have signed contracts with the national oil companies of Azerbaijan and Kazakhstan to develop their subterranean wealth. The reserves are estimated to be tens of billions of tons, more than twice those of the North Sea, and perhaps many times more. Oil companies are preparing to invest $30 billion to explore and exploit these reserves over the coming decades.

To export this cornucopia of 'black gold', Georgia, Azerbaijan and Turkmenistan have signed an agreement that is intended to allow the construction of a pipeline under the Caspian Sea, linking Turkmenistan to Turkey via Baku and Georgia. This pipeline, projected to cost an estimated £1.5-1.8 billion, is one of many proposed for the area. Whichever are successful, they will hopefully bring an end to the bitter civil wars in the area (fuelled in part by a desire to control the coming bonanza).

DOCTORS	HOSPITAL BEDS
(per 1000 inhabitants)	
3.23	8.1
Armenia	
3.64	8.1
Azerbaijan	
5.49	10.53
Georgia	
3.75	6.3
Kazakhstan	
3.30	10.4
Kyrgyzstan	
4.4	13.1
Russia	
2.26	9.6
Tajikistan	
3.03	7.2
Turkmenistan	
3.23	8.5
Uzbekistan	

▲ HEALTH SERVICES

Index

Page numbers in *italics* denote illustrations. The letter and number
references in brackets are the co-ordinates for places in the map section, pp 136-45.

Acknowledgments

Abbreviations: t = top, m = middle, b = bottom, l = left, r = right

FRONT COVER: A summer camp at Kyzyl Bel pass (Kyrgyzstan), A. CHENEVIÈRE. BACK COVER: Chess players in the park, CORBIS-SYGMA/B. Koshanak

4/5: ASK/M. Barlow; 6: COSMOS/SPL/T. Van Sant; 8tl: EXPLORER/C. Monteath-N. Zeal Hedgehoghouse; 8bl: BIOS/F. Suchel; 8/9: A. CHENEVIÈRE; 10/11: ANA/ V. Gippenreiter; 11tr: EXPLORER/E. Chrétien; 11br: BIOS/ R. Seitre; 12t, b: A. CHENEVIÈRE; 12/13, 14tr: ALTITUDE/ E. Alesin; 14/15b: RIA-NOVOSTI; 15tr: RIA-NOVOSTI/ A. Bouchkine; 16/17: ANA/V. Gippenreiter; 17tr: ALTITUDE/ E. Alesin; 17br: ANA/V. Gippenreiter; 18tr: A. CHENEVIÈRE; 18m: G. DAGLI ORTI/Hermitage Museum, St Petersburg; 18b: A. CHENEVIÈRE; 19tl: G. DAGLI ORTI/Museo Nazionale della Siritide, Policoro, Italy; 19tr: ANA/V. Gippenreiter; 19m: J.-L. CHARMET/History of Old Russia 1783, Institute of Slavic Studies, Paris; 19b: HOA QUI/C. & J. Lenars/Hermitage Museum, St Petersburg; 20t: HOA QUI/W. Buss; 20ml: G. DAGLI ORTI/Monastery of St Mark, Dracevo, Macedonia; 20mr: J.-L. CHARMET/B.N., Paris; 20b: J.-L. CHARMET/Library of Decorative Arts, Paris; 21tr: G. DAGLI ORTI/Museo Correr, Venice; 21ml: THE BRIDGEMAN ART LIBRARY/Ivan the Terrible, 1989, I. Glazunov, 1930, private collection; 21b: RUE DES ARCHIVES/BCA/ Alexander Nevsky, S. Eisenstein, 1938; 22t: Archives M.L. Éditions; 22ml: G. DAGLI ORTI/Apotheosis of Peter the Great, anonymous, circa 1710, State Historical Museum Moscow; 22bl: THE BRIDGEMAN ART LIBRARY/Cosacks in a winter landscape, A. Baumgartner-Stoiloff, 19th century, Gavin Graham Gallery, London; 22br: G. DAGLI ORTI/State Historical Museum, Moscow; 23tl: G. DAGLI ORTI/Portrait of the Empress Catherine, F. S. Rokotov, circa 1770, State Historical Museum, Moscow; 23tr: THE BRIDGEMAN ART LIBRARY/Portrait of prince G. Orlov Potemkin-Tavricheski, 1790, J. B. Edler von Lampi (1751-1830), Hermitage Museum, St Petersburg; 23b: THE BRIDGEMAN ART LIBRARY/The execution of the boyarina Pajaritar Morozova, 1675, 1887, V. I. Surikov (1848-1916), Tretiakov Gallery, Moscow; 24t: G. DAGLI ORTI/Battle of Russian and Caucasian troops, G. G. Gagarin (1810-1893), Hermitage Museum, St Petersburg; 24bl: Coll. VIOLLET; 24br: G. DAGLI ORTI/Army Museum, Paris; 25tl: G. DAGLI ORTI/Museum of the two World Wars, Paris; 25tr: Coll. HARLINGUE-VIOLLET; 25r: THE BRIDGEMAN ART LIBRARY/Oil-producing country at Baku on the Caspain Sea - The Illustrated London News, 19 June 1886, English school, private collection; 25b: J.-L. CHARMET/Coll. Dominique, Paris; 26tl: Coll. VIOLLET; 26ml: L'ILLUSTRATION; 26mr: CORBIS-SYGMA/M. Garanger; 26bl: KEYSTONE; 26r: RIA-NOVOSTI/ Poster V. Korableva, 1931; 27bl: CORBIS-SYGMA; 27br: KEYSTONE/Archives l'Humanité; 28tl: RIA-NOVOSTI; 28tr: CORBIS-SYGMA/M. Garanger; 28b: AFP/D. E. Curran; 29tl: AFP/B. Swersey; 29tr: AFP/EPA; 29m: SIPA PRESS/ Milstein; 29bl: AFP/O. Prasolov; 29br: CORBIS-SYGMA/ A. Gyori; 30/31: A. CHENEVIÈRE; 32/33: ALTITUDE/Y. Arthus-Bertrand; 34t: O. SPRUNG; 34b: ANA/N. Rakhmanov; 35t: DIAF/B. Simmons; 35bl: O. SPRUNG; 35br: ANA/ N. Rakhmanov; 36tr, b: CORBIS-SYGMA/J. Langevin; 37tr: BIOS/Klein-Hubert; 37m: BIOS/G. Dif; 37b: ALTITUDE/ F. Latreille; 38tr: ANA/N. Rakhmanov; 38m: CORBIS-SYGMA/ J. Langevin; 38/39b: ANA/L. Weisman; 39tr: ALTITUDE/ C. Sappa; 39ml: O. SPRUNG; 40bl: BIOS/B. Lundberg; 40/41b: ANA/V. Gippenreiter; 40t: ANA/L. Weisman; 42t: JACANA/R. P. V. Glutron; 42b: RAPHO/R. S. Michaud; 43t: COSMOS/C. Sattlberger-Anzenberger; 43bl: RAPHO/ R. S. Michaud; 43br: ANA/V. Gippenreiter; 44t: BIOS/ P. Prokosch; 44b: BIOS/J. J. Alcalay; 45t: ANA/L. Weisman; 45bl, br: CORBIS-SYGMA/J. Langevin; 46tr: CORBIS-SYGMA/ P. Parrot; 46m: CORBIS-SYGMA/F. Gosset; 46b: CORBIS-SYGMA/T. Orban; 47t: CORBIS-SYGMA/A. Rogov; 47bl: AFP/ J. Robine; 47br: CORBIS-SYGMA/EPIX; 48t: A. CHENEVIÈRE; 48b: RIA-NOVOSTI/Y. Kaner; 49t, m, bl: A. CHENEVIÈRE; 49br: BIOS/R. Seitre; 50/51: AFP/A. Nemenov; 52tr, b: ANA/ N. Rakhmanov, 52m: CORBIS-SYGMA; 53tl: RIA-NOVOSTI/ F. Soubbotine; 53ml: AFP/A. Nemenov; 53b: RIA-NOVOSTI/ S. Ptitsyne; 54t: CORBIS-SYGMA/P. Andrews; 54m: CORBIS-SYGMA/B. Roshanak; 54b: CORBIS-SYGMA/R. King; 55t, m: CORBIS-SYGMA/B. Roshanak; 55b: CORBIS-SYGMA/ R. King; 56tr, m, b: CORBIS-SYGMA/B. Bisson; 57t, b: ANA/ V. Gippenreiter; 57mr: ANA/N. Rakhmanov; 58t: M. LANGROGNET/Old Tbilisi — G.W.S. Comp. Ltd Tbilisi,

Georgia; 58mr: EXPLORER/Ph. Roy; 58ml: RAPHO/ J. Wassman; 58b: SIPA PRESS/Johannes; 59tr: CORBIS-SYGMA/R. King; 59m: HOA QUI/C. Sappa; 59bl: DIAF/ Maximilien Stock Ltd; 59br: CORBIS-SYGMA/P. Andrews; 60t: A. CHENEVIÈRE; 60bl, br: CORBIS-SYGMA/Reza; 61t: ASK/TRIP/V. Kolpakov; 61bm: CORBIS-SYGMA/ L. Zylberman; 61br: BIOS/STILL PICTURES/T. Hjalte; 62/63t: CORBIS-SYGMA/A. Gyori; 62ml: RIA-NOVOSTI; 62m: A. CHENEVIÈRE; 62/63b: RIA-NOVOSTI/Y. Kguidine; 63tr: RIA-NOVOSTI/F. Grinberg; 63m: HOA QUI/C. Sappa; 64/65: RIA-NOVOSTI; 66tr: L'ILLUSTRATION; 66m: ANA/ A. Mokletsov; 66b: CORBIS-SYGMA/CNES/C. André-Deshays; 67tl: ANA/A. Mokletsov; 67tr: CORBIS-SYGMA; 67m, b: ANA/ A. Mokletsov; 68t: CORBIS-SYGMA/VOSTOK NEWS/Sauchenko; 68/69b: CORBIS-SYGMA/RPG; 69t: CORBIS-SYGMA/ V. Sumousky; 69r: CORBIS-SYGMA/R. King; 69b: CORBIS-SYGMA/A. Nogues; 70t: CORBIS-SYGMA/RPG/L. Yakutin; 70bl: RIA-NOVOSTI/S. Kompanitchenko; 70br: CORBIS-SYGMA/RPG; 71t: RIA-NOVOSTI/S. Soubbotine; 71bl: RAPHO/S. Petrukhine; 71br: ANA/V. Svartsevitch; 72tr: CORBIS-SYGMA/RPG; 72ml, bl: RIA-NOVOSTI; 72br: CORBIS-SYGMA/I. Wyman; 73tr: RIA-NOVOSTI; 73m: ASK/TRIP/A. Tjagny-Rjadno; 73b: RIA-NOVOSTI/ V. Tchernov; 74/75: A. CHENEVIÈRE; 76tl: GIRAUDON/Woman with a cigarette or Self-portrait, N. S. Gontcharova, 1881-1962, Museum of Art and History, Serpoukhov/ADAGP, Paris 2000; 76tr: CORBIS-SYGMA/J.-P. Laffont; 76bl: BIOS/OKAPIA/ J. Cancalosi; 76br: RIA-NOVOSTI; 77t, bl: ANA/N. Rakhmanov; 77br: ANA/A. Goriaïnov; 78tr: AFP/S. Chirikov; 78bl: AFP/ A. Vitaly; 78bm: AFP; 78br: CORBIS-SYGMA/G. de Keerle; 79tr: RIA-NOVOSTI/T. Mikhalev; 79m: CORBIS-SYGMA/ S. Bassouls; 79b: ANA/Shakhverdiev; 80t: COSMOS/ G. Buthaud; 80bl: HOA QUI/F. Charel; 80br: CORBIS-SYGMA/ I. Kostin; 80/81t: BIOS/G. Gunther; 81bl: AFP/Y. Kochtkov; 81br: BIOS/G. Gunther; 82t, b: CORBIS-SYGMA/G. de Keerle; 83tl: COSMOS/COLORIFIC/J. Hill; 83tr: CORBIS-SYGMA/RPG/ V. Velengurin; 83b: COSMOS/IMPACT VISUALS/J. Eskenazi; 84t: DIAF/Valdin; 84m: HOA QUI/C. Sappa; 84b: RIA-NOVOSTI; 85t, m, bl: ASK/M. Barlow; 85br: ASK/TRIP/ B. Turner; 86t, m, b, 87t, ml, mr, b, 88t: CORBIS-SYGMA/ J. Langevin; 88bl: BIOS/R. Seitre; 88/89b: HOA QUI/R. Manin; 89t: CORBIS-SYGMA/J. Langevin; 89m: RAPHO/R. S. Michaud; 90tr: RIA-NOVOSTI/A. Poliakov; 90ml: ANA/N. Rakhmanov; 90mr: HOA QUI/W. Buss; 90b: RIA-NOVOSTI/A. Poliakov; 91t, bl: ANA/N. Rakhmanov; 91b: COSMOS/COLORIFIC/ J. Hill; 92tl: RIA-NOVOSTI/A. Sverdlov; 92ml: HOA QUI/ B. Perousse; 92mr: ANA/J.-J. Sommeryns; 92b: DIAF/ G. Simeone; 93t, m.: A. CHENEVIÈRE; 93b: METIS/L. Choquer; 94t: PHOTOTHÈQUE CULINAIRE/Hamot; 94m: RAPHO/ G. Sioen; 94b: RAPHO/J.C. Bourcart; 95tl: GIRAUDON/ A merchant's wife taking tea, 1918, B. M. Koustodiev, 1878-1927, State Russian Museum, St Petersburg; 95m: AFP/A. Nemenov; 95b: COSMOS/Anzenberger/R. Haidinge; 96t: SIPA PRESS/ Sichov; 96bl: RIA-NOVOSTI; 96br: RIA-NOVOSTI/ D. Korobenikov; 97t: CORBIS-SYGMA/B. Roshanak; 97bl: CORBIS-SYGMA/R. B. Mermandez; 97br: Coll. HARLINGUE-VIOLLET; 98tr: CORBIS-SYGMA/EPIX; 98m: ANA/ N. Rakhmanov; 98b: EXPLORER/R. Mattes; 99t: COSMOS/ COLORIFIC/J. Hill; 99b: ANA/Steinbock; 100tr, m: RIA-NOVOSTI; 100bl: VANDYSTADT/DUOMO/S. Sutton; 101tl: VANDYSTADT/G. Vandystadt; 101tr: VANDYSTADT/ ALLSPORT/S. Botterill; 101bl: VANDYSTADT/ALLSPORT/ T. Duffy; 101b: RIA-NOVOSTI; 102/103: HOA QUI/C. Sappa; 104tr: ANA/V. Gippenreiter; 104m: RIA-NOVOSTI; 104b: ANA/ V. Gippenreiter; 105t: HOA QUI/ISIP; 105bl: ANA/ V. Gippenreiter; 105br: EXPLORER/R. Mattes; 106/111: DIAF/ SIME/Gräfenhain; 106tr: RAPHO/NETWORK/B. Lewis; 106bl: EXPLORER/Ph. Roy; 106br: ANA/A. Goriaïnov; 107tr: ANA/N. Rakhmanov; 107ml: RIA-NOVOSTI/ B. Prikhodko/Gorky Museum - Architect: F. Chekhtel; 107mr: ASK/TRIP/N. & J. Wiseman; 107bl: ANA/N. Rakhmanov; 107br: HOA QUI/W. Buss; 108hl: ANA/N. Rakhmanov; 108tr: RIA-NOVOSTI/V. Fedorenko; 108bl, br: HOA QUI/ F. Charel; 109t: ANA/Maxhmlenkov; 109/110tr: ANA/ A. Goriaïnov; 109mr: ASK/TRIP/A. Tjagny-Rjadno; 109bl: HOA QUI/T. Borredon; 109br: ANA/N. Rakhmanov; 110t: RIA-NOVOSTI/S. Soloviev; 110ml: HOA QUI/Th. Borredon; 110mr: ANA/A. Goriaïnov; 110bl: HOA QUI/F. Charel; 110br: ANA/A. Goriaïnov; 111t: HOA QUI/W. Buss; 111bl: HOA QUI/F. Charel; 111br: CORBIS-SYGMA/P. Vauthier; 112t: ANA/ J. J. Sommeryns; 112bl: COSMOS/Anzenberger/G. M. Schmidt;

112br: ANA/J. J. Sommeryns; 113t: HOA QUI/W. Buss; 113mr: HOA QUI/P. Escudero; 113b: COSMOS/ASPEN/ J. Aaronson; 114ml: ANA/N. Rakhmanov; 114m: ANA/ N. Rakhmanov/Lithograph by Jacottet and Reganiev; 114mr: HOA QUI/W. Buss; 114b, 115t: ANA/J. J. Sommeryns; 115m, bl, br: ANA/N. Rakhmanov; 116tr: RMN/F. Raux/Musée du Louvre, Paris; 116ml: ASK/TRIP/W. Jacobs; 116b: HOA QUI/W. Buss; 117t: RIA-NOVOSTI/A. Sokolov; 117ml: CORBIS-SYGMA/ P. Robert; 117mr: EXPLORER/C. & J. Lenars; 118t: CORBIS-SYGMA/Th. Orban; 118m: CORBIS-SYGMA/J. Armineh; 118bl, br: ANA/V. Gippenreiter; 119tr: COSMOS/FOCUS/ R. Bezjak; 119m: HOA QUI/R. Manin; 119b: COSMOS/ FOCUS/R. Bezjak; 120m: RIA-NOVOSTI/G. Ratouchenko; 120bl: RIA-NOVOSTI/B. Manouchine; 120br: RIA-NOVOSTI/ A. Varpolomev; 121tl: RIA-NOVOSTI/V. Viatkine; 121tr: COSMOS/G. Buthaud; 121b: HOA QUI/W. Buss; 122/123: ANA/N. Rakhmanov; 124t: GIRAUDON/Roosen/ Archives Larousse, Paris; 124ml: RIA-NOVOSTI/ S. Rachmnaninov, K. Somov/Tretiakov Gallery, Moscow; 124b: RIA-NOVOSTI/The Group of Five, Makovski (1839-1915) - Collection of the Theatre Museum, Bakhrouchine; 125tl: RIA-NOVOSTI; 125tr: CORBIS-SYGMA/L. Stone; 125m: CORBIS-SYGMA/STM CONCEPT/F. Dugowson; 125ml: THE BRIDGEMAN ART LIBRARY/Set for The Buffoon, scene 2, S. Prokofiev (1891-1953) Library of the Opera, Paris; 125b: ENGUERAND/Ch. Masson, Eugene Onegin, production by W. Decker, musical direction by G. Bertini; 126tr: RIA-NOVOSTI/The Swan Princess, A. Wroubel (1856-1910) - Tretiakov Gallery, Moscow; 126bl: THE BRIDGEMAN ART LIBRARY/GIRAUDON/The Old Testament Trinity by A. Roublev (1360-1427), Trinity Monastery of St Sergius, Zagorsk; 126br: RIA-NOVOSTI/A Backyard in Moscow, 1878, V. Polenov, 1844-1927 - Tretiakov Gallery, Moscow; 127tr: GIRAUDON/The Sportsmen, (1928-1932), K. Malevitch, 1878-1935/State Russian Museum, St Petersburg; 127ml: GIRAUDON/The Volga Bargemen, 1870-1873, I. E. Répine, 1844-1930/State Russian Museum, St Petersburg; 127mr: RIA-NOVOSTI/Samovar, 1913, A. Lentoulov, 1882-1943; 127b: EXPLORER/C. Lenars/Worker and the Female Collective Farmer, 1937, Véra Moukhina; 128tr: RIA-NOVOSTI/Portrait of F. M. Dostoyevsky, 1872, V. G. Pérov (1833-1882/83)/Tretiakov Gallery, Moscow; 128ml: CORBIS-SYGMA/S. Bassouls; 128m: RIA-NOVOSTI/ S. Soubbotine/Pasternak Museum; 128mr: RIA-NOVOSTI/ A. Pouchkine, 1827, O. Kiprenski/Museum of Literature, Moscow; 128b: ANA/N. Rakhmanov; 129t: RIA-NOVOSTI; 129m: CORBIS-SYGMA/P. Le Segretain; 129mr: M. LANGROGNET/Nouvelles, Nina Berberova, © Sabachnikoff, Moscow, © Actes Sud; 129b: RIA-NOVOSTI/The Cherry Orchard, A. Chekhov, Taganka theatre; 130t: ANA/ N. Rakhmanov; 130m: G. DAGLI ORTI/Bibliothèque des Arts décoratifs, Paris; 130bl: RIA-NOVOSTI/Younost folklore group, Volvograd; 130br: CORBIS-SYGMA/G. Rancinan; 131tr: RUE DES ARCHIVES/CS/FF — The Cranes are Flying, M. Kalatozov, 1958; 131ml: RIA-NOVOSTI/Ivan the Terrible, 1944, S.M. Einsenstein; 131mr: COLL. CAHIERS DU CINÉMA/Taxi Blues, P. Lounguine, 1990; 131b: RUE DES ARCHIVES/CS/FF — The Barber of Seville, N. Mikhalkov, 1998; 132t: RIA-NOVOSTI; 132mr: RIA-NOVOSTI/Gouchtchine; 132ml: ANA/ N. Rakhmanov; 132/133b: ANA/J. J. Sommeryns; 133t: CORBIS-SYGMA/J. Armineh; 133b: G. DAGLI ORTI/Bibliothèque des Arts décoratifs, Paris; 134/135: COSMOS/G. Buthaud; 148: HOA QUI/C. Sappa; 149t: HOA QUI/Rotondo; 149b: ANA/L. Weisman; 150t: ANA/ N. Rakhmanov; 150b: RAPHO/C. Sappa; 151t: CORBIS-SYGMA/J. Langevin; 151b: RIA-NOVOSTI/V. Choustov; 152: AFP/S. Chirikov; 153: RIA-NOVOSTI; 154: RAPHO/ J.-C. Bourcart.

Printed and bound in Europe by Arvato Iberia
Colour separations: Station Graphique, Ivry-sur-Seine